C000139709

LONG-DISTANCE CRUISING

Bobby Schenk

LONG-DISTANCE CRUISING

——— The Ocean Sailing Handbook ———

David & Charles

All photographs by Carla and Bobby Schenk except: Amel
26–7, 35, 52; Autoflug 152 right; Ballonfabrick Augsburg 149
below, 220; Baltic 28; Jean Paul Basseget, 155, 170, 183;
Bavarian Yachten 14, 47, 74; Dantronic 232; Dehler 5, 12;
Henk van de Weg 148, 149; Kadametic 150, 152 left; Najad 13,
50, 51; Pictor International 32, 39, 42, 59, 100; Schöchl 12, 46;
Volkmann 243, 244, 252, 253; ZN-Technik 81, 83, 234
Illustrations by Helmut Hoffman
Jacket photography by Patrick Roach

A DAVID & CHARLES BOOK

Translation copyright © Peter Davison, 1994
First published in German as *Fahrtensegeln*
Copyright © BLV Verlagsgesellschaft mbH, Munich, 1993
ISBN 3 405 14589 9

English translation, *Long Distance Cruising*,
First published 1994

ISBN 0 7153 0245 0

Peter Davison has asserted his right to be identified as
translator of this work in accordance with the Copyright,
Designs and Patents Act 1988.

All Rights reserved. No part of this publication may be
reproduced, stored in a retrieval system, or transmitted, in
any form or by any means, electronic or mechanical, by
photocopying, recording or otherwise, without prior
permission from the publisher.

A catalogue record of this book is available from the British
Library.

Typeset by Ace Filmsetting Ltd
and printed in Italy by LEGO SpA
for David & Charles
Brunel House   Newton Abbot   Devon

Contents

The Cruising Boat

Electrics and Electronics

Contents

Wind, Weather and Waves

Contents

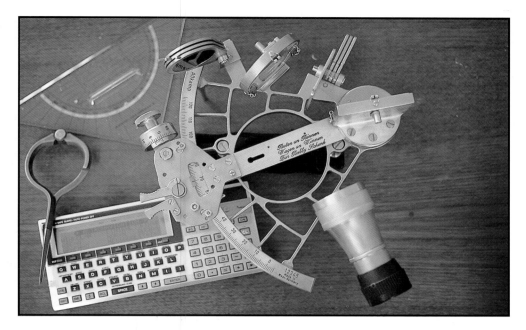

Navigation

Contents

Important Notes

Preface

Nowhere is there so much freedom as on the sea, so it is no coincidence that more and more sport-minded people are crowding onto the water, even in the age of space travel. With a small sailing boat they are looking for the independence lacking in the confined surroundings of their everyday life. Does this explain the attraction of offshore cruising? Or is the reason more romantic, as, since time immemorial, the wind drives the boat towards its destination, which the skipper has calculated with the help of a small magnetic needle – regardless of whether this destination is a few miles along the coast or on the other side of an ocean.

Although the tenets of seamanship have remained unchanged for centuries, in the last few years technology has made things so much easier in racing boats with modern materials and new developments in electronics, that today anyone regardless of their age or gender can undertake any journey in the right boat at no risk, if they have the right information at their disposal.

This book tries to give just that information. I have therefore tried to explain problems as easily as possible, so that anyone can gain the necessary understanding, even without previous technical knowledge. In so far as it requires the reader's collaboration in the Navigation section, the book contains all the necessary documents (maps, nautical charts etc).

I would like to thank Dr Walter Dirr and Dr Gerhard Meyer-Uhl, who as seasoned and experienced sailors wrote the chapters on 'Health' and 'Avoiding Collisions'.

Since its first edition this book has appeared in several languages, and as a result I have been been approached with important suggestions for improvement, particularly from England and the USA – countries with a strong sailing tradition – all of which I have been able to work into this edition, as I have the technical developments, especially in the area of navigation (satellite sounding and Decca navigation). Numerous yachting friends have helped by sharing the wealth of their experience with me in endless conversations in picturesque anchorages all around the world, experience which I am now able to pass on. Suggestions from readers of this book are also welcome.

Bobby Schenk

The Cruising Boat

Choosing a boat

Over the last few years, the demands made on an ocean-going yacht have changed drastically. Earlier one would have referred to either a 'coastal' or an 'ocean-going' yacht. Today one rightly makes no distinction, as every sailing yacht can easily come across such bad weather that it must prove its capacity for extreme conditions exactly like an ocean-going yacht. I believe along with many other sailors that it is much easier, for example, to cross the Atlantic on the trade winds, than to go on a successful short sailing trip for a few weeks in the North Sea. Boats only 6m long have proved their ocean-going qualities, even if only on single occasions which are not necessarily worthy of imitation.

The size of the boat you choose must in the first instance depend on your financial resources. If one only wants to sail along the Adriatic coast on holiday, and spend every evening in harbour, I should imagine that a 7m long boat would be suitable for a couple. It is mostly a question of personal taste and certainly of sportiness. A friend of mine sailed from Canada to Australia with his wife and two-year-old child on a 7m long boat. This is definitely not everybody's cup of tea, but it does show that you can live in very little space, if need be. In the tropics, where you live more in the open anyway, this is more easily possible.

Those who can only afford a small boat should not feel disheartened: small boats have a few advantages which should not be underestimated. Firstly a small boat is much easier to handle both on water and on land, where it

Opposite page: The wind doesn't care if it is driving a 6m or 16m long sailing boat over the stretches of the oceans.

The whole world lies before this couple in their Dehler 31.

A Sunbeam, a high-quality yacht from Austria, most suitable for open sea.

can be transported behind a truck. Apart from that, there is much less maintenance to do. From a certain size (eg 13m and up) maintenance can easily become a full time job, depending on the yacht's age, equipment and condition. And finally, when buying you should bear in mind that the financial risk involved in a small yacht will be much lower. If you want to resell your boat, there is a relatively large market wanting to buy even in bad times, and the percentage loss you would make is substantially lower.

When buying a cruising yacht you should basically look out for two things:
- Safety
- Comfort

Speed plays a less important role, and this should on no account be a priority at the cost of safety or comfort. If you return to harbour from a day trip an hour earlier or later it's not the end of the world. Of course it is fun to be faster than other boats – what sailor hasn't been gripped by racing fever – but success at regattas alone should never influence your decision to buy a particular boat. One consolation is that even the fastest boat will have to come to terms with the fact that other newly built boats are even faster.

There are however two arguments which one should put forward in favour of a faster boat, which are probably the reason why in the last few years sailing boats have increased in size significantly: comfort and safety. In the past, sailing too big a boat has always been warned against, because it could not be controlled by a small crew. That could well have been so, when one put heavy cotton sails on big booms without winches. The size limit has gone right up because of efficient winches and modern synthetic sails. On a large yacht, setting and furling the sails obviously takes longer, and turning takes more time. Everything happens more slowly. But on the other hand the crew has more room in which to work, the movements of the boat are much calmer, and you don't have to hold on in such a cramped way. This all goes to show that a small boat is possibly more difficult to sail than a larger one with easy movements.

Larger yachts are safer. A few years ago this would have been a provocative thing to say. However, this has unfortunately been proved by the fateful Fastnet race in 1979, which cost 17 people's lives. Most of the disasters in winds over force 10 happened in the smaller classes. The fateful statistics of this regatta lead you to a definite conclusion: the smaller the yachts, the more numerous and serious were the accidents. You will reach the same conclusion if you duly consider that the biggest classes had been back in harbour long before the actual hurricane passed through.

Buying a boat

Buying a boat usually begins with the prospective skipper falling in love with a particular yacht (although this is a non-fiction book, the comparison with a pretty girl is allowed). Following that, one thinks of all sorts of reasons why this particular boat is so practical, safe, profitable and above all such unbelievably good value. In this pitiful state one is hardly open to sound and rational reasoning, but nevertheless I will try to give some advice here, and perhaps I will catch the reader still in a 'normal state'.

Don't buy too small a boat! Always remember that in offshore cruising a boat is not only sailed but lived in. In one's initial enthusiasm for a yacht it is easy to overlook the minimum requirements needed, especially in the living space. It is better to save on equipment, and suppress your urge at the beginning for the odd toy such as a wind direction finder or a spinnaker. Go to your financial limit for the boat size. You can make a bad buy with equipment and it won't be a disaster, but if you make a bad move on the size of the boat, it will be a very difficult mistake to rectify.

Even though it would enable you to get a larger boat, you should avoid group ownership. You want to go offshore cruising to enjoy a certain freedom. With a partner, even if you get on well at the beginning of your shared dream, you are making yourself dependent on them, which in my experience always leads to friction. Group ownerships only work very rarely.

Don't count on using the boat for commercial purposes as well so that you can get back part of the costs of

A Najad. Their owners commend them as safe and comfortable yachts with nordic workmanship.

buying or maintaining it. I have known many tragedies in my circle of friends where the charter company which was calculated into the cost has not got off the ground. This market is hotly contested (as can be seen in the advertisement section of yachting magazines) and there is no room left for newcomers. There is hardly a country left where a yacht can legally be chartered privately without the government cashing in on it too.

If you want to have a boat built, go to a reputable shipyard and ask for the addresses of previous customers, and ask them for their advice too. If the shipyard doesn't produce any addresses, then spare them your address as well. But if you have decided on a particular firm, don't underestimate their technical capacity. You, as customer, may

A Bavaria sloop which can also be sailed by a small family.

have hundreds of good ideas which you want to see put into practice in your boat; but the shipyard will add many years of experience gained from mistakes with earlier customers. It would be a shame not to benefit from their experience.

Be extremely suspicious when it comes to the financial side of buying a boat. Hardly a single shipyard has become rich from selling boats. Even very sound firms have collapsed in the recent past, almost always leaving a string of customers brought down with them. With that the dream of owning their own boat often disappeared for ever. Unfortunately practice is such that part of the cost (usually a third) has to be paid when the job is started. This is understandable for the shipyard, as they have to buy materials first, but the customer becomes dependent on them as they have the money and the beginnings of the boat.

It remains like this until the boat is handed over, which only happens after the rest of the money has been paid. If the shipyard isn't well disposed, any complaints about the quality can only be pursued by means of the law. You will therefore have to be prepared to work with bank securities, blocked accounts, or withholding the outstanding amount, and the expensive advice of a solicitor can pay off.

The more your boat is built to individual specifications, the longer you should stay in the area of the shipyard. Don't plan a trip straight away which will take you away from the shipyard for ever, just sail on trips from the shipyard for a few weeks. A boat cannot be compared with a car, where the experience of thousands of newly built cars lies behind every model. Faults in a cruising yacht are therefore quite to be expected. It is disappointing for the beginner to discover that his beloved also has faults!

There is an easy way to eliminate the financial risks, which I believe are considerable these days, and that is to buy a second-hand boat or a boat from an exhibition. If you are buying with cash you are holding all the trump cards, and look around in the advertisements under the 'For Sale' section. There is always something wrong with a finished boat, as you would always have preferred something some other way. However, the slogan which you see bandied about on the used boat market 'Better than new' is more often right than one would care to think.

Finally comes the serious question of whether we really need our own boat for offshore cruising. Is it just as good to charter a yacht every year with the family? If you calculate all the costs of your own boat with all its problems (such as moorings, transport, repairs and insurance), for a yacht about 10m long, you will reach amounts which would bring in enough interest to pay for chartering a yacht every year in the sailing waters of your choice anywhere in the world, footloose and fancy-free. It is therefore not so sensible to think about getting your own yacht. But what sailor wants to be 'sensible'?

Hull and keel

The development of types of hull and keel over the last few years is the best example of why it is not always right to let yourself be guided by regatta sailing. The short keel which is usual in most boats doesn't have many advantages for offshore sailing. I will freely admit that better manoeuvrability and a sensitive, lively rudder – characteristics of modern hulls – are indispensable in a good many waters. Many offshore sailors often take part in regattas anyway, and have little success with an old-fashioned long keel.

The greatest disadvantage of a short keel is however its directional instability. Sensitive to the rudder, the yacht will tend to go off course, particularly downwind. A short keel will also have an effect on space, as the ballast is kept there and the natural storage space for fuel and water is therefore not available. When you lay the boat up you will have problems, because few shipyards are adapted for a yacht with a short keel.

The rudder suspension is considerably weaker hung on the transom or skeg than if it were attached on a long keel, and this is an enormous disadvantage. If this sensitive part of a yacht is damaged it is an extremely serious matter, much more so than losing the mast for example. Unfortunately the Fastnet race in 1979 is proof of this. The first sign of most disasters was the

free-hanging rudder on the modern regatta yachts simply breaking off, and the stricken vessels being left at the mercy of the elements. If the mast breaks you can always make do by rigging up the boom or another spar, or simply using the engine if it isn't too far from the next harbour.

If the rudder is lost, building an emergency rudder is often impossible, particularly for a bigger yacht over 10m long. Many books will tell you that a yacht can be steered with the help of the sails, which might well be the case in the smooth waters of a protected area for a short time, but is mostly impossible on the open sea with swell. You need only to set the tiller and try it.

For an offshore sailor, the question

A 25m long yacht from the golden age of the sport of kings shows its classical form.

This hull and keel has good properties for sailing in bad weather.

A short keel.

A typical long keel for a reliable and safe cruising yacht. Held in high regard by the author, but too slow for those who like speed. The overwhelming advantage of this under-water shape is its capacity to carry large volumes of drinking water and fuel.

A round section, expensive to manufacture, looks good, but doesn't have any great advantages for offshore sailing.

A hard chine works more firmly on the open sea, and is cheaper to manufacture particularly in a steel boat.

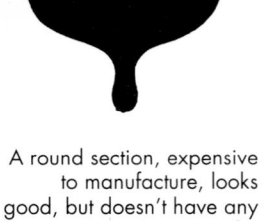

A type of motor sailer with a solid, not very fast hull and keel. It tries to combine the advantages of a long keel (the rudder is protected, and soundly attached) with those of a short keel (less surface area therefore faster).

of a hard chine or round section is no alternative. Granted, a chine doesn't look as good as a round section, but apart from that nothing is as good as a chine or double chine: quite the opposite, this type of boat is much cheaper to manufacture, particularly in steel as it is easier to produce smooth surfaces.

A monohull yacht should not be capsizable. It should therefore carry enough ballast to right itself in extreme circumstances if it is thrown flat on the water. Ideally, a cruising yacht would be unsinkable too, ie it would not sink even when fully loaded. However this is only possible for very small yachts with the help of buoyancy bags, and is not possible at all for boats 10m long and bigger unless you give up a lot of your storage space. Only the person who constructs the boat can

decide how high the proportion of ballast should be. It should never be as high as it is in racing yachts (50% and above of the weight), because the ship's movements become so violent that your boat will not be comfortable at all. The ability of a racing yacht to carry maximum sail even in strong wind, when the heeling factor is at its greatest, plays only a secondary role for a cruising yacht. In the swell of the open sea, the incredible courses into the wind which some racing yachts manage are not sailed any more. A cruising yacht can be happy if it is running a course of 50°. It is incidentally very easy to check at what angle a yacht is going into the wind by reading the compass first on one and then on the other tack. The difference divided by 2 gives the angle you are making.

Construction materials

Synthetic materials

There has been a real revolution in yacht construction over the past 20 years. Wood has disappeared completely as a construction material for sea-going yachts. This development is due to the tremendous progress which has been made in chemistry. Synthetic materials such as polyester and epoxy resin have such impressive properties that they were immediately adopted for use in boatbuilding whilst wood as a material has many disadvantages. Firstly, wood is an organic substance which can decay and rot. Pieces of wood can never be joined together homogeneously, and must be either stuck together which means that it is 'working', or the cracks between the planks must be caulked in the age-old way to make the boat watertight. Over and above that, a wooden boat would cost a lot more to manufacture, because of the labour costs involved, than a synthetic boat with all its major advantages. Apart from that wood is particularly at risk in southern waters from the gribble worm (including parts of the Mediterranean), and must be specially protected from it under water.

A synthetic yacht has in comparison a couple of decisive plus points. First of all the synthetic material is watertight, which you can only expect from very few wooden boats. The synthetic material in question is not pure polyester or epoxy resin, which is much more expensive and less pliable, but glass fibres which have been soaked in polyester – fibreglass. Polyester serves only to bind the fibres together. The more glass which can be introduced into the material the stronger the boat will be. In racing yachts nowadays carbon fibres have replaced the glass, which gives even greater strength.

However, fibreglass is not completely insensitive to water. It is a slow process but nevertheless water dissolves polyester if it isn't covered in an outer layer of paraffin-based gel. If this layer is damaged, water forces its way along the fine glass fibres due to the capillary structure of the material, and slowly dissolves the polyester (a process which can take years). A good layer of gel coat should last for 6 years, and a synthetic yacht need only be repainted when little cracks start to show. Nowadays paints are of such good quality that you don't need to worry about this again for a couple of years.

Over the last few years, words like 'blister disease' and 'osmosis' went the rounds and made the fibreglass scene uneasy. The so-called blister disease made itself known by little bulges, usually a few square centimetres large and near the waterline, which became blisters. The cause was water vapour which had forced its way through the tiny cracks in the gel and expanded in the warmth, raising the protective outer layer. At first the shipyards were held responsible for apparently sloppy work. But when osmosis appeared even in the most expensive boats, it was established that shipyards only remotely had anything to do with it. The chief responsibility lay with the manufacturer of the material. This 'disease' is increasingly rare these days as shipyards are in a position to eliminate the consequences of osmosis cosmetically and mechanically, and are gradually gaining control of it. In any case there is no cause to get upset if you find a blister on the underpart of the boat when it is laid up for the winter.

Another problem occurs time and again with synthetic boats. Unfortunately many shipyards are so sloppy about screwing on fittings and screwing together the deck and the hull that the synthetic material's advantage of being watertight is again put on the line. You should therefore make sure when the boat is built that every screw

The rung on this new ladder hung in the water for only five weeks; this gives you an idea of what the gribble or ship worm can do with a wooden boat.

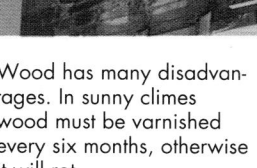

Wood has many disadvantages. In sunny climes wood must be varnished every six months, otherwise it will rot.

Synthetic material and wood which has been painted as opposed to varnished cannot be told apart by the naked eye.

Water seeps drop by drop into the boat and spreads evenly between the berths and the cupboards. It is virtually impossible to tell where it is getting in.

30 – 50 cm

hole is sufficiently protected with silicone rubber, to avoid water seeping in. The biggest headache in this respect is the join between deck and hull. Both parts are usually stuck together and then screwed in short sections.

This method has not proved itself a success mainly because many shipyards rely just on glue on sections of 30cm and more between screws, to keep costs down. If the ship is working on the open sea, the relatively brittle glue gives way, and water can get into the inner boat through the hairline cracks. Nowadays a different path is taken and a durable elastic mixture is used. You should pay particular attention to the watertightness of your boat since the crew's well-being on a long trip depends largely on the people and their belongings staying dry.

I must acknowledge however that I have never come across a really watertight material. A friend of mine had a good idea, although I doubt whether it could be put into practice. He thought that if he bought a boat again, he would have it stated in the contract that before he took the boat away it would have to be subjected to spraying with a fire hose for 30 minutes, particularly the hatches and the windows. Unfortunately in many cases, places liable to leak will only show themselves on the

open sea or if the boat heels over, and a fire hose will not protect against that.

Steel

There is no doubt that steel is the most robust material for a yacht if there is a collision or you run aground. Many sailors will gladly accept a string of disadvantages to have this one advantage. Today corrosion is no longer the biggest drawback of steel. There is an old saying which goes 'A steel yacht is always red, whether from rust or from red lead.' Nowadays there is almost unanimity about the treatment of steel.

The steel must be sandblasted inside and out in the shipyard, until any traces of rust are completely eliminated. The first layer of protective paint must then be applied within a few minutes. It usually takes only 10 minutes for a corrosive layer to form on the steel surface. This goes too for Corten steel, which is partially resistant and is used a lot in yacht building. The advantage of Corten steel, along with its strength, is that although it rusts like normal steel, the rust acts as a protective layer.

Steel nowadays is relatively problem-free, which is due mainly to excellent tar-epoxy-paints which give the steel a protective layer similarly reliable to the paraffin gel coat on synthetic material. This is where the similarity between the two construction materials lies: if the protective layer is damaged, something has to be done, as with synthetic material.

The problem with building steel boats is corrosion. If two different metals are connected together electrically in seawater (which is an electrolyte) or are held very close together, the more reactive metal will be affected, meaning that ions will travel from the more to the less reactive metal. This is the principle on which a battery works (electric current is only the movement of ions). If you drop a couple of copper screws into the bilgewater of a steel yacht, the steel would be corroded, being the more reactive metal.

If you want to use one metal throughout, this electrochemical process will unfortunately still occur. Even construction parts from one and the same metal get a different 'stress potential' through processes such as welding. Special protective measures must therefore always be taken against corrosion.

Passive corrosion protection: The aim here is to keep the electrolyte (seawater) away from the steel, using particularly thick paints (tar-epoxy-paints), without which the dreaded electrochemical process of corrosion would take place. It is a good and cheap method, which doesn't raise problems of adhesion between the paint layers. But if after mechanical damage the steel is not covered with this layer, it is left open to corrosion.

Active corrosion protection: Here the base metal zinc is brought into conductive contact with the sandblasted steel by the process of galvanisation (hot bath, which is very expensive; or the less adhesive cold-spraying process) or in the form of zinc-epoxy-paint, and the seawater is kept away as with non-active protection with tar paints. If the paint layers are damaged, the zinc reacts, protecting the steel.

It is difficult to be clear about which method is the best. The steel boats belonging to most offshore sailors (eg the old and new *Cairo* of the Koch couple) or from the Dutch shipyard Noord Nederland where my *Thalassa II* comes from, are actively protected, but on the other hand the Jongert yard is satisfied with non-active protection. With both methods we must protect our boats additionally by applying small bits of base metal to the areas at risk, which will deflect from the steel. Usually you use small pieces of streamlined zinc as 'sacrificial anodes'. It isn't easy to find out the areas at risk on a yacht, but they are are generally astern near the propeller. I think it is a good

idea to put the yacht into the water as a test and then dive down for the first few days and weeks to observe on the underside of the ship where the first signs of electrolysis are showing, in order to attach the pieces of zinc in exactly the right places.

Some sailors believe that a boat made of pure stainless steel would solve all your problems. This is not true at all. A few years ago, one of the most experienced offshore sailors in the world, the Frenchman Marcel Bardiaux, who already has 350,000 sea miles under his belt, achieved the dream of the ideal offshore boat. He had a boat made completely of stainless steel. It says a lot for this great sailor that he readily admits that his dream boat *Inox* was a flop (and who is willing to say bad things about his own yacht?). He would have had to use hundredweights of zinc anodes to protect the underside from corrosion damage.

Stainless steel doesn't rust away reddish brown like normal steel but it is at least as susceptible to electrolysis. We can see that very well if we look carefully at our stainless steel propeller after a couple of years in seawater. You will easily be able to tell corrosion in the metal parts of a synthetic boat. It is therefore usual to fix zinc anodes onto synthetic and wooden yachts in the par-

Steel too can be so evenly built by good shipyards that the construction material can only be recognised by a couple of traces of rust at the most when it is laid up for the winter.

At the Jongert yard tar paint is applied straight after sand blasting, as passive protection.

Instead of the less reactive steel, sacrificial zinc anodes are eaten away.

A hard-chine hull looks less elegant than a round section, but apart from that has only advantages. It should be better value and sail at least as well.

Zinc anodes should especially be placed near the propeller where lots of different metals meet to their mutual destruction. This position is also effective in boats not made of steel.

ticularly active waters of the tropics.

Apart from the question of cost (steel is normally the cheapest construction material for boats), the complete watertightness of a welded joint is an advantage. It is not necessary at all to bolt through the fittings on a steel yacht, as you can cut them open from the inside with an oxyacetylene torch. In this case the boat builder should naturally be completely clear about the deck plan already. The places which are most at risk from rust, by the way, are on deck, where blocks can rub the paint off or the anchor chain is pulled over a sharp edge. A yard which has any pride in itself should be easily persuaded to weld on little stainless steel sheets on these places, and then this problem would also be solved.

On a steel yacht every little corner should always be easily accessible with a wire brush, in order to get rid of the rust if need be and paint it again. This is probably not necessary at all with the protection of tar-epoxy-paint, but

a hole the size of a pinhead in an inconvenient place in the protective layer would create just such a problem. One should therefore be consistent in other points, and never make the foot rail out of wood. It is absurd to put teak planking on a steel deck even if teak does look good on a boat. In hot areas a brightly painted steel deck is much cooler than a teak deck.

While we are on the subject of the disadvantages of steel, many people think that condensation forms very easily inside a steel boat. This can only happen if there is a big difference between air- and water temperature, as in spring on the North Sea when you can get a hot day and the water is still only 12° or 13°C. Generally speaking the danger of condensation building up is overestimated. The way to get round it is efficient ventilation of the boat or good insulation, for which modern plastic foams are good. I am not particularly keen on foam insulation, for the same reasons that I would not have a teak deck on a steel boat. You should try it first without insulation.

Aluminium

Aluminium has never become really popular despite its advantages. This expensive boatbuilding material is lighter than steel, gives almost the same strength and doesn't rust. Aluminium does of course corrode but it forms a protective layer which reliably protects the material from further damage. Unfortunately, it is by far the most sensitive metal to electrolysis. On the scale of electrical voltage, aluminium stands almost at the top and so we must be particularly aware of this problem when we instal things in our yacht. It is recommended that you insulate electrically winches and other fittings, but I doubt whether this can be carried out consistently without compromising strength of construction.

However there are many very well-known aluminium yachts which have sailed on the seven seas for years and are still in excellent condition today. As with all areas of sailing, the choice of the right material for the boat is an entirely personal matter. The owner of an aluminium yacht whom I asked about his experiences told me once 'I am quite content, I couldn't imagine a better boatbuilding material. You just need to be a little careful, and I avoid mooring in a harbour next to a steel boat under any circumstances, as that would definitely damage my yacht'. As an offshore sailor I see another disadvantage of aluminium in that it cannot be repaired everywhere as can steel and synthetic materials: it oxidises so fast that any welding needs to be carried out in an inert atmosphere.

Reinforced concrete

Reinforced concrete was very popular in recent years because it is suitable for amateurs to build their own boats with, unlike any other material. You don't need any lavish mould, as the reinforced concrete is held by a steel framework encompassed with wire.

The main advantages of this cheap boatbuilding material are its strength and the almost complete absence of electrolysis problems. Mind you, compared with steel it has the disadvantage of being relatively brittle, and springs leaks much sooner when grounding or in a collision. Reinforced concrete is only suitable for yachts at least 9m long because of its weight. It seems that the 'concrete-boom' is dying down.

Aluminium yachts have many advantages (metal but no rust), but are very sensitive to electrolysis problems.

Multihulls

When the first catamarans and then trimarans were built shortly after the war, the sailing world was in a state of excitement, mainly because of the unimaginable speeds, of which the good old monohulls were not capable. After a few accidents when people died as catamarans capsized and could not be righted, the initial enthusiasm was somewhat dampened. If you look at the international boat market today, it is noticeable how few multihulls are still available and for sale. But it is a completely different picture when you come across anchorages occupied mainly by warm water sailors. Everybody who has decided on a multihull is filled with enthusiasm for their boat. Sailors who have spent half their lives on monohulls and then changed over often feel that they have only then discovered the real joy of sailing.

The main problem with multihulls, as conservative sailors see it, is the fact that they can capsize but cannot right themselves as monohulls can. But it would be wrong to conclude that catamarans or trimarans are therefore worse. They are just different. Catamaran fans point quite rightly to the fact that their boats have the advantage that they cannot sink. So, in the same way that a major leak spells the end of a yacht, catamaran sailors have to do their best to avoid capsizing.

There is only one way to do this, and that is:

reduce the surface area of the sails in time.

It is not easy to recognise this moment with a multihull. There is no alarm signal of heeling over excessively. If a float lifts out of the water it can already be too late, depending on the type of boat. I therefore think that a wind speed indicator is imperative on a multihull.

The sheets should never be set so that they can't be freed in seconds. Automatic cleats have been designed for this purpose which open and let the

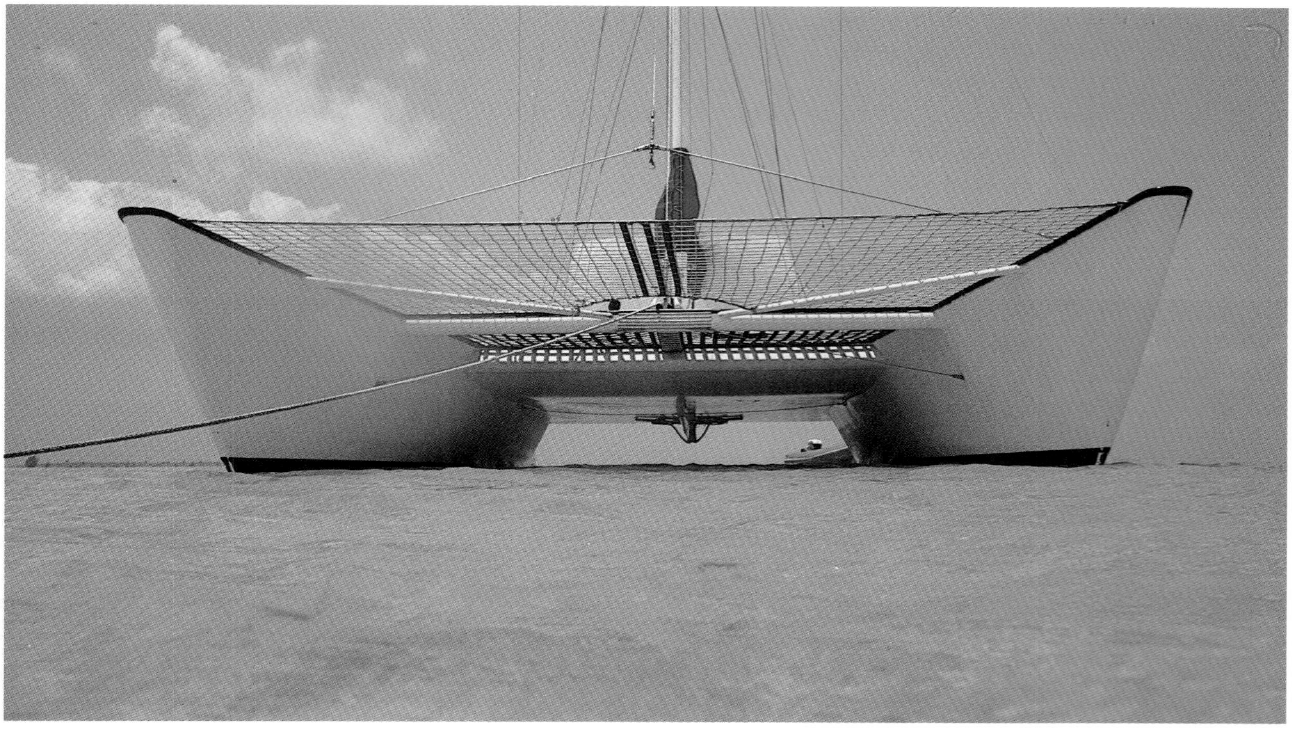

With huge catamarans like this it is advisable to put a trampoline between the hulls for reasons of safety and weight.

The 17m long catamaran *Taboo III* belonging to the round-the-world yachtsman Wolfgang Hausner. It is made of laminated plywood. The catamaran has an engine on the bridge deck, and the hydraulic propeller can be raised.

sheet free at a heeling angle of about 20°. Of course the mainsheet must in this case be so coiled and led so that it can also run freely through the blocks and not ruin the entire work of the automatic cleat because of a kink.

Wolfgang Hausner, one of the most experienced catamaran sailors in the world, thought up an irresistibly simple and above all cheap device, which works along the same lines. When he had established that his automatic cleat opened with no wind pressure, but only because of gliding down steeply from a large wave, he simply trimmed the main boom fully with the aid of a normal fishing line which he wound round several times. He had already set the mainsheet so that the boom would not crash into the shrouds if the fishing line broke, but would be caught by the (stretchy) main sheet. Everyone has to try for themselves how many times the fishing line has to be wound so that the point at which it should break is measured properly.

I don't altogether trust Ernie Hampton's method of preventing his trimaran from capsizing. He calculated the rigging of his *Soraya VIII* so that the mast comes down before the boat capsizes. I cannot imagine that the actual (as distinct from the calculated) unbreakability of your rigging can be estimated so exactly. Today there is still no method which would allow an ocean-going catamaran (Wolfgang Hausner: 'Ocean-going cats under 10m are criminal') to be righted without someone else's help. We just have to accept this, even if brilliant methods are constantly being 'invented' at someone's drawing board.

The aids designed for this such as balloons and parachutes have never worked in practice. You see lots of catamarans fitted with a disc-shaped buoyancy device at the top of the mast to avoid turning turtle. Hausner rightly finds this method unsuitable, and even dangerous. The disc would have to be

quite large to work, and this would present a target in strong winds. When the boat heels over, this streamlined disc, at the most disadvantageous point of the entire rigging, extends its surface area facing the wind quite considerably, thereby helping the boat capsize.

Forget all this. The best thing on a catamaran or trimaran is to do absolutely everything you can to avoid a capsize. But if this starts to happen, look at it as distress, which isn't a desperate situation if you are prepared for it. There should therefore always be a survival kit packed in a watertight container on the underside of the catamaran, in which you should have an axe, so that you can get into the lower hull without having to dive down.

If you wanted to build an extremely stable and therefore heavy catamaran, you would put its quite outstanding speed at stake. A multihull should always be built as a light-displacement-boat, so that it can display its great potential for speed. The catamaran *Wanderbird* from Devon (LOA 12.20m) turned out to be too heavy and was overloaded anyway, so that it achieved distances of only 120 miles a day. This wouldn't be too bad for a monohull, but is disappointing for a catamaran. As long as a cat is no longer

The catamaran's trump card is the amount of space on deck . . .

On the *Taboo III* the hydraulic propeller system is raised with the winch. There is no water resistance when under way!

The 17m long catamaran *Taboo III* can put into the shallowest coves with its draught of barely a foot.

than 13m, it shouldn't be made of steel or solid wood. It is best to stick with plywood, which is used today only in its laminated form.

I don't see the bad manoeuvrability of a catamaran as a real disadvantage. You spend most of your time on the open sea and rarely in confined harbours, so you don't need to be influenced by that. Neither should you be worried by the fact that a cat tacks more slowly. You will always have the opportunity on the open sea to make a lengthy turn or simply to wear round, a manoeuvre which doesn't present a catamaran with any great difficulty. However, it should be mentioned that given the increasing popularity of sailing as a sport, wide catamarans do cause inconvenience in marinas, as places are in short supply. On the other hand you can crawl into the far corners of a harbour with your shallow-draught catamaran, into places where no keel boat can drop anchor given its depth.

The weight of a multihull becomes a major problem when you install an engine in a catamaran or a trimaran. A cat with its restricted manoevrability would especially need a good engine in harbour. Most cat sailors make do with outboards, which should only be a temporary solution. Wolfgang Hausner actually lost his catamaran *Taboo* on a reef in New Guinea, and interestingly he thinks that a good inboard motor would have saved his boat. But an inboard motor raises a whole lot of problems for a catamaran. On the one hand it should be fitted amidships for weight reasons, so that a lavish propeller system would have to be installed between the hulls.

Wolfgang Hausner has fitted his new *Taboo*, a 17m cat made of laminated plywood, with an engine on the bridge deck, in the middle between the two hulls. The propeller sits on the end of a long shank between the hulls, and is driven by a hydraulic system. This comes quite near to the ideal solution, as long as Hausner can lift the propeller out of the water so that it doesn't slow him down under sail. The deep freeze and his diving compressor are also run off the engine.

You can only afford yourself the luxury of an inboard engine in each hull with really big catamarans. You can either use a normal propeller system as with a monohull, or – and this is the common solution – instal a so-called Z system. This isn't ideal either when you look at the cost and the technical problems, as the Z system has to be able to swivel.

I have met a lot of friends through sailing whose main argument for a catamaran is the fact that its movement is gentler on the stomach. Those who don't suffer from seasickness might laugh at the fact that choosing the right boat depends on reasons like this. But if you have experienced what it is like to lie about feeling like death on the deck of a rolling and pitching monohull boat, you can understand that for people like this a multihull is their last hope.

Sailing on a catamaran is of course slightly different, and its handling in a storm is particularly so. Whilst the drift anchor in monohulls is a useless and even dangerous tool, it so far seems to have proved very worthwhile on catamarans. You can put this down to the fact that multihulls almost always travel very flat in the water, and are much easier to hold head to wind above a specific point, ie the drift anchor, than a deep keel yacht with the high wind resistance of the bow.

The arguments I have used for and against multihulls so far are almost exactly the same for trimarans. It can generally be said that catamarans achieve greater speeds, but that they can capsize more easily. The floor plan in a trimaran should be easier, particularly if the cabin roof extends over all three hulls. A boat builder called Piver

Catamaran

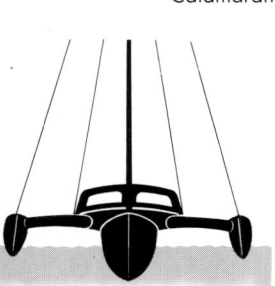

Trimaran

Multihulls need twice as large a berth as a monohull. This will eat into your money in marinas.

made a significant contribution to the distribution and development of trimarans by designing 'build-your-own' trimarans (out of plywood) which were so cheap that they caught on in America particularly with hippies as cheap floating accommodation. This didn't exactly lead to the Piver trimarans' popularity in harbours. One of the most interesting yacht clubs in the world, the otherwise sensible Seven Seas Cruising Association, stopped taking on any more multihull sailors into its club as a result.

Arguments for or against multihulls

- multihulls can capsize (the smaller, the sooner).

- multihulls are unsinkable.

- multihulls must be built light. Steel and GRP are too heavy as construction materials in yachts of 'our size'.

- multihulls offer a lot more space for the money than monohulls.

- multihulls are weight-sensitive, and space can often not be used.

- multihulls are more difficult to manoeuvre.

- multihulls are problematic in cramped harbours.

- multihulls are a lot faster.

- multihulls cannot sail so close to the wind.

- multihulls can be brought to anchor at sea in a storm.

- multihulls sail upright and have a more pleasant movement.

- installing an engine causes problems.

- self-steering systems are problematic because multihulls gain such speed in surf that the apparent wind direction changes.

An offshore boat of one's dreams, the ketch *Super-Maramu* belonging to the brilliant boat-builder and transatlantic sailor H. Amel.

The rig

The ketch

The ketch is a two-master, where the smaller mizzen mast stands forward of the stern, unlike the yawl. This rig used to be necessary on larger yachts, in the days of block and tackle and cotton sails. You had to subdivide the surface area of the sails because a sail over 30m² could not be managed by just one person. In my opinion, the only advantage of a ketch rig is the ability to divide the sails over the boat better in heavy weather. If the skipper of a single-masted yacht has to reef the mainsail carefully in an increasing light wind, he can furl it quite easily on a ketch and leave the foresail and mizzen instead.

The problems start with downwind courses. An otherwise well-trimmed sailing boat will tend to luff too much downwind and a mizzen sail is then even more problematic. Many warm-water sailors who have gone for a ketch rig agreed later that the mizzen was seldom of any use for this reason. Most of the time they sailed the ketch like a single-masted boat, so the yacht was naturally somewhat under-canvassed. Ketch rigging is not ideal when sailing dead downwind either, if you sail goosewinged, ie moving the mizzen and mainsail to different sides with the boom preventer. The mizzen sail casts so much tiresome wind shadow onto the mainsail that the latter greatly loses forward thrust.

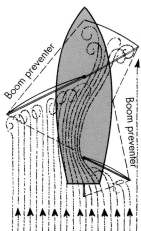

Ketch goosewinged; only the wind in the mizzen is not disturbed by eddies.

27

The sloop

Of the many types of rig, such as schooner, yawl, junk or lateen sails, apart from the ketch only the sloop has been successful. It is the easiest, cheapest and also the most versatile rig. With the high quality of stainless steel today even the tallest mast may be effectively stayed. This is why over 95% of all cruising yachts under 12m prefer sloop rig. I would arrange this single-mast rig as simply as possible, running just the shrouds and stays which are necessary for the mast's safety. You don't need a second forestay, even when it might seem as if a double forestay would make operating the boat easier. On a cruising yacht, the few minutes we would gain at the very best are irrelevant. The disadvantage of two forestays is the fact that the two wire cables never hold the same tension, but always have to be set with variable slack. Experience shows that this leads to strong vibrations in the cables, which weakens stainless steel in no time at all. A double forestay never contributes to safety. If we are beating, the luff of the jib acts as a 'second forestay'. On the other hand, I would have a double backstay for safety reasons. If there is only one and it breaks under the spinnaker, the mast

Round the world with one mast!

has no more support at all and will definitely be lost.

A second forestay in the form of a cutter-stay will give you additional safety. A cutter-rigged sloop seems to me ideal for yachts over 13m long with a small crew. It is possible here to divide the naturally large foresails. Where you might use the genoa in a light breeze, in a force four to five you can set the number one jib on the front forestay, and a smaller storm jib on the cutter stay. From force seven you take the outer jib or the storm jib away completely. And if turns really rough, bring the mainsail down and leave just the small jib on the cutter stay.

However, the cutter stay has the disadvantage that backstays have to be used, at least in high winds. This is because the cutter stay joins the mast some distance below the masthead, often at the height of the upper spreaders. It pulls the mast forward at this point, so the backstay is needed to provide a balancing tension. However, if you set the backstay at the same height as the cutter stay, it would get in the way of the mainsail. To avoid this, twin backstays are used, one run to either side of the stern. The windward one is tensioned, while the leeward one hangs loose. This type is also called a running backstay.

A Baltic sloop for the most demanding owner, built to international standards.

Rigging

Roller foresail and roller mainsail

These have such impressive advantages that they have been successful in cruising yachts. One tug on a rope and the jib is wound up and doesn't act as a target for the wind any more. There is space on the foredeck for anchor manoeuvres and you can become manoeuvrable in a matter of seconds with the aid of the jib. Roller foresails have been around for decades, but they are triumphing only slowly. Sailors have been let down too often in difficult conditions on a boat by these sensitive mechanisms. But in the age of stainless steel and synthetic materials these problems are being overcome. Precautions just have to be taken, so that if it does fail, it can be replaced by conservative sails.

A common cause of problems with the rolling mechanism is that the tack bearing can tilt over without enough tension. When you use a roller jib, you must ensure that the roller mechanism at the jib luff, rather than the forestay, bears the tension between mast and bow. Our synthetic sails are particularly sensitive to ultra violet light. With a roller, to which the sail is fixed constantly, it is therefore necessary to protect the sail properly with the help of a cover reaching from the foot to the top of the mast.

Today there are special roller foresails which can be used in different sizes. In high wind, you don't haul the jib out completely. An ideal shape for all courses can obviously not be expected with that sort of scaled-down sail. However, it should be sufficient for offshore cruising, mainly when not beating, where a well-cut sail is particularly important. The systems that have not proved themselves are the ones where the special sail is simply wrapped round a wire forestay, which ruins the sail on the stem fitting. Instead of this, a pole should be used with a slot into which you can run

The teething troubles of roller foresail systems have long since been overcome. It is a great idea, not only for small crews. One pull and the genoa is up.

1 The mainsail is rolled into the mast
2 The mainsail is wound onto the boom
3 Electric reefing system for the mainsail
4 Electric reefing system for the foresail

the luff boltrope (see also Hubert Raudaschl's view on page 34).

Rigging strength

Stainless steel is the only material used today for shrouds and stays. For standing rigging, use wire cables consisting of 19 single wires. The following thicknesses are recommended:

Standard rigging	
weight of boat in tonnes	diameter in mm
up to 1	4
up to 2	5
up to 4	6
up to 6	7
up to 10	8

This cable is not suitable for halyards. Cable made up of 133 wires is used here.

Halyards	
weight of boat in tonnes	diameter in mm
up to 2	4
up to 6	5
up to 10	6

It has always been disputed whether the terminals should be pressed, rolled or screwed on. Personally I have always had the most trust in Norseman terminals, which, although they aren't as strong as roller terminals, can be fastened with things you have on board and are much easier to monitor.

The most common bottlescrews are made of stainless steel, but there is also nothing wrong with bottlescrews made of atlas bronze. They should have more or less the same breaking point as that of the wire cable.

Designed breaking point of stainless steel wire cable			
4mm	1.5t	7mm	4.7t
5mm	2.4t	8mm	6.1t
6mm	3.4t	10mm	9.5t

Bottlescrews should be equipped with a toggle, which avoids the wire

twisting and breaking. I don't like locking nuts for securing the bottlescrews. They actually weaken the bottlescrews because they exert extra pressure when they are screwed up tightly enough to fulfil their purpose. The same security can be attained through using an 8mm stainless steel wire, run around the casing of the shrouds. Bend the twisted end of the wire inwards and protect it with gaffer tape, so no-one can cut themselves on it.

The weakest part of the rigging determines its strength. This is why the feet of the wire cables, the chainplates, have to have the right dimensions. This is one of the points you should look out for when buying a boat. Never accept chainplates which are merely bolted onto the deck. The chainplates should be laminated into the side of synthetic boats. It is stupid on a cruising yacht to use inner shrouds, which are attached to the deck structure and not the side of the boat. The angle of tension to the mast is less favourable here, and the cabin structure is rarely super strong anyway.

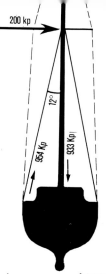

Under a pressure of 200 kN, at 3m width there is a pressure of 933 kN on the foot of the mast and 954 kN on the lower shrouds.

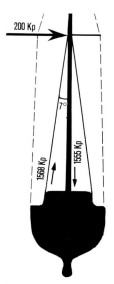

The same boat but with the lower shrouds further in 1555 kN on the foot of the mast and 1568 kN on the lower shrouds. The cabin construction is under a lot of pressure.

Top: The shrouds are attached on the very edge, the chainplates are long enough to spread the tension over a broad surface.
Left: Clamp terminals
Centre: Bottlescrew, secured by a clevis pin
Right: Toggles, used to avoid destructive shear stresses.

An impressive cruising yacht. You can see thousands of sea miles in the mainsail, and in the skipper, who knows what he's doing. He has reefed the mainsail at the right time and not even used a smaller foresail. That comes next. For the moment, the old girl is moving at maximum speed. Six or seven knots? Does it really matter?

Tension of the shrouds

The correct adjustment of the shroud tension seems to present great difficulties for many sailors. You shouldn't be talked into a flexible rig, which is so popular with regatta sailors. It is particularly dangerous to put variable tension on stainless steel. It will break much more easily than if there is a constantly high tension on it. My old teacher Eric Hiscock has three rules for shroud tension, which make work extremely easy as long as you stick to them rigidly.

1 All opposite pairs of shrouds should have the same tension
2 The forestay should have the strongest tension, then both the mainstays, then both the pairs of lower shrouds, and finally the backstay (in this order)
3 The shrouds should be so strongly tensioned that in a position of 10° heel you can just feel the slack in the leeward shrouds. But you should not be able to see the slack

With these adjustments the rigging is well under control. You will often have to make adjustments to it at first, but the tension should then remain constant. On older wooden boats it is difficult to achieve this relative tension, and every synthetic and steel yacht must be in a position to withstand such tension. The mast should stand up straight, which can only be plumbed from land. It can lean slightly forward, but must not be curved, which you can easily tell if you look up at the top of the mast from the bottom. The last and final adjustment is carried out at sea, when the yacht is heeling at 10°.

Maintaining the rigging

Luckily you don't have to worry much about stainless steel. However, any rust should be removed as it can dam-age the steel. I found a cheap synthetic cleaning material worked very well for this purpose and was much more effective than special steel cleaner which is extremely expensive. The bottlescrew threads are greased before use; sprays like WD40 are not suitable because they evaporate very quickly. It is important to check the wire cables and terminals regularly, as well as those in the mast. This should be done at least every 1,000 sea miles. A single broken strand in a halyard doesn't weaken the wire cable, but it does show that either the diameter of the blocks is too small or that it isn't turning smoothly on them.

Lightning protection

The likelihood of being struck by lightning is extremely low. However, I felt more at ease after I had attached a 3m long, 5mm diameter copper wire to all the shrouds and the stays as well as the foot of the mast with a rubber clamp. I then simply towed the wires after me in the water if there was a storm. But I would strongly advise against keeping these wires in the water all the time, because the rigging can then suffer electrolytic damage. On a steel yacht you don't need any lightning protector. You are completely protected by the Faraday cage principle.

Sails

I would see the following sails as usual for sloop rigging: mainsail, genoa, working jib, no 1 jib, and a storm jib. You might be able to persuade the sailmaker to cut a mainsail which doesn't need any battens. It doesn't look as good, but you will have a lot less trouble. On all courses it is quite all right to furl and set the mainsail. I don't think a storm mainsail, or trysail, is necessary. If you were to need it because of the wind strength for sailing to windward, the conditions are guaranteed to be such that you aren't able to beat any more. On any course

Backstay tensioner to control the mast curvature. Not entirely necessary on a cruising yacht, but who would say no to a bit of extra speed?

Balloon, asymmetrical spinnaker, blister, genoa, reacher, etc. These are all particularly light sails for free wind, and are a good substitute for heavy spinnakers on a yacht with a small crew.

Cutter rigging is well suited to a cruising yacht. On the high seas you don't often gybe so the strains on the outer jib through the cutter stay are rare.

you will be able to manage well with just a foresail. Boom-less sails can't cause any great damage.

I strongly advise against a boom jib. Its only advantage is the fact that it doesn't need to be handled when turning. There are however a lot of disadvantages; the unwieldy boom takes up a lot of precious space on the foredeck. In swell and light wind, working on the foredeck can be extremely dangerous because of the boom. It is almost unusable when sailing downwind, if you don't want to run the risk of an unintentional gybe. It is very difficult to attach a boom preventer for safety. Hubert Raudaschl from St Wolfgang in Austria, who is an Olympic medal winner and one of the most successful sailors in the world, is not only an enthusiastic sailor in his free time but quite an expert sailmaker too. He is well qualified to give us a few extra tips on our sails:

'It is well worth considering your sailing equipment or roller

reefing system when you adjust it, and particularly when you are buying it new. An offshore sailor should be quite clear about whether he is going to race and run certain risks in bad weather such as changing the sails on the foredeck, or if he would like to have easy sails and safe handling of the yacht under sail despite an unpractised crew.

'Firstly, the racing sailor who has qualified crew to hand and at the same time wants to keep the financial expenditure on sails within limits, should go for conventional sails such as number one genoa, number two genoa, number three genoa with a reef or number four genoa as storm jib (the above-mentioned genoa, jib, small working jib and storm jib would also do). A mainsail with two or three rows of reefs and a storm mainsail, or trysail, are enough.

'For ocean sailors, specialist downwind sails such as a big boy, two similar genoas or a double booster are useful. Specialist downwind sails are useless in the Mediterranean because their area of use is small.

'Secondly, for 15 years there have been firms manufacturing advanced jib reefing systems. The reef-foresails themselves have been developing fast over the same period. Every sailor who decides on a roller reefing system is recommended to get a good quality rolling-reef genoa. Standard genoas delivered by shipyards are made of poor quality fabric for price reasons, and sails like this are often more similar to a spinnaker than a foresail when reefed. Sailing close-hauled is almost impossible with sails like this.

'Before getting a mainsail reefing system, everyone should ask themselves whether they want maximum sailing comfort or optimum boat speed.

'Roller reefing systems on the aft side of the mast or integrated in the mast are very comfortable to handle, but impair sailing quality. The sail can only be fitted with a small roach despite vertical battens. The profile of a sail like this should be significantly flatter than a conventionally cut and battened sail anyway, because the sail can only rolled into the mast if it has a flat cut.

'The sailtrainer mainboom reefing system is a good alternative, which makes a full-cut and battened mainsail possible. The performance of this sail is so good that it is suitable for the demands of regattas. The only loss of speed, which is extremely low anyway, stems from the somewhat flatter cut on the foot, to ease the reefing.'

If you use twin staysails on a long voyage, you can make the difficult procedure of setting and furling much easier if you can open both sails on one roller stay. The foot of this double roller stay should be about 20% of the ship's length from the mast.

Finally, be careful: It almost goes without saying, but I will reiterate the fact that everything in your rigging is better over- than undersized, and that you must not be influenced by regatta sailors. Regatta sailors will always go to the danger limit when measuring their rigging, for weight and wind resistance reasons. This plays no part at all for the offshore cruiser. Stronger rigging is of course a shade more expensive. Changing it later would naturally be expensive, so you must consider this when you buy it to avoid too high an extra cost in the long term. Be careful: unpredictable strain can occur in a storm (eg falling into the trough of a wave!).

Specialist downwind sails like these on H. Amel's *Fango* are typical for ocean-going cruising yachts.

The engine

Outboard or inboard

This alternative only exists on boats up to an overall length of 7m. The disadvantages of an outboard engine make a short list:

1 Petrol on board is a fire risk.
2 It can become impossible to use the engine in high seas because the propeller comes out of the water.
3 High fuel consumption.

In spite of these disadvantages, using an outboard on very small yachts can hardly be avoided because there isn't enough room to instal an inboard with a lavish propeller system. The decisive disadvantage as I see it is the fact that the propeller won't sit deep enough in the water, even using a long-shafted model, to guarantee in thick swell that the propeller stays in the water all the time. Of course it does no harm if it surfaces for a moment and the engine roars, but this lowers its effectiveness considerably. If surfacing became the rule, it could cause great damage to the bearings.

If possible, it is best to use the outboard in a shaft. When you hang it up on the stern, there is the danger that a following wave will flood your precious engine. The fact is, unbelievable though this may seem, that many established firms instal parts in outboards which are only seawater-tight to a degree and will be worn out after three or four years. The engine should therefore be painstakingly protected against seawater.

If you order an outboard engine for your boat, you must make it clear that you don't need it for a speed boat but for a slow displacement craft. Many firms will then fit the engine with a special propeller and you can better use the power available at your low speed. I would see the lower limit for coastal waters as about 5PS.

The grating protects the engine from foreign objects being sucked in through the cold water inlet, such as plastic bags, ropes or fish.

I would recommend the following engine capacities:

weight of boat	engine capacity
up to 700kg	c. 5PS or c. 4kW
up to 800kg	c. 8PS or c. 6kW
up to 1,000kg	c. 10PS or c. 8kW

It should be pointed out that the engine capacities shown are not enough to be able to travel against a very strong wind or storm. An outboard motor isn't suitable for this, and raising the engine capacity wouldn't make it any more suitable.

Inboard petrol engine

The main disadvantage of a petrol engine is the risk of explosions and fire that go with it. Even if you fit the engine with protection devices to reduce this risk, you can never really rule it out. A compressor should at least be fitted, which when the ignition key is used, will suck out the engine room until the engine can be started. A gas detector is worthwhile in any case, as long as no sparks occur when turning it on or off. This would cause the mixture of petrol and air to explode (only this explodes, petrol itself just burns) before the detector has had time to indicate anything is wrong. However, this disaster can occur if there is an unnoticed leak in the fuel pipes.

As long as you have petrol on board you must be extremely careful, and never show it the same indifference that car drivers do. Leaking petrol systems in cars are not dangerous in comparison, because the petrol vapour escapes into the air, and no dangerous mixture of petrol and air can occur.

The reason why some sailors decide to go for a petrol engine even so is not so much the price but the low weight. This is one of its main advantages compared with a diesel engine. The higher fuel cost is hardly a matter worth considering given the small quantities used on small boats. Another recommendation for a petrol engine is of course that it is considerably quieter than a diesel engine.

A big disadvantage though is the sensitive ignition system without which no petrol engine can function. An ignition system like this is a problem on a boat, where the air is always full of damp and seawater corrodes contacts. It is a wise precaution to start the engine up every morning, as long as you are out at sea, because the heat this produces will dry out the engine, particularly the spark plugs, distributor etc.

Diesel engine
This has only advantages, apart from its weight and considerably stronger vibration. Fuel consumption is lower, diesel is cheaper, it doesn't vapourise at normal temperatures so that it can't result in a dangerous mixture with air, and there are hardly any sensitive parts.

The installation of a diesel engine can only be carried out by experts. Nowadays flexible mountings are normally used. The vibrations transferred to the body of the boat should be as low as possible. If you fit an engine in a rigid position, the life of the whole boat – particularly if it is synthetic – will be significantly shortened.

Installing a single-cylinder diesel engine is particularly troublesome. You need a certain skill, and luck with it, to manage to instal it so that it runs quietly. The result is not always satisfactory in all engine speed ranges, even with two cylinders. The vibration of the entire boat is nerve-wracking, particularly in neutral. You should therefore set your normal 'slow ahead' speed not only for reasons of economical fuel consumption, but also taking into account the engine vibrations, if you have any respect for your boat. The more cylinders the engine has, the less of a problem this is.

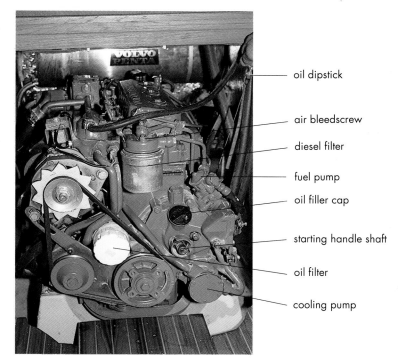

oil dipstick

air bleedscrew

diesel filter

fuel pump

oil filler cap

starting handle shaft

oil filter

cooling pump

How powerful an engine do you need for your boat? The most common view on this is that 3PS of engine capacity per ton is sufficient for a sailing boat. I don't agree, and see this as the lower limit. You want to use your engine not only in calm, but also when leaving a harbour in strong winds and current, and in high seas. My yacht was motorised at 3PS per ton, which gave it a speed of 6 knots in calm water. Against a force 4 wind and a corresponding swell I managed only 2 or 3 knots.

It is interesting how badly informed even so-called experts can be. Before I started my world tour, I went to my boat's engine-manufacturers. One of the managers couldn't believe that this enormous engine only brought my 6 ton boat up to a speed of 6 knots. He firmly believed that you would reach 9 knots at least with 20PS. He had never heard of a maximum displacement speed (2.2 x square root of the length of the waterline for sailing boats). If I had to choose an engine again for a sailing boat, I would go to 4PS per ton, and for a motor sailing boat much more.

You should have a spare drive for the water pump amongst your spares. Changing it is easy. Get the dealer to show you.

Problems You are obviously going to have to do some work on your engine, even if you don't think you are very gifted mechanically. You just can't go to a garage every time there's a problem, and you will have to carry out repairs at sea yourself with what you have available on board.

One comfort is that with a normal diesel engine, the only problem you can have is with the fuel pipes. The most common causes of this are a dirty filter or diesel pipes, or air in the fuel pipes. You can recognise this by the engine not running smoothly, or if it only runs for a few seconds after starting, dies and won't restart. You should be able to manage here with what you have on board, although it isn't as easy as it seems.

The manufacturers will have given you a set of gaskets. It is always advisable to throw away the old gaskets. Copper gaskets should never be used twice, but if you haven't got any new copper gaskets to hand, you can anneal the old ones on the stove. They will then get back their old flexibility and through this their seal. You should therefore make sure everything is always clean. A small piece of dirt or a spot of paint can ruin the seal.

All parts of a diesel engine should be cleaned in the fuel itself before putting them together. Diesel is itself a penetrative oil like the ones you use at home or on the boat to loosen rusty screws (such as WD40). The engine must be bled after work has been done on the fuel system. Lots of engines have a special air bleed screw for this. The only thing you have to do then is pump some diesel by hand using the lever on the fuel pump until there are no more bubbles at the bleed screw, just pure fuel. If there is no bleed screw, the engine manual will tell you how to bleed the pump.

You should always try to get as much documentation as possible for your engine. Even if you can't follow the repair manual instructions, working on the cylinder heads for example, you may end up finding a skilled mechanic in an isolated harbour who will be able to follow these instructions much more easily. Ask the manufacturer for the torques of the different screws. You can cause a lot of damage to your engine by turning screws too tightly. The ideal solution is to work with torque spanners so that you don't have to rely on the feel, which unmechanically-minded people like ourselves don't have anyway.

You can generally go on the principle that it can do no harm if you have too many tools and spare parts on board. The tools supplied to you by the manufacturer are definitely not sufficient, particularly on a long voyage. For a petrol engine, I would have the following spares: a set of gaskets, spark plugs, spark coil, points, and perhaps even another carburettor. For a diesel engine, you should have spare seals, oil filters and injectors on board. You can't do work on the latter yourself, so if a problem arises, the only thing to do is to change all the injectors (two in the case of a two-cylinder engine).

If you have the choice of having your engine painted in different colours, go for as light a colour as possible. You will then be able to see when there is a fuel or an oil leak, and follow up the cause immediately. It is particularly important to keep the engine compartment easily accessible. You should consider this when the engine is installed, as the length of its life and its ability to function are extremely dependent on this. Ideally, all the casing around the engine should be removable so that you can easily carry out the necessary routine work from any side. A smaller diesel engine (up to two cylinders) has the advantage that it can be started by hand if need be. This possibility should be taken into account when the engine is installed, so that there is enough room to turn the crank.

Opposite page: Those who like plenty of space for sunbathing and are susceptible to seasickness are best off with a trimaran. It is a boat for the South Seas.

38

It can only do a diesel engine good to be run as often as possible. Rust will therefore not be able to set in on the piston rings in the cylinder compartments, which would considerably shorten the engine's life. This should also be taken into account when you lay it up for the winter. The position of the pistons during the winter should always be changed slightly, by hand.

If you look after your diesel engine properly, it should have a running life of about 5,000 hours. That is almost once round the world, with the engine running. Without wishing to advertise them, the following firms produce reliable diesel engines, given the experiences of my friends: Sabb, Fayrman, Mercedes, Peugeot, Renault, Yanmar and Perkins. For yachts over 15 tons, the MAN ship's engine 'Bavarian power' is good, or the wickedly expensive Gardner.

Cooling There is divided opinion on this. On paper, an air-cooled engine would seem trouble-free. This type of system is only possible with an engine over a particular size. Ventilation shafts have to be painstakingly designed, which ensure the engine is efficiently cooled. When you consider how expensive each square metre of your yacht is, the space lost for ventilation shafts makes it a very costly solution. It would of course have to be protected against water flowing in, and apart from that you would hardly be able to get round water-cooling the exhaust, which heats up to over 400°C.

Personally, I would therefore always go for a water-cooled engine. You can spend a long time deliberating whether you use a single- or a dual-circuit cooling system. In the former, seawater is pumped into and around the engine's cooling system and exhaust. This is a simple system, which needs only a pump. The disadvantage of it is that lime and salt begin to precipitate at engine temperatures over 65°C, which will sooner or later block the cooling

system. You can therefore only use the engine running cool, ie 60°C. Consumption is higher because of this, and the engine's life is reduced.

Dual-circuit cooling avoids this disadvantage. The engine is connected to a closed cooling system similar to that of a car, which can work on fresh water. The engine is run near to boiling point in much more favourable temperature conditions. The task taken on by the airstream on a car radiator of cooling down the cooling system, is left to a second cooling circuit in a dual-circuit system, which uses seawater.

The disadvantage of this system is that you need a second pump. But a dual-circuit cooling system should in the end be safer, because if one pump breaks down, the temperature will only rise slowly and the engine won't be ruined.

With a single-circuit system, if the pump breaks down or the ventilation shaft blocks up, you only have a few seconds to stop the engine. Single-circuit freshwater cooling systems have been successfully used on steel boats. The pipes are welded inside onto the side (or in the steel rudder), so that the heat from the hot water can be given off through the wall of the boat into the seawater flowing past. Cooling the exhaust still presents a problem though, or the exhaust remains uncooled, and needs to take up a lot of space.

Instruments are necessary to monitor your engine properly. The most important one is a thermometer, even if a thermostat has been installed in the engine which keeps the temperature within the required range. The thermostat can break down, which you can only tell by the thermometer. Secondly, you need an oil-pressure gauge which will tell you whether there is enough oil in the engine or if the oil pump is working properly. The oil pressure gauge usually shows a very high reading when starting the engine, whilst it drops off during the journey. It is best to ask the manufacturers how low it can sink without the engine being endangered. You will also need a rev counter of course, to stick to the optimum rpm.

In practice there are only two dangers for a diesel boat engine: overheating if the cooling system breaks down, or loss of pressure in the lubrication through a leak in an oil pipe. Both of these spell death for the engine. If the instruments haven't been watched as carefully as they should have been at sea, you will usually only notice an impending disaster when it is too late. I would therefore strongly recommend an acoustic alarm system, which goes off if the water temperature oversteps a certain mark or if the oil pressure drops beneath a certain limit.

Tanks These should be installed so that the fuel is drawn in by a pump. A mechanical pump is best for a diesel engine, so that you don't have to rely on electricity in an emergency. With diesel you should be particularly careful that the tank is kept as clean as possible. For this reason a copper tank for diesel fuel is out of the question because a sort of rubbery mass is secreted which would quickly block the filters. A fuel tank must always be fitted with a breather pipe opening onto the deck.

Condensation always builds up in the tank, depending on how much air is in it. For this reason it is best particularly with diesel to run the engine with the tank as full as possible. In regions where the water and air temperatures vary greatly, the condensation must be removed from the tank from time to time. Water is heavier than diesel fuel and therefore drops to the bottom of the tank. It would be ideal in this case to let the water run out from the bottom of the tank using a valve that can be turned on and off. You can tell by the colour when the diesel itself starts

to come out. The pipes leading into a diesel tank should obviously not go right to the bottom, because water and dregs would often be drawn into it. A diesel tank should never be completely emptied, to avoid having to bleed it all the time. Even if the nozzle doesn't go to the bottom, it is possible because of the boat's movements that either dirt (usually algae, which thrive in condensation) or water is unsettled in the tank and is sucked in. You will notice this immediately by the engine spluttering. The engine won't generally stop because of this but will be far less efficient.

A lot of boats have a so-called 'day tank'. This doesn't look very good but is actually a very reliably functioning if crude piece of apparatus. In this case the engine isn't reliant on a pump any more. The principle behind the day-tank is simple: a relatively small tank with only a few litres' capacity is installed above the engine, which you either fill with fuel yourself or pump it up from the main tank. The tank should either have an indicator or be transparent, so that you can avoid running it dry, and getting air in the engine.

In normal use, a diesel engine will consume roughly 0.1 litres per PS per hour. It should use hardly any oil. It will only improve the running of the engine if you change the oil as often as possible. The manufacturer will usually stipulate which type of oil you should use, and you should definitely stick to this recommendation. If HD 20 oil is called for no matter what the time of year, whatever happens you should try to get this thin oil in hot areas as well, which is often not so easy. You would do well to stock up with supplies accordingly, but don't overdo it. Oil can go off like any other organic substance including diesel, so two years should be taken as a rough limit for stocking up in advance.

Propeller and gearbox As a rule, the engine's power is still transferred to

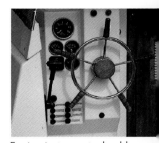

Engine instruments should be readable from the steering position or from the rudder. Water temperature is the most important.

When the wind drops in the evenings, there is a great temptation to press the starter. But who would spoil nature with the roar of a diesel engine? We will just have to wait till tomorrow to reach harbour. Nights alone with the sea are one of the thrills of offshore cruising.

the propeller via a mechanical gear-box, which should definitely have a reverse gear. It is the only way to 'brake' your boat. But don't forget that the gearbox also needs an oil change, even if not as often. A propeller shaft is flanged onto this which usually enters the water through the boat just behind the gearbox. Nowadays it usually rests on rubber seals. In southerly regions you should not only run the engine often, but also ensure from time to time that the propeller is turning. This is because rock-hard little mussels attach themselves between the rubber seals and the propeller shaft, which will badly damage if not ruin the seals if they aren't removed in time. This rubber seal is lubricated with water. Water must be prevented from forcing its way into the inner boat over the propeller shaft.

The stuffing box fulfils this task, and must be watched particularly carefully. Inside it is the so-called stuffing box gasket, which is pressed hard onto the turning propeller shaft depending on the pressure on the two seals. The stuffing box gasket is only a piece of cotton cord soaked in grease. There is usually a grease nipple on the stuffing box which should be turned a bit further each time after the engine has been running, so that these cords are greased again. The pressure can be changed by just altering the position of the nuts. The art of installing the stuffing box correctly lies in not letting it run dry but on the other hand allowing as little water to get into the boat as possible. Try to adjust it so that one drop of water every 5 to 10 seconds filters from the stuffing box into the inner boat with the propeller running. Care must be taken not to tighten the seals more on one side than on the other, because otherwise one of the two screws will certainly break. It is therefore better to be patient and tighten the left screw half a turn, and then the right screw half a turn etc. If the correct adjustment is found at last, the position must be fixed with the locknuts. At regular intervals (20 run-

Only on a very big yacht should you consider having two engines. You get double the trouble with few advantages! These propellers are far too close together to give you the theoretical gain in manoeuvrability which should come from using them in opposite directions.

Installing a drive shaft.

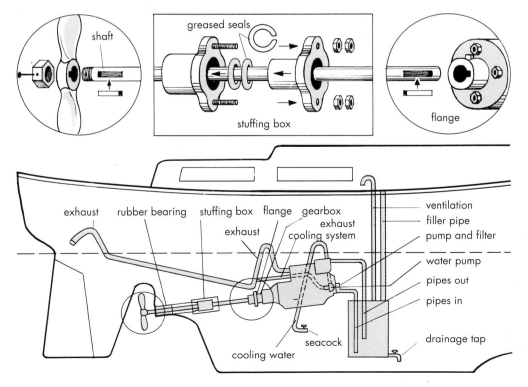

It is a good idea to keep the engine running for safety reasons when entering a narrow fjord or along a mountainous shore. The squalls shown here can disappear in seconds or even veer through 90°.

ning hours), you should check to see if the stuffing box needs adjusting. If it has already been tightened as far as it will go, it must be packed again. You can also do this when the boat is in the water. When you have got the new casing ready, it is a matter of seconds before the cord seals are put on and the minor 'water invasion' is stopped.

You will have to rely on experts when it comes to calculating the propeller's diameter and slope. On a sailing yacht a double-vaned one is generally preferable because of its lower water resistance. It is a little-known fact that a double-vaned propeller running at a low rpm creates quite considerable water resistance, so that it is far preferable to take the clutch in and immobilise the propeller blades, aligned vertically behind the skeg. The 'correct' position of the propeller screw can be marked with a

piece of tape on the shaft in the engine room. Doing this will also put less wear on the bearing and the stuffing box.

I am not keen on folding propellers, which create little resistance even if they are situated behind the skeg. Barnacles or dirt all too often prevent them from starting automatically, and they are very bad for reversing. Propellers like this therefore have no justification on cruising yachts, where a tenth of a knot difference in speed is not important. An adjustable propeller would be much more useful. With these you can change the slope of the propeller with a support. You can even save yourself the mechanical turning mechanism, because it is possible to turn the propeller blades to 'reverse'. But even if you are sailing with the engine running, you have the advantage that the slope can be adjusted so

44

that it is a bit steeper, and the engine, which is under an extra burden from the sails moving the boat forward, will work more effectively. The smaller the system the lower the efficiency unfortunately, so with boats under 13m they aren't ideal. In addition, you have to get a second stuffing box because the support for the propeller blades also has to lead outside to the propeller.

The only advantage of folding propellers is their low water resistance. How much difference does this make – 0.1 or 0.2 knots? If barnacles have grown on the propeller, it sometimes doesn't open, and is not very effective in reverse.

Checklist	
Every week	Battery acid level and seals
Before every trip	Oil level in the engine
At the start of every trip	Stuffing box with the engine running (one drop every 10 seconds) Exhaust seals (leaks recognisable by black spots; hold white paper over suspect areas, which would turn black)
During the trip	Temperature and oil pressure (every 10 minutes)
After every trip	Turn the grease nipples on the water pump and the stuffing box; with the propeller in gear press the throttle in fully
Every 20 hours	Water level in the dual-circuit cooling system
Every 50 hours	Oil level in the engine, oil change (depending on the type of system), clear the ventilation shafts
Every 250 hours	Change the oil filters

The interior

Layout

The interior will naturally be determined by the size of the boat. It would be awkward on small yachts to divide further what already limited space you have with partitions. On large yachts (10m and up) I would actually go for dividing up the space because I believe it best meets man's cavedwelling instinct and makes the boat more cosy.

The normal division of a small offshore yacht will always be living area and fo'c's'le. If you want to use the fo'c's'le as a living room, stow as little as possible in that space, and particularly no sails. These belong in the lockers in the fo'c's'le, or simply on deck, which is certainly not the worst alternative. The fo'c's'le is the least com-

fortable part of a boat when under way. The bunks can become practically unusable in a rough sea, and the crew will live largely in the bunks next to the companionway anyway.

Wide beds can be comfortable in harbour, but disadvantageous on the open sea. A double bunk might seem like a good prospect but in reality is ridiculous in an offshore yacht, as you will hardly be able to sleep well there when on reaching or windward courses. The bunks must of course be fitted out so that you are protected from falling out. You can do this by rigging up a lee cloth or with bunk boards. On our world trip we used bunk boards which were secured to a hinge under the mattress in harbour, so that they only needed to be folded out on the open sea. They proved worthwhile. The hood of a pram over the

High living in Sunbeam 32 from Schöchl!

companionway extends the living area of our small yacht quite considerably. You only have to shut the hatches occasionally (in rain and in a force 8 gale), and so you do at least get the feeling of a larger space.

On bigger yachts we can afford a cabin in the stern. This is ideal if you are sailing with several friends who can then have their own self-contained area. However, it must be big enough not to be a 'rat's nest', as a well-known boatbuilder once said of a small cabin aft.

You can even build a centre cockpit in boats over 12m long, which I particularly like, although it has a string of disadvantages. The greatest disadvantage is the fact that it is by far and away the wettest part of the whole boat. Apart from that we are then 'wasting' the most comfortable part of the

The 'living room' in the Bavaria 320.

The beautiful Bavaria 42. But what does such a plush living area look like draped with oily things or wet swimming gear?

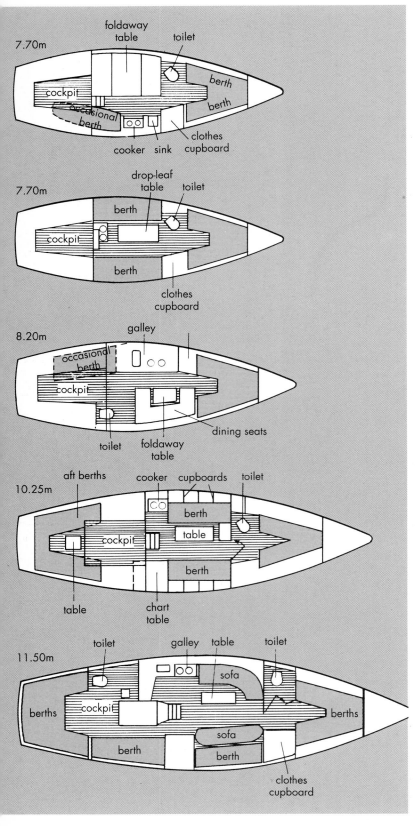

7.70m — foldaway table, toilet, berth, berth, cockpit, occasional berth, cooker, sink, clothes cupboard

7.70m — drop-leaf table, toilet, berth, cockpit, berth, clothes cupboard

8.20m — galley, occasional berth, cockpit, toilet, foldaway table, dining seats

10.25m — aft berths, cooker, cupboards, toilet, berth, table, cockpit, berth, table, chart table

11.50m — toilet, galley, table, toilet, sofa, berths, cockpit, berths, sofa, berth, berth, clothes cupboard

boat when the boat is moving because of the engine underneath.

Ideally the boat would be so big that you could get from the living area through the centre cockpit into the stern, without having to open the companionway hatches at all in bad weather. If the engine is underneath the centre cockpit, you can get right up close for overhauling or repair work. You must be extremely careful though that any water that gets into the cockpit escapes down the bilge pipes and can't get into the engine-room. This is a tough task but feasible.

An important requirement on a seagoing boat is of course that the cockpit drains itself, and over and above that a **bridge deck**. Designs with only one normal wooden bulkhead in use on the open sea to prevent water from the cockpit getting into the cabin are extremely dangerous. If a lot of water gushes in, the cockpit is usually brim full for a moment. Even though most of the water will be thrown out again immediately by the boat's movement, hundreds of litres will remain which could be in the cockpit for some minutes and with a wooden bulkhead would easily find their way into the cabin. Quite apart from the discomfort this would cause, for safety reasons it must be avoided at all costs.

It is a matter of taste whether you allow for a so-called **wet cell** near the companionway, where the toilet, shower, galley and oilskins cupboard are installed. Experience shows that unbelievable amounts of water are brought into the inner boat with oilskins, even without water coming aboard in bad weather, and this can spoil things completely. You can prevent this to a certain extent if the crew member changes in this wet cell after the companionway and leaves their wet oilskins in there. This sort of facility is only possible on big yachts though, where it doesn't matter if living space is lost at the widest part of the boat.

The **navigation area** with its precious instruments should be near the companionway, but well protected against spray. Designing the chart table big enough that there is room for a normal sea chart on it is of course easier said than done. We will seldom have that much room on our yacht and a surface area of 70 × 50cm is plenty. I would even say that a chart table is unnecessary on a round-the-world yacht. In this respect it must always be remembered that yachts are so expensive that there really can be no reason to waste space. When you are under way out of sight of land you will have no need for a chart at all, or at the most once a day to establish your noon position. However, this will never happen if the table is already covered, and you can also use the dining table as a base. Near land I can hardly imagine anyway that anyone would be navigating from the chart and eating at the same time. You can usually only sit down in peace to eat when the all-clear has been given.

I have had excellent experience of **hanging tables**, but I also know a lot of widely travelled offshore sailors who will say only negative things about them. The main advantage for me is not that I can eat at the table without having to worry about plates and salt pots flying all over the place, but that there is a place on the rolling boat where the ship's cook can put all his things for cooking at any time. A hanging table will rarely work perfectly from the start. You will usually have to experiment for a while until you get the swinging movements to match the rolling of the boat by adjusting the hanging bits with pieces of elastic. It doesn't do any harm with a table on single gimbals to fit it with a small rail which you have to take off in harbour, otherwise eating becomes a struggle.

If you do without a hanging table, you will have to resort to a whole list of less-than-ideal solutions when under

Living inside the Hausners' catamaran *Taboo II*. This picture doesn't show even half the living area. The 'bedroom' is in the other hull.

way. A rail at least 5cm high around the edge of the table helps of course. A wet underlay spread on the table prevents the crockery from slipping about to a certain degree. In very bad weather conditions eating and sleeping is actually most comfortable on the floor. It is first and foremost a matter of personal taste whether the table is in the middle of the saloon or in a special dining area. I prefer a dining area (particularly in yachts 9m long and up) because I think they make the space more cosy. If you are a sociable person and like to have a lot of visitors on board in harbour, then I would recommend the more conservative arrangement with the table in the middle, as you can then hold larger gatherings. Mind you, the table is in the middle of the passageway.

The galley

I've got something against plastic plates and don't find them at all practical either. The only advantage is that they don't break. Apart from that they get scored by knives and they attract dirt. On our world trip we had normal porcelain and not one piece was broken. It is however a prerequisite that the cupboard in the pantry is fitted with the necessary shelves and sections to prevent the crockery from slipping back and forth.

Be careful with cutlery as frequent washing in salt water can badly damage silver electrolytically, and the steel

A hanging table is suspended on single gimbals. Even in rough weather it should not throw its contents off. It works too. The table and the red wine will stay horizontal even in gale force 6.

Oysters don't demand great cooking ability of the ship's cook. However, the galley on this Najad is also equipped for the most sophisticated cook.

This table on a Najad gives free access to the fo'c's'le for a small crew. If it is opened out there is enough room at it for eight people.

in your knives (even if they are stainless steel) will be weakened through electrolysis and they will soon be as sharp as a razor edge. If you buy mugs so that you can give hot cups of coffee to the person freezing at the helm, you should try them out beforehand: they shouldn't conduct the heat so well that the helmsman can't hold it in his hands at all. We found that enamel soup bowls were no use as we kept on burning our fingers on them. Enamel saucepans are dangerous because the enamel flakes off.

Many experienced ship's cooks can't do without a pressure cooker, for the following reasons: they avoid the annoying problem of steam which then precipitates and makes the cabin damp, they greatly reduce cooking time, and in places where you can't get tender fillet steak you can make a goulash from tough meat by pressure cooking it. Fears of explosions are unfounded with today's fool-proof pressure cookers, as long as you stick to the instructions.

Stoves

Propane gas It is only a matter of time before there have been so many accidents that propane gas is banned on board yachts. Only very few people are aware of this very real danger. Propane gas is heavier than air and therefore sinks out of a leak in the supply or a bad screw thread and collects in the bilges waiting to be set alight one day. You can smell escaping gas, but not if you've got a cold. You can also get gas detectors which will reliably indicate if there is gas in the bilges, as long as they are working and switched on.

I could even understand that someone might prefer this sort of fuel if there were tremendous advantages to it. It does give off a lot of heat, and maintaining this kind of stove is easy, but that is all. Installing it must be done very carefully, and must even to some extent be taken into consideration when constructing the boat. The gas canister should best be kept outside. The canisters have to be filled from time to time, which can be a great performance especially abroad. Taxi drivers in some Spanish towns refuse to take sailors carrying gas canisters as passengers. And then the valve must fit that of the filling station, which hardly ever happens abroad. Many sailors have found it cheaper to throw their own canister away and buy a new one each time.

Methylated spirit or paraffin If we have any respect for the lives of our crew members and for our own, we are left simply with methylated spirit or primus, as the electricity supply on an offshore boat will never be plentiful enough. Meths is the least dangerous fuel, however it gives out relatively little heat. It is adequate to fry a piece of meat in a pan even if not crisply. Methylated spirit cannot explode, but it will burn. If some has been spilt and a fire starts, there is no need to panic. Even substantial spirit fires can be put out easily with a bucket of water. In my opinion primus is the most suitable for use on board. It gives off about the same amount of heat as propane gas and maintaining the stove presents no difficulties when you are used to it.

The burners of a primus stove must be heated up before use so that the paraffin vapourizes as soon as it pours out. You heat up the burners by pouring methylated spirit over them. Of course you must do this before you allow any paraffin to pour into the burner, with the control on low. If it isn't hot enough yet, a tall flame will be thrown upwards which is completely harmless as long as there isn't a curtain hanging over it. If you turn the control off again, the flame will die down within a short time. This sort of mishap makes paraffin unpopular as a fuel with certain ignorant sailors, but it need not occur at all if you are patient

51

The cutlery on H. Amel's *Fango* is ready to hand where it is needed – in the base of the table. And it is cosy inside . . .

about heating up. Small canisters of meths are available for this purpose, which hold exactly enough spirit for heating up. If the flame goes out on you, wait patiently until the burner has cooled down before beginning the procedure again. If there is a draught inside the boat the amount of fuel you have measured out might not produce enough heat so the burner is still too cold when the paraffin is poured on. In some countries you can only get low-concentration spirit (70% and under) so you would in this case have to use more.

Paraffin stoves, which are made by Primus and are available all over the world, have two or three burners, on gimbals or solid, and with or without an oven. The latter is not necessary on a yacht jaunting from harbour to harbour, seldom spending longer than three days on the open sea. But if we want to cross an ocean, an oven can enrich our menu immensely. Think about being able to bake your own bread! If we have a luxury yacht with a freezer (see below) an oven is a must.

Our stoves can be used for heating as well, and are really effective in small cabins. We must take care though that enough fresh air is allowed into the cabin as stoves burn up unbelievable amounts of oxygen. Headaches are the first alarm signal.

Fridge

This could be one of the most valuable pieces of equipment for well-being on board. But if we think about it sensibly and study brochures carefully, it is obvious that it would be madness to have an electric fridge on board. A simple calculation will show this. One brochure states: 'Economical consumption: 5 amps, and only 3 amps when the food has cooled down.' Modern electric fridges which work on the variable compressor principle also need 2 to 3 amps. If we allow 3 hours for cooling down, we have already used 15 ampere-hours (Ah) out of our 72 ampere-hour battery, and after a further 10 hours overnight we have already reached 45Ah. If our battery gives out about 55Ah in practice, it will almost completely have run out by morning because of the fridge alone, and we will have to run the engine for 10 hours to recharge it (see Electricity on board, p75).

However, we could also run a fridge on gas, primus or spirit (petrol is obviously out of the question on our boat). We mentioned the danger of gas on board with our stove and it is even more lethal with our gas fridge. A draught can put out the flame behind the fridge, and if there is no safety device, allow the gas to flow out freely, without there needing to be a leak in the supply. A paraffin fridge would be preferable: these function brilliantly in harbour. Nevertheless, you should never overlook the fact that on small yachts a paraffin flame can heat the area around the fridge quite nicely. If the boat heels underway, neither a gas nor a paraffin fridge will work.

Over recent years American sailors have found a good solution to the problem as I see it. Let's take a look at the energy path of a normal compressor fridge: the energy in the fuel is transformed through burning into mechanical energy (the engine), and then into electrical energy with the help of the

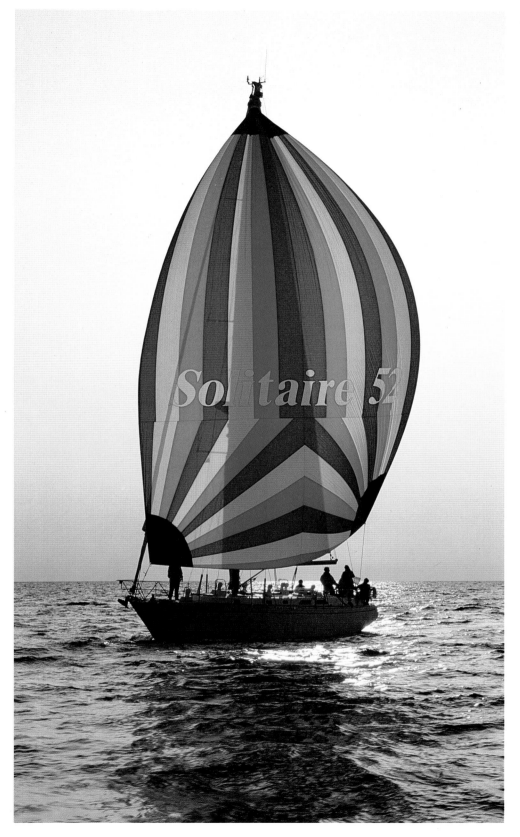

A 16m (52-foot) Solitaire 52 sloop; easy to sail and a fast and comfortable offshore yacht.

alternator. The alternator stores the resulting electricity in the battery, which then emits only a part of the stored energy into the hungry electric motor of the fridge. The latter then drives the fridge's compressor. Energy is lost at every stage. The Americans have taken a diferent, and surprisingly economical, tack. Its main advantage lies in the fact that we are not burdening the weakest part of our electrical supply system, the battery. We are instead using mechanical energy from the engine which easily satisfies the demands of the little fridge compressor. But there is a difficulty with this: while the fridge's thermostat turns the engine on and off in short bursts to prevent the temperature rising, we obviously can't turn the main engine on every five minutes to keep the temperature down.

This problem is overcome with 'cold banks', flat metal tanks filled with a mixture of alcohol and water, which are built in around the food in the fridge. With the help of the compressor, which is driven by magnetic coupling off the main engine, we only need to cool down the cold banks which store the cold, and won't have to use the main engine again until the next day.

However, results like this are reached not only by excellent insulation, but also through applying the principle of freezing. For example, if you use one calorie of energy to cool down a certain amount of fluid by one degree, then you will need 50 to 80 times the amount of energy to bring the liquid near to freezing point from a liquid to a solid state (ice!). Conversely, a certain amount of coldness is 'set free' when the ice returns to its liquid state when it melts. It is exactly this principle that you put to use in the cold banks. You need a lot of energy to freeze the freezing liquid, which is no problem for the ship's engine (at 20PS, 2 to 3PS are hardly crucial). If the

The unspeakable! Every sailor should not only use it but know how it works. Nothing will spoil a trip on the open sea more than a broken toilet.

liquid thaws again when the cold-compressor is turned off, the coldness which it now contains is set free again and can keep things cool in the fridge for a long time. It is however clear why you can only use this cooling principle if the freezing liquid has been cooled down so far that it is frozen. For a first-class installation, it is useful to know the following: the engine needs about 5 to 6 hours to bring the fridge coolant to minus 32°C; after reaching this temperature the engine will only need a daily running time of 60 minutes.

However, from the beginning the installation must be designed like a fridge or freezer. If for example the freezing liquid in the cold banks (eutectic solution) has a freezing point of minus 18°C, the installation will only work economically once the solution has frozen, ie when at least minus 18°C has been reached. In this case you will need a bigger compressor than for a normal fridge which works around 0°C.

The individual components, which also include a capacitor cooled by seawater, must all be matched exactly to one another. It just is not possible to convert an existing fridge by tinkering around. You would be better off getting one from a company which specialises in making fridges like this, which are simple to operate, and cost from about £1,500 ($2,250) and up. Adler Barbour Yacht Services Inc. have been involved in making fridges for yachts for 15 years. Their address is: 43 Lawton Street, New Rochelle NY 10801, USA .

The toilet

The ship's toilet is nothing but a container (bowl) with two pumps. One pump takes care of getting rid of the contents, whilst the other introduces the seawater to flush the bowl. Nowadays these toilets have become much more robust, because diaphragm pumps are used almost exclusively.

But these are also sensitive to a point, so it is wise not to use toilet paper which is too soft, and to make sure that the pump never has to deal with any synthetic, solid objects. If the pump is situated on the bottom of the bowl under the water-line, both the rubber pipes for drawing in and pumping out must be secured with a swan-neck.

To avoid one of these hoses turning into a siphon which will automatically draw water in, an outlet must be built in at the top of the pipe at the bend, which will allow air to get in so that the water column can break because of the resulting air bubble. The pump is usually assisted by moving a longish stick about and, depending on the position of the outlet, pumped out without flushing out the contents or additional flushing. It is interesting to know that a single membrane pump usually undertakes both pump functions: to flush it forces the water into the bowl with its underside, and it forces the contents out with its upper surface. Everything from the toilets on board has to be forced outside through a narrow tube, and this leads to problems.

Problems!

- The lever is very difficult to operate. This is usually because the seacocks are not open or a pipe is blocked.
- If small scraps of the flushed-out contents come back up, there is a tear in the diaphragm.

The neoprene diaphragm has a limited lifespan, as with every diaphragm pump, and in seawater this is not much more than a year. You would therefore be wise to get a set of spare parts when you buy the toilet. Changing the diaphragm is a very unpleasant process, although not very difficult, and anyone can do it on their own using the tools on board and after first closing the seacocks.

It is probable that in the future you will only be allowed to use toilets on board which don't empty into the sea but into special waste tanks. These chemical WC systems do have some disadvantages, despite what some people say. The tanks use up a lot of space and must not leak odour, which is not so easy with the ventilation you need. You can't use untreated steel tanks because the contents of the toilet will quickly corrode it.

A further problem is emptying the tanks. As long as there are no waste management facilities in marinas, using waste tanks is no great help to the problem of pollution. That is why I would still always prefer the old-fashioned ship's toilet. But I would always make sure with a new boat that it would be possible to convert it in the future. You must already allow for a waste tank.

Pumps

As well as the bilge pump which is responsible for the boat's safety, we need a whole string of other pumps on board. We ought also to have enough spare parts that we can manage easily if there are problems. A foot pump is best for the wash basin in the toilet, so that you are free to wash your hands. If you can only work the water pump with your hands, there is no point to it. If we want to do the washing up in the basin, we must attach a pump with a check valve at the outlet, even if the basin is situated above the waterline. It is wrong to think that the water will run out of its own accord.

On boats 10m long and up it is advisable to fit a shower. It is always a great relief to wash the seawater off you, and the beds will stay dry longer. The reason why our bunks are so cold and damp is that we inadvertently bring a lot of salt into bed with us. Incidentally we don't need to worry about the amount of water we use, except on very long trips. A short shower only

Every yacht needs a canvas hood. For very little money you will get an extra space where you can hide from the spray or take off your oilskins in the rain. The wet will stay 'outside' under the hood.

actually very easy. All the same, a heat exchanger should be fitted in the engine's cold water system, which draws fresh water from another tank and pumps it into the shower with the help of an extra pump in the engine. However, there are firms manufacturing installations like this today and the only problem with them is connecting them to the engine. If you are planning to instal a hot water system for later on, make sure when the boat is being built that the water pipes are made of copper and not plastic.

Cooking

Cooking is of considerable importance for the crew's well-being and the safety of the boat. First of all it must be said that we are working with naked flames and that the danger of injury is therefore not slight. Burns must be taken extremely seriously on board a boat, and extreme care must therefore be taken to avoid this happening. This is why the ship's cook should never mess about in shorts at the stove, even in hot climates. You must always have ovengloves to hand to hold hot saucepans with. Stoves are usually fitted with a small rail which is adaptable to the size of the pan, but it can do no harm if big pans are also secured with rubber loops.

uses up about 5 litres of water, about half a bucket. Try it if you don't believe it. As an exception I would recommend an electric pump for a shower, which does use a lot of electricity but is seldom in use for longer than a minute and is therefore hardly crucial.

Personally I would rather not take a shower at all than have to use a foot pump to operate it. It is all right for the water from the shower to run into the bilges; it is expelled in a few pumps of the over-sized bilge pumps.

In cool regions a hot shower at the right time is a great relief. But this causes quite considerable problems if you aren't used to the gas, which is dangerous to use. I'm not aware of a continuous-flow water heater run on paraffin which works as efficiently as the ones at home which run on gas. The smaller models would be sufficient for a modest shower on board our boat, but it must be stressed that they are extremely dangerous because of the fuel used.

Another solution is to heat the water up with the engine, although this isn't

For those who are planning a long voyage, the drinking water supply poses a particular problem. In reality there are hardly any problems with this, if you remember a couple of principles. If you avoid using a lot of water to wash, and are reasonably careful about using water for other things, you will need about 1.5 litres per person per day. If you drink canned fruit juice and soft drinks, and use seawater wherever possible, you can reduce this amount to 1 litre without suffering. Washing up must then be done in seawater, which is all right. You can boil eggs in seawater, and pasta and potatoes in a mixture of half seawater and half freshwater. You can also wash yourself with seawater if you use special saltwater soap. If you can't get this kind of soap, bubble bath will do.

Many freshwater tanks are not suitable for drinking water, which you usually only discover long after buying your boat. Galvanised metal tanks are particularly unsuitable as they give the water a bitter aftertaste. Synthetic tanks are generally more problem-free, and normal plastic canisters can be used just as well.

Bad drinking water will not be improved by keeping it in a suitable tank. The best thing therefore is to stash away as much good quality water as possible in every harbour.

When I sailed around the world I never boiled any water or put any additives in the tanks. Hygiene-conscious Americans would never drink water like mine. I did find a build-up of algae when I cleaned the tanks, but this didn't affect the colour or the taste. If possible I would always collect rainwater rather than use doubtful water from shore. If you have a suitable arrange-ment for collecting rainwater, a single downpour can fill the tanks, particularly in the tropics. An awning or a cabin roof with edges for this purpose are especially good for collecting water. Always wait until the salt has been washed out of it though. If the quality of the water is doubtful and there is nothing else to use, take the precaution of boiling the water for at least 10 minutes before use. On my last world trip however, I treated the water with Micropure and it kept very well on this 4-year trip. I had a stainless steel water-tank and didn't need to clean it once, which I put down to the taste-less additive Micropure.

If we are spending an extended holiday on board and endeavour to run a perfect household, it is worth going through granny's attic for old kitchen implements, such as a hand whisk, baking tins for bread and cakes, a paraffin iron or even a hand sewing machine.

Provisions

I have often seen even experienced people rushing around in a state before a long trip, anxiously looking at their shopping list to make sure that

Under the hot sun of the Mediterranean, food often tastes better in the cockpit than inside at table.

they haven't forgotten anything. There are only a few things which are really necessary: fuel for the stove, matches, salt and pepper, oil and vinegar. If you haven't got any pasta on board there are always potatoes and rice. It just is not worth getting excited about. If we go round a large supermarket carefully, it is almost impossible to miss anything. There are unfortunately very few good tinned meats on the market, and none at all outside Europe. So on our big trip, lacking a deep freeze, we got out granny's recipes and unwrapped and salted food, and even dried or smoked fish and meat. A well-smoked entire ham is a good fresh fish substitute, especially in the tropics. It keeps for weeks, and if you soak a couple of thick slices overnight you can even make a passable fry-up. Freeze-dried food is expensive but always better than corned beef. Our American friend Dawn knew 148 recipes for preparing palatable meat for breakfast, although palatable is a flexible term!

One of the main problems for European stomachs is always bread. There is no way of keeping bread fresh for very long, so you will have to make do with bread substitutes such as crispbreads, pumpernickel, crackers and rusks. You can cut white bread in slices and let it dry out completely in the sun on deck. Even after a few weeks it can be toasted over a naked flame if you spray it lightly with water first. We can bake our own bread if there is an oven on board, as fresh bread is a delicacy on long trips.

Eggs are a very important food for long voyages. They keep for several weeks if they are bought really fresh. You can significantly extend the length of time they will keep if you cover them with vaseline or put them in boiling water for two seconds, but you must do this no later than a day after you buy them. If you want to avoid breaking open a rotten egg in the cabin

Opposite page: If you have a strong crew who also know enough about sails, you can run up a marvellous spinnaker on a cruising yacht on a downwind course.

later on, you can test it by immersing it in a bucket of water. If it sinks it is definitely still all right.

Nowadays it is quite difficult to get fresh fruit and vegetables in big towns. Frozen foods are not much use to us as they go off very quickly, as do milk and other types of food. On a long trip aim to have fresh fruit and vegetables on the menu at the end if possible. You must therefore buy them as unripe as possible. For example, tomatoes keep no longer than 10 days, but on the other hand oranges, grapefruit and cabbage (which I don't normally like but find really delicious after crossing the Atlantic!) are still all right after 4 weeks. Apples (for the night-watch), lemons, potatoes, onions and garlic will last for months. An appropriate place is obviously required for storing your food, and you must check it regularly. Rotten food must be picked out and rotten parts taken off in time (such as the outer leaves of a cabbage). Containers made of wire mesh like the ones you see in self-service shops are particularly good for storing fruit and veg. But buy bananas when they are green and hang them in the fo'c's'le until they ripen, which they unfortunately do all at once.

On long and boring journeys the menu should at least be varied. It helps if you have enough spices, ketchup and other sauces, mustard, capers, olives, gherkins etc on board.

People often recommend that you mark tins or even paint them to prevent rust. This is unnecessary on our relatively dry boats today. If a tin is lying half in seawater, it will be at least six months before it rusts through. If you are worried that the paper labels are going to dissolve, it is enough to write M (meat), F (fruit) or V (vegetables) on them in waterproof pen. On long trips you should have chocolate, dried fruit and biscuits for the night-watch. Plain biscuits are the best thing to start off eating after being sea-sick.

The Monitor-autopilot is the successor to the legendary Aries-autopilot which has at least a hundred circumnavigations to its credit. The Aries is no longer being built. The new Monitor works on the same principle and is finished in stainless steel. It is available from Scanmar Marine Products, 298 Harbor Drive, Sausalito, CA 94965, USA.

Autopilot

Briefly, autopilot systems on small yachts work on the following principle: a windvane is allowed to find its own angle, so that it stands exactly in the wind. Then it is joined to the tiller which is fixed straight ahead. If the yacht now runs off course, the vane will no longer be standing in the wind and will meet with so much resistance that it will turn the pivoted windvane back into the wind. After the windvane has been joined to the tiller with a hinge or with cables, it will move the tiller, and the yacht will change its course (relative to the wind) until the windvane is standing in the wind again and the tiller is straight ahead at the same time.

You need quite big windvanes for this, and you can't use this system at all on a big cruising yacht. Instead of transferring the force of the windvane to the tiller, you use an auxiliary rudder which can still be moved by the windvane because it is small. The drawback of the latter system is the fact that in light winds the system is just not sensitive enough to serve the rudder. On the other hand, this arrangement has the great advantage that you have got a second rudder in an emergency.

Autopilot systems which work according to Hasler's revolutionary idea don't have the above disadvantages. Instead of transferring the force from the windvane directly to the rudder, Hasler uses a thin, narrow board on the stern of his yacht which reaches about 1m into the water. It is pivoted, but also rigged up so that it can hang like a pendulum to starboard or to port. Let's assume that the yacht is travelling at 4 knots. The servo rudder will be turned by the windvane at the same time. It therefore can't come to a standstill amidships in the current, but is pushed to one side by the water current. The force with which this happens is quite considerable, particularly if the servo-blade is suitably long. If

The big windvane acts directly on the tiller.

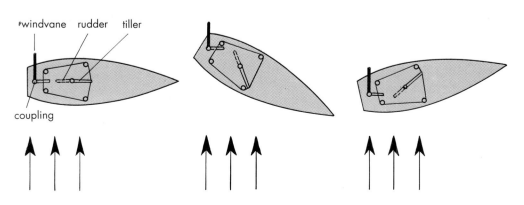

then you simply either fasten a rope at the lower end of the servo-blade or extend it up above the pivot and attach two ropes there, you can transfer this power quite easily over the blocks and onto the tiller.

In other words, when the windvane is not standing in the wind, the servo-blade will always swing out to one or the other side and move the tiller. The force of the wind is not used to steer the boat but simply to turn the long, thin servo-blade, whilst we use the force of the current to steer. The main advantage of this system is that the windvane only needs to be very small as it only has to turn the servo-blade. Its effectiveness depends not so much on the strength of the wind as on the speed of the boat. I used a Hasler system on my round the world trip, and it happily worked at just 1 knot. Incidentally I steered only about 100 sea miles of my 32,000 mile voyage by hand. Hasler's brilliant masterpiece took over the rest of the journey.

If our yacht has heavy weather helm, we should help the system out with taut pieces of shock cord on the tiller. (The shock cord can equally well be led round a drum on the wheel.) When you instal a system like this you obviously have to remember that it can sometimes be necessary to disengage the system. This is important because the force produced by the servo-blade is so strong that you can't steer against it by hand. I have a pair of rustproof scissors ready to hand in my cockpit locker in case such an emergency arises.

The return effect is important especially with systems like this. This means that as soon as the wind pressure on the windvane has dropped, the servo-blade swivels back of its own accord into the centre position. This is easy to achieve so long as the struts which the servo-blade should turn are not in line with the pivot (see diagram on following page). If it was exactly in the

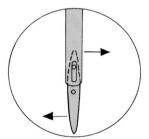

Electric autopilot systems need a lot of electricity but can stick to a compass course. Installing small systems is not complicated. They work directly on the tiller or even the wheel.

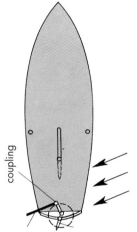

coupling

windvane   auxiliary rudder

An auxiliary rudder is used here to increase the effect of the wind; the windvane only needs a little power to turn the auxiliary rudder.

centre, the pendulum would have no reason to return to the starting position on its own, but would first need a push from the other side from the windvane. Our yacht would follow an extreme zig-zag course.

If you believe that this brilliant idea is perfect you are wrong. Yachties who are good with their hands could make improvements on the Hasler system. Stick with the basic idea of using power from the current for the tiller, but you could change the windvane. Early models turned on a vertical axis like the racing flag at the top of the mast, but modern systems (Aries) now turn on a horizontal axis.

However, the windvane must have a counterbalance underneath it in order to stand vertical without being influenced by the wind. If the wind strikes directly onto the edge of the wind vane, it can't bring it down because it is blowing exactly parallel to the axis of rotation. The counterbalance keeps the windvane vertical. If the yacht now runs somewhat off course, the wind immediately has a target and will turn

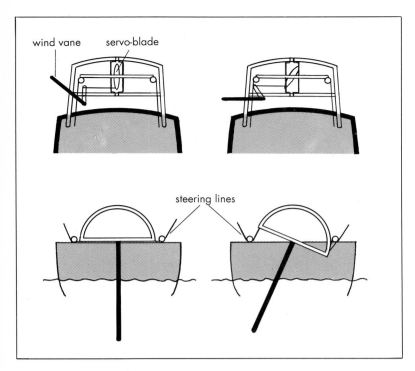

wind vane   servo-blade

steering lines

The Hasler system: the windvane moves a swinging rudder which is forced sideways when it is off centre, by the boat's motion.

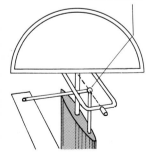

The joint is exactly on the turning axis, so there is no return-effect.

This doesn't work if the pendulum doesn't go back of its own accord.

the windvane round swiftly. This movement is transferred to the servo-blade via a complicated design. This arrangement allows us to manage with an even smaller wind vane, which is a great advantage in a storm (see diagram right).

Unlike an electric system, the system of steering with the wind vane obviously doesn't stick to a compass course, but alters course when the wind veers, for example. This also happens if the wind gets stronger or dies down, because the apparent wind direction will then change too, and it is this alone which is decisive for us on board. The advantage is that our sails will sit at their optimum once they have been rigged, and the disadvantage is the change of course.

Electric autopilot systems stubbornly stick to their compass course. This can also be a disadvantage, because when the wind veers the sail trim is not right any more. But the main disadvantage is, as we mentioned at the start, the high use of electricity. Manufacturers may court sailors with

meaningless claims like 'low power consumption' or 'little strain on the battery', but it must be remembered that even well-meaning makers of such equipment can't turn the laws of physics upside down. An electric engine is turned on and off through commands it receives from a scanned steering compass. The more heavily the yacht resists rudder movements, the more power the electric motor must produce, and this costs power from the battery.

There are now systems which are steered by a small wind vane instead of with the compass. Because the wind vane hardly has to produce any power, but simply passes on information which is transferred electronically, it doesn't need to be bigger than a few square centimetres, like the ones we see used as wind direction indicators. However, I fail to see why I should achieve an effect with precious battery current when I can achieve it mechanically just as well, thanks to Hasler's brilliant idea.

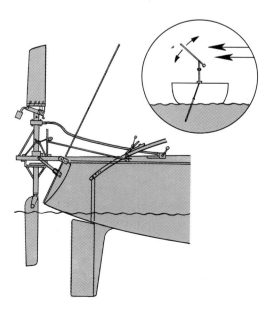

Offshore sailors are often asked 'Why sail round the world?' The answer lies in this picture – Fatu-Hiva, perhaps the most beautiful anchorage in the world. There is nowhere more romantic in the South Seas than here in the Marquesas Islands in the Pacific. One thing is missing from the photo: the strong smell of tiara blossom and the sweet air of copra.

The dinghy

The dinghy is part of the sailing boat's basic equipment. You should always allow for the likelihood that you will find only one anchorage; that once a line has been let out or you have berthed 'Mediterranean style' (see pp.131–3), the conditions will be so bad that the yacht's stern cannot be brought near enough to the jetty for you to climb directly across.

Inflatable or rigid?

This question does not even arise for a boat of 7 or 8m in length, because there is too little space to keep a rigid dinghy on deck. You would have to go for an inflatable. Of course, that does not mean that you should buy one of the cheap single-compartment sort which you can get in department stores for about £30 ($45). For years now, firms have manufactured extremely good inflatable dinghies which are so robust that they can survive even the most violent landings on rocks. If they get a hole in them, the tear is comparatively easy to mend. However, after six years

of use, the rubber becomes so brittle and cracked that it is better to get a new dinghy.

A rubber dinghy is more stable in heavy seas but is more difficult to row. Unfortunately industry has not yet managed to simplify the process of inflating and deflating so that it can be done in just a few minutes. This is the true disadvantage of an inflatable boat. If an inflatable dinghy is still damp before departure, it should never be stowed away in this state. It is considered bad seamanship to tow the dinghy behind when underway, which is only possible in sheltered coastal waters anyway. Your voyage will be slowed down significantly, and there is always the danger in following wind that a wave will fill the dinghy and the painter will be ripped out under the enormous pressure. If bad weather develops, the dinghy must be taken on board. In such circumstances you would usually have so many other important things to do that you would have hardly any time left for the dinghy.

If there is enough room on deck, either fore or aft, you should always go for a rigid dinghy. Plastic boats are unsinkable, and from a given size upwards they are almost impossible to capsize. With no mechanics to go wrong, the working life of a plastic boat is usually limited only by light sensitivity.

The advantages of inflatable and rigid dinghies are combined in the synthetic banana-boat (tri-bell GmbH, Hamburg). Up and running it has enough room for three adults and is wide and therefore easy to row. It can be motor-driven with a 3PS outboard, and can be put away in a matter of seconds. Even on small cruisers, there is room to stow a banana-boat along the rail.

If you are lucky enough to go to the tropics, it is no great expense to fit a sheet of glass or perspex in the bottom

For children the great adventure begins in the harbour, if there's a safe dinghy to hand.

One of the most popular dinghies: the banana-boat. A good compromise, it takes up very little room on board, is easy to inflate and so robust that it can be dragged single-handed up a stony beach.

of your dinghy. In clear tropical waters you can see the bottom without a snorkel and mask, to check if it is suitable for anchoring. If you stow the dinghy on the coachroof, most common on small yachts, the skylight underneath will not be obscured as the glass in the dinghy lets the light through. You can get to know the underwater world of corals with your glass-bottomed boat without having to worry about sharks!

The size of your dinghy depends on the size of the parent boat and its crew. As a rule of thumb it should only be so big that the crew can heave it on deck in an emergency without having to use the halyards.

Outboards

In the Baltic, the North Sea or the Mediterranean, an outboard motor is unnecessary for a dinghy, and would definitely not be popular due to the noise and pollution it creates. However, just across the Atlantic, jetty berths are extremely hard to come by, and good anchorages are so far from shore that a light outboard is definitely a worthwhile acquisition. With an outboard motor on your dinghy you can afford to look for the safest anchorage, even if it is further out from shore. In a headwind and heavy seas a small outboard motor is considerably more effective than a strong oarsman.

Fresh air and the occasional splash of water damages the dinghy's outboard motor less than being smothered in a tarpaulin.

Left: Every dinghy is a compromise. An inflatable boat can be deflated and folded up, if you can be bothered . . .
Right: . . . It's obviously such an effort that you might want to save yourself the trouble over the winter!

The 'ideal' cruising boat

The great attraction of sailing must lie partly in the fact that there are strict rules for only very few things and there is therefore room for very individual views and opinions. For this reason it would be presumptuous and against the spirit of the sport to lay down to a fellow sailor how his boat should look. In the same way that I think a steel boat is the ideal, another fellow sailor might think a plywood yacht is the best for reasons just as important. It is however interesting to hear very experienced sailors' views and get some ideas from them.

The magazine *Yachting World* made a significant contribution to sailing by organising a questionnaire amongst offshore sailors including members of the Ocean Cruising Club and the Royal Cruising Club. One of them, T. H. Carr, has for example logged the almost unbelievable figure of 100,000 miles under sail in his lifetime. Great names such as Robin Knox-Johnson, Sir Alec Rose or Roderick Stephens have almost as much experience. Behind the bare percentages, if you want it, lies knowledge which has been gained on voyages over more than a total of 7 million sea miles on the open sea and in coastal waters.

The results of the questionnaire are still valid today, even if there have been further developments in a few details over recent years. The trend is going strongly away from wooden boats and towards bigger yachts. The two-master has further lost ground, and on the subject of equipment, the Global Positioning System (GPS) has gained a strong place today whilst Omega and high frequency transmitters have been replaced almost completely by satellite navigation and VHF-transmitters (see page 68).

Opposite page: the author's *Thalassa II* against the picturesque South Seas backdrop of Bora-Bora.

OCEAN CRUISING CLUB SURVEY RESULTS – PERCENTAGES

type of hull	%
single compartment	95
catamaran	4
triple hull	1

overhang	
long	1
medium	71
short	28

structural material	
wood	24
composite (wood & iron)	11
cold-moulded wood	8
GRP	15
GRP (sandwich)	13
steel	15
aluminium	10
reinforced concrete	4

deck	
flat deck	34
short cabin roof	28
long cabin roof	18
cabin roof and wheel-house	20

deck surface	
teak	65
plywood	3
synthetic	17
painted	3
non-slip cover	12

keel	
long keel	81
short keel with separate rudder	10
bilge keel	1
centreboard	6
other	2

rigging	
sloop	14
cutter	17
ketch	47
yawl	16
schooner	3

downwind sails	
spinnaker	15
twin staysail	20
big boy	4
whisker pole & jib	61

reefing	%
roller reef	66
tied reefs	30

overall length	
under 7m	0
7 – 9m	1
9 – 12m	58
over 12m	41

steering	
tiller	37
wheel	63

autopilot	
with sheets	6
wind vane moved horizontally	32
wind vane moved vertically	44
electric	10
no autopilot	8

autopilot operation	
directly on tiller	32
separate servo-rudder	44
trim tab on main rudder	24

cockpit	
centre cockpit	28
stern cockpit	72

sea anchor	
necessary	12
useful	26
unnecessary	62

auxiliary engine	
none	0
outboard	0
inboard on centre line of ship	94
outside centre line of ship	1
2 inboards	5

PS	
under 10	2
10 – 30	44
30 – 60	43
over 60	11

fuel	
petrol	1
diesel	96
paraffin	3

range	%
0–200 miles	16
200–800 miles	70
over 800 miles	14

draught	
under 1.50m	12
1.50 – 2m	80
over 2m	8

generator	
on main engine	39
separate generator	22
powered by wind	1
combination of methods	38

electrical system	
6 volt	2
12 volt	69
24 volt	27
32 volt	2

navigation lights	
electric	87
paraffin	13

anchor lights	
electric	45
paraffin	55

main anchor	
CQR	60
Danforth	27
Fisherman anchor	12
other	1

anchor with	
chain only	66
cable & chain forerunner	44
cable only	0

how much chain?	
40 – 80m	46
80 – 100m	41
over 100m	13

cable length	
60 – 100m	23
100 – 150m	56
over 150m	21

ballast	%
iron	11
lead	80
other	4
no ballast	5

dinghy	
rigid	33
inflatable	67
none	0

dinghy size	
under 2.5m	14
2.5 – 3.5m	84
over 3.5m	2

operation of dinghy	
oars	52
outboard	42
sail	6

dinghy material	
wood	16
metal	2
GRP	34
other synthetic materials	48

cooking fuel	
paraffin	31
gas	52
methylated spirit	11
electricity	2
diesel	2

would you equip your boat with:	
life raft	95
radar	16
Decca	4
Loran	5
Omega	6
radio direction finder	91
short wave transmitter	12
medium wave transmitter	25
VHF transmitter	31
high-frequency transmitter	49
echo-sounder	96
wind speed gauge	51
wind direction gauge	43
radar reflector	80
towed log	72
freezer	18

Thalassa II <u>almost</u> became the dreamboat. The broad deck (up to 4.70m) made working with the sails easy. The boat's movement was pleasant on the open sea. The waves seldom found their way into the cockpit or the fo'c's'le, even in the Roaring Forties.

The 'dreamboat' and what became of it

The word 'dreamboat' betrays the fact that we are dealing with something personal, a dream, and that other people's opinions are not easily adopted. This is why I always accept other opinions, so long as they are technically tenable. The *Thalassa II* is a steel sloop, about 16m length over-all. The builders, Elsenga, originally conceived her as a ketch, and my mast was simply taken aft by 1m compared to the twin-mast design. This was strictly speaking a cutter rig, because the 65m² genoa jib is changed for an outer jib in force 4 and over. In following wind up to force 4, a big boy of 120m² is run up instead of the genoa. There are twin staysails for frequent following winds, which are attached together to the forestay. The booms are run tightly against the mast.

The halyards have a wire fore-runner and are operated over strong winches which are fitted on deck. They run outside; on my first round-the-world trip they ran <u>in</u>side, and caused no problems, but I never felt totally at ease.

The ground tackle consists of an 80m long chain and various other cables for the 75 pound Standard-CQR and 35kg Danforth. The chain runs across a strong 12 volt Simpson and Lawrence winch.

In the engine room there is an 80PS MAN, which operates at angles of heel up to 25°. On the main engine there is the compressor for the freezer and two 55 amp 12 volt alternators. They run two separate batteries, 240Ah for the starter and 480Ah for electricity supply generally. The boat doesn't have a generator, and everything is therefore geared to the main engine. Apart from the luxury of a deep freeze, the boat is rather spartanly equipped. There are no electric pumps, no hot water system, no heating (the boat was planned for warm climates from the start), and no air-conditioning, which would only be possible if there was a generator running all the time.

The ventilation is through four big hatches – very expensive. Two further ventilator shafts were also installed. The deck, and indeed the entire boat was painted white to keep the temperature down. I decided against a teak deck for this reason. Another hatch was built in the cockpit to venti-late the galley with its hot paraffin stove, which is situated in the passage-way between the saloon and the stern.

The steering works through a hy-draulic system which has to be short-circuited with a valve when switching over to the Aries auto pilot system, because the Aries system puts more force on the tiller in a boat of this size. The navigation was spartan from the beginning, apart from an Omega sys-tem. Compass, echo-sounder, towed log and sextant were the next and only pieces of navigation equipment.

The construction was taken on by the Noord Nederland shipyard, and was trouble-free, with not a cross word spoken. Blomhoff, the manager, was always able to give me good ideas, and was not at all self-opinionated.

After sailing about 40,000 sea miles, our dreamboat can prove how it fared in practice: I had previously feared that this boat weighing over 20 tons could not be sailed by two people, but this was proved wrong. However, the *Thalassa II* is not a yacht you would use for a few quick trips. There are only two things which must never go wrong: the electric anchor winch and the engine. Neither of these has given me cause to worry to date. Apart from that, this cosy double-chine hull with a long keel is not at all slow. 150 nautical miles in 25 hours at force 4 is normal under both stay sails of 40m² each. Apart from 2 days when we were almost becalmed, we took only 19 days to cross the Atlantic (although with a larger crew) and on two days covered over 180 nautical miles. The record day is now 196 nautical miles, which is quite considerable for a steel construction with no spinnaker. The Aries, good value when it was bought at £600 ($900), steered this record day and it is a system I can only strongly recommend to owners of boats over 8 metres long. Only the external halyards caused me any trouble, as they were always hanging in the wrong place. Next time I would take refuge again in internal halyards.

There is a rust problem but not nearly as great a one as I had feared. A box of paint pots was always ready to be used in the odd five minutes. During the first year in the tropics, the amount of time spent on this – apart from time on the slip – was about ten hours in total. The white deck with all its hatches also proved itself. In the tropics the *Thalassa II* was so nice and cool inside that we were able to do without the sunshade, which would otherwise have been indispensable. The ventilation shafts were unnecessary as they never let any air in, but sometimes water from high waves. The boat has remained watertight to this day, even after a rough trip round Cape Horn. I can still

vacuum in the bilges, and there are cobwebs under the engine.

She has no oil leaks either, which is unfortunately a rarity for a ship's engine. The MAN diesel engine is naturally the heart of the boat. It had to run for an hour every other day to generate the electricity and cool the freezer, and used about 3 to 4 litres for this and 6 litres per hour when motoring steadily at 7 knots. Since the entire energy necessary on board the *Thalassa II* was produced through this, the prospects of further fuel price increases don't worry me unduly. With this energy supply, and 1,000 litres of diesel and 1,000 litres of water in the tanks, we never had to turn to onshore power. The paraffin stove with the primus burners defied all prophecies of doom. It was used at times to feed 8 people, who could all use it perfectly well after getting used to it over a short while.

After the first foggy trips in the North Sea, a radar system (Decca 060) was added to the navigation system, which meant a short and ugly radar mast for the *Thalassa II*. This was a small sacrifice for the advantages it brought. I would never again sail without radar, even if there were no fog. It makes navigation so easy and safe. Omega didn't prove worthwhile, which is strange because this hyperbolic navigation system works well for flying. In future I will have a GPS on board.

Roller-jibs were also originally planned for my dreamboat, which unfortunately I went without in the end for financial reasons. This doesn't bother me so much any more, since I have so often witnessed serious problems with these mechanisms, as they are susceptible to jamming on long voyages. Even so these things would of course greatly facilitate sailing on a large boat, so long as they work. Although content, one dreams on!

I have purposely put my friend Dr Bullmer's remarks at the end of my report on my 'dreamboat'. He has

The *Thalassa II* was the floating home of the Schenks for four years. Its home port: Cook's Bay, Moorea, in the Pacific.

arrived at quite a different 'dreamboat' after returning from the first German round-the-world trip in a catamaran. By doing this I want to show how diverse and delightful offshore cruising is. Dr Ernst Bullmer, an ex-dinghy sailor and later owner of a single-hull yacht, writes:

'My ideal boat for sailing round the world? A catamaran not less than 12m long, light but very strongly built, with ketch rigging, very little technology, a light diesel engine just sufficient for harbour manoeuvres and going through canals (on my world trip I spent 275 engine hours going through the Panama Canal!), a small diesel generator, water supplies in 20-litre canisters, a garden hose as shower, pumping the pressure tank up by hand, a small 30-litre cold box with a compressor so that the butter stays cold...'

The cutter rig proved its worth most of all in the storms on the southerly ice limit. The crew, which was weak in numbers, used the many variations offered by this rig. Roller jibs would have been better if . . .

The *Thalassa II* was always troublefree to sail, whether by two people over 72 days on the open sea, or by eight people over 19 days under twin staysails across the Atlantic.

Electrics and Electronics

Electricity on board

There are technical problems involved in having electricity on a boat. This does not mean that a skipper should be frightened of the problems: rather, it means that time spent on getting to know the boat's electrics is time well spent.

We have two sources of power: the engine alternator and the battery. The on-board battery will be a lead-cell battery. One cell gives a potential of almost exactly 2 volts. Car batteries normally have 12v batteries, made up by linking 6 cells (occasionally only 6v, with half as many cells). In an ideal world, the higher the battery potential, the better, since 12v electricity fed into a long wire comes out as slightly less than 12v at the other end. This is known as voltage drop or voltage loss. The lower the voltage and the thinner the copper wire, the more voltage will be lost.

It follows that a 24v battery would be ideal for your yacht's current. However, you would then find that you could not use all those convenient (and cheap!) 12v items of equipment developed for hooking up to car batteries. You might not even be able to find an appropriate starter motor for the engine, since almost all starters are designed for use in 12v systems. You end up plumping for 12 volts; but you should be aware that this is a compromise solution. In order to minimise voltage loss, you should install the thickest possible cable to major items of equipment. This may work out expensive in the short run, but cable should be regarded as a capital investment. I would regard 2.5mm diameter as the ideal lower limit.

Formulae for calculating cable diameters	
cable diameter =	$\dfrac{\text{length of cable}}{50 \times \text{resistance (Ohm)}}$
resistance (Ohm) =	$\dfrac{\text{acceptable voltage loss (Volt)}}{\text{current (Amp)}}$
current (Amp) =	$\dfrac{\text{power consumption (Watt)}}{\text{voltage (Volt)}}$

The formulae shown should allow you to calculate the minimum diameter for your cables. You should reckon on allowing a maximum voltage loss of 5% for most equipment (but only 2% for navigation lights). Remember also to include both wires in two-core cable.

Battery

You must care for your battery and maintain it, so beware! Do not leave your battery on board for long periods unless it is fully charged: a run-down battery left alone will be damaged.

You will need to do a careful periodic check of the battery charge. A hydrometer is used for checking the specific gravity of the battery acid. A recently charged battery will reach a value of 1.28. Once the specific gravity gets down to 1.15 you know the battery needs recharging.

Yachts which are being used exclusively in hot climates such as the Mediterranean or in the Tropics need the battery acid kept at a lower specific gravity. A fully charged battery should not get above 1.235 to 1.245, or its life will be unnecessarily short. If you are moving a yacht to a hot region, you can adjust the battery acid using the following technique (recommended by the battery manufacturers Hagen AG): empty the acid from a fully charged battery into a container and add distilled water to reach a specific gravity of 1.22. When you tip the acid back

into the battery, you will find that the value rises to 1.235–1.245. Adjust by the addition of more distilled water or pure battery acid at a gravity of 1.28.

You can tell an old battery easily: even when it is fully charged, values as high as 1.28 cannot be reached. Most batteries will have to be scrapped after four years. All the cells should show the same reading. If a single cell shows a markedly different reading, that cell is probably no good, and the whole battery will be useless.

Check the acid level frequently. The plates should always be covered. If they become uncovered, do not top the battery up with sulphuric acid: normally all that has happened is that some water has evaporated away. You should top up with distilled water (though rainwater will do at a pinch).

You must have a voltmeter on the battery (just as you must also have an ammeter) though the voltmeter is not much use for checking the charge. The reason is the shape of the discharge curve, which rapidly goes down to 12 volts (2 volts per cell) then stays at or around this level for a long period. The charge declines dramatically at the end of the constant phase. No voltmeter will tell you how far along the flat part of the curve you have gone.

Lead batteries can discharge themselves. Nickel-cadmium batteries do not have this irritating habit. They are effectively maintenance-free, and last about ten times as long as a lead battery. Unfortunately they also cost about ten times as much. They also have a steeper discharge curve: an unattractive feature which their fans tend to overlook.

Electrical appliances need at least 12 volts, and the NiCd battery will only deliver this for a short period. In effect, you would need a further (very complicated) piece of equipment to switch extra cells on stream as your consumption demands.

Not all 12v batteries have the same

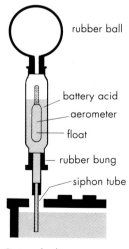

rubber ball

battery acid

aerometer

float

rubber bung

siphon tube

Battery hydrometer.

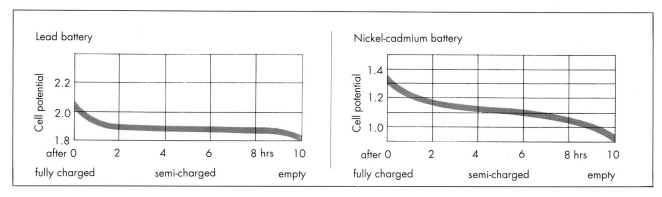

Lead battery

Cell potential

2.2
2.0
1.8

after 0   2   4   6   8 hrs   10

fully charged   semi-charged   empty

Nickel-cadmium battery

Cell potential

1.4
1.2
1.0

after 0   2   4   6   8 hrs   10

fully charged   semi-charged   empty

capacity. Some carry more 'juice' than others. If you look at the 12v, six-cell battery of an electrically powered boat, you will find it is enormous compared with a car battery of the same potential, simply because the boat motor is uneconomical and draws much more current. The capacity of a battery is calculated in ampere-hours (Ah). If we have a cabin light which draws 1 ampere, and leave it on for an hour, we use 1Ah. In theory, a 100Ah battery could power the light for 100 hours; in practice the battery would run down before then, probably at about 70% of the nominal capacity.

Car starter motors, as normally used on board, are far from ideal for marine conditions. They are designed to deliver a high current for a very short time, just long enough to start the engine. Marine batteries, on the other hand, are required to store a lot of electricity and release it over a longish period evenly distributed to all the appliances on board. Car batteries are not designed for this requirement: the demands made on their capacity by marine use tend to reduce their functional lifespan and effectiveness considerably.

There are few firms, so far as I know, which have tackled this problem seriously for the cruising community. Hagen AG have developed a battery with extra-thick plates, tested both in the lab and in practical use, specifically for applications which demand a lot of capacity. This battery, known as

a 'Multicraft', operates at heel angles of up to 60°, and may also be used for starting the engine. Ideally, though, you would use a normal car battery as the starter battery. One is often advised to take two batteries on board, but safety reasons are a secondary consideration in this context: the conflict between short, high-current bursts and long, slow release of capacity to appliances is the real reason. You want to be able to charge both batteries from the main engine, so you need either two alternators, or an electronic current distributor which separates off the larger battery and allows both to be charged at the same time.

You must bear in mind that the chemical processes involved in battery discharge are very precisely controlled. There is no point hoping for

Discharge curve of a lead versus a NiCd battery.

You can measure the potential of the whole battery or of a single cell, using a simple voltmeter. Each cell of a lead battery gives about 2 volts, irrespective of the size of the battery.

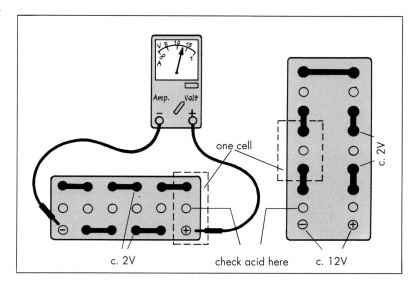

one cell

c. 2V

c. 2V   check acid here   c. 12V

more than arithmetic dictates you are entitled to. If your battery has a capacity of 72Ah, it will be flat in practice after about 50Ah. A fridge using 5A per hour will leave you with a flat battery after 10 hours. You will usually find the power consumption of an appliance given by its wattage. This can be converted as follows:

$$Amp = \frac{Watt}{Volt}$$

If you are using a 20W navigation light with a 12v supply for one hour, you will consume 1.7Ah. With the three lights required for any boat of over 7m, consumption becomes 5Ah, so the above battery will not allow you to show lights for longer than 10 hours.

You might not worry about this if it was easy to recharge your flat battery the following day. However, you not only need a powerful alternator to deliver the charging current; recharging a battery can actually damage it if more than a tenth of the capacity is recharged per hour. Put another way:

A completely flat battery takes 10 hours to recharge.

The alternator

Once upon a time, it was unusual to find anything other than a dynamo attached to a boat engine as an electrical power source; nowadays, alternators are much more common. Alternators not only allow the use of alternating current, but they produce higher currents, and are usable from lower engine revs (though an inboard engine is usually used somewhere in the medium rev range, so this final advantage is largely academic).

These days, you can get alternators which produce 90A. Alternators are generally rated for power rather than current however. A 400W alternator gives (400W divided by 12v) about 35A. The 35A supply may be used to feed a large family of hungry electrical appliances; and we saw earlier that a battery should not be recharged at any more than one tenth of its capacity. No-one has space for a 350Ah battery on board a small cruiser. This brings us to the conundrum faced by the alternator owner: what do you do with all this excess power supply? On a larger vessel, no problem: always plump for as much battery capacity on board as your boat can sensibly accommodate, as the example at the top of the next page shows.

The alternator has a regulator attached which ensures that you are not pumping too much juice into the battery. The regulator will normally reduce the current to the battery to only a few amps after a certain time. You should not read into any of my earlier remarks any dissatisfaction with this state of affairs. The regulator is simply responding, automatically, to the state of charge of the battery. I advise against overriding the regulator with a manual potentiometer or cutting the regulator out of the circuit. If the regulator reduces the current after a short while, this can only be because the battery is already fully charged, or is too old to take a full charge. You can check which by measuring the acid. If the meter tells you the battery is flat but the regulator will still not send any more juice to the battery, then you must wave this battery goodbye. Batteries often last no longer than three or four years on board, especially in the tropics.

Generator

If you need only to recharge the battery, it seems a waste to use the boat's large, powerful engine. Many boats

Dream switch bank on a 52ft yacht. Equipment like this gives the skipper an excellent overview of today's complex electrical systems.

YACHT A		YACHT B	
Alternator	400W	Alternator	400W
Daily consumption	35Ah	Daily consumption	35Ah
Battery capacity	70Ah	Battery capacity	350Ah
Engine needed	5 hours per day	Engine needed	1 hour per day

The same alternator running the same appliances. What a difference the size of the battery makes!

therefore have a special small generator on board just for battery charging. This arrangement does have some disadvantages:

1 Engines of the appropriate size, such as an ED 250 Honda, are usually petrol powered, and thus there is a risk of explosions
2 All generators are much too loud to be used in enclosed harbours
3 Fuel costs pretty much the same as for the main engine
4 Just one more engine on board to break down and be looked after

On-shore electricity

Most marinas these days can connect you to electricity at your berthing spot. You can convert the supply to 12v direct current using a battery charger.

Of course the availability of your usual power supply means it would be possible to use your normal domestic appliances. However, you should not forget how well 'earthed' your boat is in the water. This earth connection caused the tragic death of the Austrian yachtsman Joe Paschernagg, who received a fatal shock from a faulty drill. It is also worth noting that a reliance on on-shore electricity puts you at the mercy of the local power supply: 220v and 50 cycles in most of Europe, but 110v and 60 cycles virtually throughout America.

If you have an unexpected need for 220v AC electricity on board, you can make your own using a transistorised current inverter. Modern inverters lose very little current and can handle power loads of up to 500W.

The search for power supplies which are quieter than a generator or more economical than the boat's engine continues. Experiments with wind vanes and towed propellers have all been more or less fruitless. They might work, but at very low levels of performance. A solar cell which might cost £600/ $900 will produce 6W, or 0.5A. Add to this the requirement that the cell needs to be kept out of any shadow. In essence, a shadow falling on any part of the cell battery is likely to reduce the potential across the whole set to, say, 11V rather than the designed 13V. When this happens, the solar cell battery produces no current at all. The only realistic use for a solar cell is to top up the battery when the boat is not being moved at all for long periods, such as in the harbour.

Many dreamers have great hopes of wave-powered electricity production. But you don't get something for nothing, even on a boat. The theory sounds neat enough. As the boat moves forward, it produces a wave, which can in turn be used to drive a generator. Thus far, it works. However, you tend to need the current mostly when you are anchored. And to make matters worse, the drive shaft of the engine is the part which wears out fastest, it makes an infuriating noise and it slows the boat down. Quite frankly, when the engine can give you 40A, and the wave generator 4A (at 5 knots), why bother?

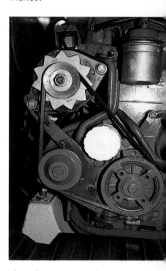

This alternator produces plenty of current even at low engine revs.

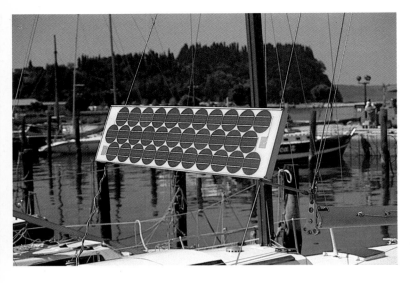

Solar panels are still very expensive. To work well, they need to be large; they also need constant and even sunshine.

Wind generator. This model is too small to be anything other than decorative.

This wind generator will develop more current, maybe as much as five to six amps, in a strong wind. It is noisy, and dangerous if you get too close.

One can use a towed propeller shaped like a log, which serves as a starter motor for the generator. This is a fair compromise: it does not wear out the drive shaft and it does not need to be built in. When you are anchored, you can use the same propeller, but power it with the wind.

You should check your electrics (the whole set-up, not the individual appliances) with a simple and cheap meter, one of those with a needle rather than a digital display. We amateur electricians use these to measure current loss (switching it to 'resistance'), to check that a connection or a light bulb element is intact or has not been shorted. If we want to check the battery voltage, we switch to 'potential', using a range higher than the potential expected (say, 20V for a 12V battery), then bring the black negative wand into contact with the negative terminal of the battery, followed by the positive wand to the positive battery terminal. Normal dry cells, such as torch batteries, can be checked using the same gadget. If a nominal 1.5V battery is giving 1.4V, throw it away.

Electronics on board

Echo sounder

The echo sounder is your most vital instrument. It helps you navigate, and is virtually essential when you come to anchor. We can use the sounder to check the length of the anchor chain and line, and we can estimate the radius of any swing at anchor. The only thing an echo sounder cannot realistically be used for is avoiding the occasional accidental grounding, precisely because these are accidental and tend to come about when the water gets suddenly shallower. The echo sounder is not an early warning submarine radar. The ideal echo sounder can be used on a variety of ranges, ideally even beyond 100m.

You can buy them with needles, lit crystal displays and digital readouts. Digital readouts are the simplest, but LCDs have the advantage that they can also recognise false echos from schools of fish and other underwater oddities. Any echo sounder will give you a surprisingly accurate reading, much better than a hand-held lead. They use tiny amounts of current.

I do not believe depth contour printers are necessary on a cruising yacht; apart from anything else, they do not produce the sort of scale drawing you would need for taking bearings on a chart. Depth alarms are handy, though: you can set the sounder to give a signal when you encounter a minimum depth. Obviously, the measurements must be calculated to take account of the depth below the waterline of the sensor. Do not paint the sensor, and do not use sharp metal scrapers on it to remove barnacles.

Log and speedometer

These two items are generally made in one combined box. They can be precise and reliable, if they have been calibrated over a measured course (this is all too rarely done). The transmitter is usually a small plastic paddle wheel which revolves like the wheel in an old petrol-pump glass: there are no mechanical parts, as the wheel has a magnetic strip which produces an impulse when it passes a magnet in the hull. The wheel and sensor need to be absolutely clean in order to work properly, so you must have a device for retracting them while the boat is in the water. Although the speedo does not appear to use much electricity, on a long uninterrupted trip such as a transatlantic cruise it can end up making considerable demands on your battery.

The famous Walker towed log works without electricity. I have never found it to be satisfactory, though the Hiscocks have used one to travel several times round the world. I must just have been unlucky.

Anemometer

I used to believe an experienced sailor could estimate wind strength. I think differently these days: one is so influenced by mood (loneliness, fear . . .). A proper wind gauge adds objectivity to your decision whether to reef or not. Mostly, they work on the principle of a dynamo coupled to a revolving cross driven by wind cups. The more wind there is, the faster the cross turns, and the more electricity is produced. No current is drawn from the battery.

Modern super-yachts appear to need a forest of aerials.

Retractable log sensor with weed-catcher. Excellent!

Left: LCD echo sounder showing fish shoal
Right: wind direction indicator and digital echo sounder.

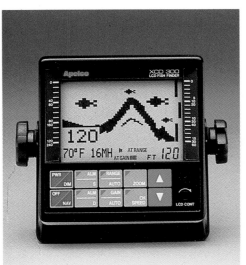

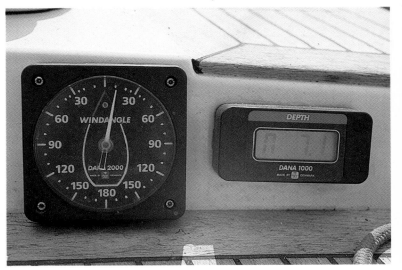

Wind direction indicator

Cruising yachts do not need one of these. The autopilot vane does the same job. Beware: some wind gauges hamper radio reception when in operation. If yours does, get help!

Radar

If you can afford the space, money and drain on your battery, radar is wonderful, however much of an eyesore it may be. Aesthetics against that much added safety: no contest! The radar range depends on how high up you put it. On a ketch, the radar dish goes on the mizzen spreaders. On a sloop, there is no ideal spot for it. Depending on its range, radar will draw at least 10A. The installation will cost £2,000/$3,000.

Its application, incidentally, is not merely to increase your range of vision, but also to check your position when you are in coastal waters. The concentric circles on the screen, around the boat, give you a distance reading for neighbouring land, and the sweep line gives you an automatic bearing.

The major difficulty with radar is not that of getting it to work, but identifying the objects on the screen. Many landmarks which are clear to the eye give a faint blip on the screen, which can leave one rather puzzled by the resulting picture. Certain cruising areas now have radar charts, so you can tell what the coast will look like on screen. Colour radars are no better, since their colour display is entirely artificial and depends on the intensity of the radar reflection, not the colour of the object.

Radars with a 'screen freeze' function are handy, so you can get a complete picture of one revolution of the antenna. The need to place the sensor high up (on the mast) can make life difficult for the radar user in a swell. You need to wait for a particularly helpful image before freezing it. This characteristic of mast-mounted radars is such a problem that for most purposes, the radar is ideally mounted only two to four metres above deck level.

Installation for wind direction and speed indicator.

A good spot for the instrument panel: in the line of sight of the helm, and well protected from green water by the hood.

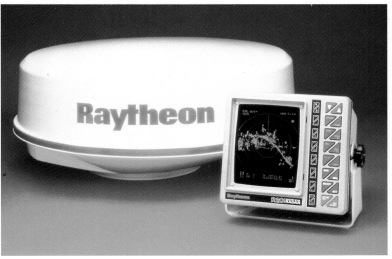

Left: Where do you put the dish on a boat? This answer is technically excellent, if aesthetically unfortunate.

Above: Radar is the most effective navigation aid you can have. Get one with a 'screen freezer'.

Centre: The dish does battle with the genoa every time this sloop tacks.

Below: Mounted sideways on a spreader: a poor compromise.

A modern receiver covering all frequencies. Like other receivers with a digital tuning mode, this one will track a signal and is easy to operate. It's cheap, too.

Radio

Good on-board radio reception

This ideal receiver has every frequency we shall ever need.

Yacht equipment manufacturers always insist that nautical radio receivers need to be built specially to survive the salt-water-laden air on board. Such special equipment is built in small numbers and therefore demands astronomical prices. In my own experience, any reputable make of receiver works just as well on a boat as do special yacht receivers. Obviously your nautical radio-direction-finding equipment can be expected to survive salty showers, while its terrestrial cousins cannot; but you should bear in mind that the transistors, condensers and other components are identical in other respects with those in your domestic radio.

Our first concern is actually less the price than the sort of broadcasts we shall need to receive, and what sort of

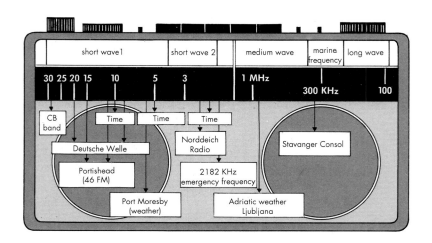

equipment this requires. A quick glance through a brochure will exclude the gadgets that are not up to the job.

The ideal would be a radio receiver with all necessary frequencies on one scale (by frequency we simply mean the number of radio waves per second). Frequencies are measured in hertz. One hertz is one wave per second. Radio waves begin at about 100 Kilohertz (KHz). One KHz is 1000 waves per second; a Megahertz (MHz) is 1000 KHz. Since wavelength is inversely proportional to frequency, the radio dial can be divided into long, medium and short wave bands. Very short waves (over 30 MHz) are those used for high-quality sound; you will also find local (weather) news on this (VHF/FM) band.

Which programmes?

Weather forecast

Whenever possible, use the shipping forecast, broadcast on frequencies which will be given in your almanac. All European weather forecasts are transmitted either on long wave or on short wave 2 between 1.6 and 3.8 MHz. There is a gradual move towards the use of short wave, but modern radios have all bands on one dial anyway, so this does not present a problem.

We might need a different wave band if we are cruising the other side of the world. Port Moresby, for instance, broadcasts on 6.405 MHz. The Italian radio broadcasts a shipping forecast in English at 06.00 UT1. Unfortunately, there are few cruising basins so well served with shipping forecasts as the North and Irish Seas and the Baltic.

Even if your radio receiver has the desired frequency on its dial, this does not always mean you will be able to pick up the broadcast you want. Some wavelengths can cover great distances; some are susceptible to atmospheric disturbances; some are best at night, others during the day. In general, higher frequencies cannot be heard more than 60 miles from the transmitter, and we need to find a low-frequency (long wave) alternative.

You will need a BFO (beat-frequency oscillator) to pick up morse frequencies like Portishead on 46 FM. These transmit energy but no sound: without the BFO which translates the energy into sound you would only notice the broadcast from the signal strength needle.

Some cruising areas of course have no maritime weather service at all. If you are lucky, you will be able to catch the usual land weather forecast after the news on the radio. This is the reason why you need medium wave and VHF/FM.

Most recently, weather fax services have become available for cruising yachts. You need a computer with the software to receive the fax, but you also need a receiver to pick up the transmission. For this, the receiver needs SSB (single side band) functions. You can pick up weather fax transmissions on a huge variety of frequencies. The British Meteorological Office's Radiofax service broadcasts a variety of weather charts covering most of the world, although at the time of writing this service is apparently under review. They transmit 24 hours a day on short-wave frequencies of 4.610MHz, 8.040MHz and 14.436MHz, and also from 06.00 to 18.00 on 18.261MHz and from 18.00 to 06.00 on 2.6185MHz. The German Deutsche Wetterdienst transmits 24 hours a day on 134.2 KHz (long wave) while Rota (the Spanish service) is on 4.7040 MHz, 5.7850 MHz, 9.3825 MHz and 17.585 MHz (short wave).

Radio programmes

These days you can listen to the latest news wherever you are in the world. Music often cheers the crew up. Any radio receiver can pick up news and music programmes on medium wave. The only shame is that medium wave

An insulated backstay makes an effective and inexpensive aerial.

transmissions rarely reach more than 600 miles. If you are crossing the Atlantic, you must reckon on a quiet patch in the middle unless you also have short wave (over 5 MHz).

Radio direction finding

Radio beacons all transmit on marine frequencies between 285 and 425 KHz. Any radio receiver which has this band can pick up their signals, and use them for navigation if it is also equipped with an RDF aerial. Consol beacons (which are more precise than RDF beacons) transmit on the same band. To use these, you do not need the RDF aerial, but you do need a BFO.

One-way radio communication

You may not have a transmitter on board. Your friends and family can still send messages to you, however. Coastal stations will read telegram messages to you on the second short-wave band (where you are listening for weather forecasts).

Time signals

If you are using astro-navigation on board, you need to know the time exactly, to the second. The radio can help. It is more exact and cheaper than buying a chronometer. Even modern quartz watches tend to lose their precision after a couple of days of severe changes in temperature, at least as far as use for navigational purposes is concerned. You can easily remember the time signal frequencies: 2.5 MHz, 5 MHz, 10 MHz, 15 MHz, 20 MHz and 25 MHz. You might wonder why such a large number are necessary. All I can say is that it is not unusual to tune in to every one of these frequencies and to find the reassuring ticking on only one of them.

Your radio receiver might have all these and a BFO and nevertheless fall short of requirements. If the dial looks like the one illustrated on page 84, it will be nigh on impossible to pick up anything on short wave. This is because each broadcaster needs a band width of, say, 10 KHz. Between 1000 KHz and 3000 KHz there is thus room for some 200 transmitters, without any of them interfering with its neighbour's signal. Just looking at the electronics, you would say there is room for another 200 transmitters between 28 and 30 MHz . . . but of course there is no room on the dial to zero in on just one of these. Even if you find the one you want, a jolt or a change of temperature can lose it for you. In a top-notch radio receiver, you should be looking for a

Opposite page: marina on the riviera.

Your all-purpose receiver needs the following bands:

European weather stations	Short wave 2 (1.6–3.8 MHz)
Overseas weather stations	Short wave 1 (4–c. 10 MHz)
FM 46 weather report	Short wave 1 (4–23 MHz)
General radio stations (Europe)	Medium wave (535–1605 KHz)
General radio stations (overseas)	Short wave 1 (4–25 MHz)
Radio direction finding	Marine (285–425 KHz)
Time signal	Short wave 1 (4–25 MHz)
Local weather forecasts	VHF/FM

decently spread out short wave band. Elite radios will use 30 mini-bands to cover the short wave spectrum; unfortunately many a 'specialist' marine receiver is inadequate in this regard.

The ideal on-board receiver is equipped as follows:

- it can tune in precisely to any frequency in the range 150 KHz to 30 MHz (not only in 5 KHz steps);
- the short wave bands are sufficiently well spread that a single transmission can be isolated;
- it has a digital display;
- it has a BFO (beat-frequency oscillator);
- it has a visual signal strength indicator;
- it can take an RDF aerial;
- it may be used as required in either SSB (single side band) or double side band mode.

Almost all transmitters have now switched to SSB (and the rest will do so soon) which means you need more expensive receivers; however, any radio which has BFO can also pick up SSB transmissions in an emergency, with the volume turned right down.

The last few years have seen the development of some receivers which are ideal for use on board. These are not specialist marine equipment: they are normal everyday radios often called something like 'worldwide' models, which allow you to type in the frequency as you would on a pocket calculator. They are built not to lose the frequency; and many of them have programmable memories so you can call up regularly used frequencies with a single key stroke. If you do buy one of these, check that it can receive all the way from 150 KHz to 26 MHz, as well as VHF. 'Steps' of 3KHz at a time are just about acceptable. SSB reception must be available. I would recommend you buy one of these radios if you need a new on-board receiver: they

will repay their purchase price of £150–£350 ($225–$525) many times over.

Aerials

Aerials are not a critical item. If you can equip the backstay with a porcelain insulator top and bottom, you should have no problems. Built-in bar aerials also work adequately, except on steel boats; however, they are sensitive to direction, so you might find you need to change course in order to get a good signal. Your backstay is an excellent wire aerial, so I urge you to use that rather than any built-in model.

Frequency guide

If you want to exploit your radio receiver fully, you will need a list of all the stations which might be of use. I recommend one prepared and published by Jörg Klingenfuss (Hagenloher Str. 14, D-74000 Tübingen, Germany) called *Guide to the Utility Stations*.

Transmitters

Until recently, a skipper thinking of buying a transmitter would end up shrugging and walking away. The equipment was unreliable, and used vast amounts of electricity to feed the valves. Today, transistors have taken over from valves, and the market is swamped with modern equipment. Do you know whether you want an eleven-metre (CB) set, an SSB transmitter, or a short wave set? Few people are certain . . . so let us try a systematic look at this whole vast area.

CB transmitters are the most tempting equipment for the lay person. You can pick up a cheap walkie talkie for not much over £40 ($60). They are easy to use and consume none of your precious electricity, as the batteries are built in. They do need to be licensed, and may only be used for transmission on the 27 MHz band. Unfortunately, their performance is as lightweight as the gear itself: you cannot rely on a range of even 5 nautical miles over open water.

Their only real application is to talk to another yacht which is close enough to be seen (and then only when the crew knows you want to speak to them). There is no emergency service monitoring transmissions on CB in European waters, so a CB transmitter is pointless for SOS calls. They are pretty toys, and no more. In times of real need, they are of no help. You will either find you are out of range of any other CB user, or there is so much traffic on the band that no-one can hear you anyway. The only use we have found for CB sets is when one crew member has been left on land for some errand, and needs to let let you know when they are ready to be picked up.

Transmitters using the wave band between 1 and 5 MHz are no longer worth buying. They are heavy, expensive, and being superseded by VHF worldwide. Their range is not terribly impressive, and these frequencies tend

only to be used where the equipment is out of date (chiefly in far-off regions). Even the state coastal radio services do not use these frequencies any longer.

SSB short wave sets are becoming ever more widely used. They work on a variety of wave bands. Their signal can be picked up by relay stations and sent on worldwide. I once telephoned a friend of mine in Germany from an anchorage off Bora-Bora in the South Pacific, and there was not much more crackling on the line than in a normal trunk call. SSB sets are getting cheaper and lighter all the time. For £2,000 ($3,000) you can buy a powerful transmitter.

Do not make the mistake of equating the transmitter's nominal power output (wattage) with its usable range. The main influence on transmission range in short wave bands is the atmosphere. Around lunchtime, when the atmospheric conditions tend to be poor, even a 1000 watt kit will not allow you to phone Europe from the Caribbean, but you could probably get through in the evening dusk on 50 watts with no problem.

Tankers and other large vessels can usually be contacted on Channel 16. Portable VHF transceivers can be carried along in the dinghy if you have to abandon ship.

Modern VHF radio telephones work across all bands. You can hook up to the domestic telephone network, and the calls are relatively cheap.

The range of a VHF transmitter depends on the height of the aerial . . . so fix it to the masthead!

The aerial is the one thing other than atmospheric conditions which will influence your range. The aerial must be electrically tuned to whichever transmission frequency you are using at the time. You therefore need a tuner. Automatic tuners can be bought, but they are not cheap. My preferred solution is to use the insulated backstay, and tune the transmitter using a 'matchbox' tuner.

VHF radio telephones work in the 156–174 MHz band. They have taken over from 1–5 MHz transmitters, for obvious reasons. They have virtually the same range, use less current, tend not to suffer from atmospheric disturbances, they do not require expensive aerials, and they can be bought for under £800 ($1,200). There has been a VHF network for some time now along the northern and southern coasts of Europe, so you can transmit from virtually anywhere, and hook up to the normal phone network easily and cheaply. Merchant shipping also uses VHF offshore, so you can call up your neighbour in that oil tanker over there, too; if you really make friends, the radio operator might even pass on a telegram for you. You need a ship licence to instal a VHF radio telephone, and a Certificate of Competence from the RYA to operate it.

One can buy hand-held VHF radio telephones. I recommend these for emergency use. They can be taken with you into the dinghy if you have to abandon ship, and the ability to transmit on Channel 16 greatly enhances the likelihood of someone picking you up.

Amateur radio sets are the most effective means of communication for long-distance cruises, in my view. A modern set will cost about £1,200 ($1,800), and will use SSB. A transistorised set is little bigger than a cigar box. It should have search functions, digital display, station preselect, signal strength monitor and so on.

Certain wave bands are reserved for amateur use. Within these bands, you can choose your frequency at will. There is enough variety between bands to ensure that you can always find one suited to the atmospheric conditions and to your purpose. Most amateurs use the 15 metre and 20 metre bands. These allow trouble-free conversations across continents (or oceans). Their one shortcoming is that there is a dead area of some 100km around the transmitter. For short-distance communication only, then, one needs to switch to the 80 metre band, which gives excellent reception. Again, the back stay, suitably insulated, is an excellent aerial. I have 'phoned' Germany direct from New Guinea using this set-up.

The disadvantage of amateur radio is that the licence is a good deal harder to acquire than a VHF transmission licence. As an amateur, using amateur bands, one can communicate only with other amateurs (i.e. not the Coastguard). Of course, the amateur radio ham who you are in touch with can easily phone the Coastguard for you in an emergency. And you would not expect to set off on a long sea journey without agreeing a regular meeting time and spot with your amateur radio shore contact. This allows you to give a daily position, so that if anything does go wrong, the search operation could concentrate on the likeliest area.

Amateur radio use is free of charge, except for the (nominal) monthly licence fee. A restriction on the use of amateur 'ham' radio is that the service may not be used to pass on news to third parties. It is thus not permissible to radio your ham contact and ask them to phone your home to check up that everything is all right with your family. Despite this limitation, a ham radio means that you never need feel entirely alone on the ocean. I would thoroughly recommend you to look into the topic of ham radio if you are considering crossing the Atlantic or going further afield.

There is a worldwide network of ham radio groups who monitor maritime amateur traffic to keep in touch: Micronesia-Net, South-East Asia Net and so on.

Ham radio set which will receive all frequencies from long wave to short wave. Unbeatable for long-distance transmission. No operating costs, but you do need an amateur radio licence.

Yacht Handling

Lines, wires and knots

There is an important difference between plaited and twisted (or laid) rope. Plaited rope is much more comfortable and more pliant than laid rope, but also more expensive. Its main use is for sheets. Laid rope is used for warps, anchor lines, and sometimes in place of wire for the main and jib halyards. Artificial fibres stretch under load to a greater or lesser extent (which can be handy in some circumstances but harmful in others). Some even stretch as much as 20%. Imagine: your 20m warp becomes a 24m warp. This is the reason why rope lines are not appropriate for use as stays or guard rails.

Pre-stretched lines are available for use as halyards. These have been stretched before leaving the factory to almost the length they would reach under extreme tension. Pre-stretched lines should not be used for the anchor or as warps, because the elasticity is an asset in these cases: a boat at anchor in a sea needs all the shock-absorption it can get!

Lines made from artificial fibre do not rot; they do tire over time, especially under strong ultra-violet light or repeated heavy tension, and they tend also to stiffen. Liros, the rope manufacturers, have researched this area thoroughly, and they recommend that rope should not be subjected to continual tension of more than one fifth its breaking strain. A little extra weight is no great concern for the average cruising yacht: always make sure your lines and warps are bigger than they need to be for the job you have in mind.

Liros Kevlar sheets are a real space-age invention which are five times as strong as steel wire, weight for weight.

This Maxi-tonner is fine for offshore cruising, so long as you take a large crew!

93

Liros's recommended line diameters (in mm) and breaking strains (in kg)					
weight of boat in tonnes	sheets	spinnaker or big boy sheets	halyards	warps and anchor line	boom uphaul
	plaited	plaited	laid, pre-stretched	laid	laid, pre-stretched
<1	8 (c. 850)	8	8 (c. 1250)	10 (c. 2100)	8
<3	10 (c. 1400)	8	8 (c. 1250)	12 (c. 3000)	8
<5	10 (c. 1400)	10	10 (c. 1750)	14 (c. 4100)	8
<8	12 (c. 1900)	10	10 (c. 1750)	16 (c. 5300)	8
<12	12 (c. 1900)	12	12 (c. 2400)	20 (c. 8100)	10

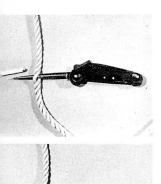

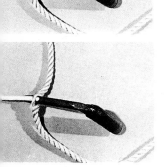

A length of copper tube turned into a marlin spike.

The down side is that they are very sensitive to being kinked or knotted, so there are few cruising uses for these ropes. They are useful as mainsheets, spinnaker or big boy sheets. They stretch very little under load (about 60% as much as polyester) so their enormous strength makes Kevlar ropes useful as backstays or as emergency shrouds.

Every sailor must be familiar with the ropes on board and able to use them. A boat genuinely ready for its first cruise on delivery is a mythical creature; and even the best material will break or wear out one day. We therefore need to have spare ropes on board, plus a few cheap, simple tools.

● Marlin spike (photos left). Hollow spikes are much the best sort, but you cannot buy them. A friendly mechanic will bend and chamfer a piece of copper tubing for you.
● Whipping thread.
● Scissors, matches or lighter.

Every rope end must be sealed and prevented from fraying. If there is nothing else to hand, melt the strands with a match, and when they have cooled so you can just about touch them, roll them to a smooth end. Such sealed ends are not terribly resilient, especially under load. A properly whipped end is the only right way to finish a rope. The Deller whipping described

Lines and halyards neatly stowed: you never know when you might need to undo them in a hurry.

opposite is my favourite for cruising yachts, since it requires no sewing, it can easily be made without tools, and it holds every time. I used one of these whippings to lengthen my jib sheets: the join lasted me all the way round the world, 32,000 nautical miles, and still looks as though it had been made yesterday.

Any loose ropes on board must be properly stowed. Make sure that they are coiled through your hand a length at a time, with no kinks and no figures of eight. If the line twists, you can easily twist it back between finger and thumb. See the photos on the next page for how to finish a coil.

When the sails are up, halyards must be stowed so that they can be made free to come down in seconds (see photos at foot of pp. 96–7).

Handling ropes

High-performance winches, blocks and cleats make it easy for even the puniest crew member to haul a sail in tight. Not much can go wrong. Even in the lightest winds the jib sheet must take three turns round a winch before it is led into the cleat. If it is fed straight in, a single squall can damage either the sheet itself or the cleat. The winch drum, incidentally, does not need to have a rough surface: the friction which holds the sheet results from the number of turns. Four turns on a winch are enough to reduce the tug from the sheet on your hand to 5% of its original strength. All the same, you should not take four turns on the winch before starting a tack: there is so much loose sheet to be pulled in that it is bound to wrap itself around the winch drum anyway.

As a general rule, you should aim to take one turn on the winch before tacking; pull with both hands while you tack; and then slip at least a further two turns on just before the sail fills on the new tack. Frequently you will find

there is a conventional cleat just after the winch, so you will have to wrap a couple of figures of eight on the cleat rather than the single pull which is sufficient in a clamcleat. The figure of eight is the same one as is used to brake the inboard end of a warp. The first turn is just to create friction, so that our frail human strength is enough to control the line. Once the line is the desired length, we wrap a couple more turns onto the cleat and finish off with a proper half-hitch.

There are those who claim that half-hitches should not be permitted on board except to brake a halyard with which we have temporarily hauled our crewmate up the mast for a repair. This was a reasonable precaution in the days of natural-fibre ropes, when damp could swell the knot and make it impossible to undo without the help of an axe. These days, artificial fibres have overcome this objection; and in this instance, the function of the half-hitch is merely to stop the figures of eight jumping off the cleat: it does not come under tension itself at all.

Here ends the first lesson in knotcraft. You can buy dozens of books full of hundreds of knots. In reality, though, there are only a very few knots anyone needs on board a yacht (certainly fewer than you need to pass a yachtmaster's exam). These few knots are such life-savers that you need to be able to tie them in your sleep.

Knots

Granny knots are not permitted on board. They come undone of their own accord; and if they ever do stay tied tight, they are impossible to undo.

A sailor's knot must never come undone on its own; but it must always be easy to undo.

A **reef knot** is for joining two ropes. It may be used in any situation where

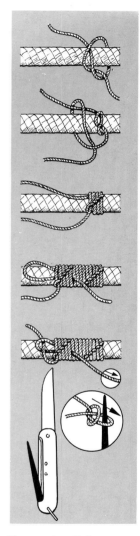

The turns in a Deller whipping are all in the same direction. They lie close up against each other, and each one is tightened individually, ideally using the marlin spike (see inset). About half way along the whipping, the turns must be made <u>over</u> the loop in the free end. The loop is tightened to finish off the whipping.

95

Left to right: Ensure that all coils are the same size, and do not allow the rope to form eights. Always make the end of the coil off in the same way: that way, any line can be grabbed from the cockpit locker in a single move.

If the line is so twisted that it makes figures of eight on its own, twist it back on itself with a finger-and-thumb roll. Try it: it works.

Left to right: Halyards must be neatly stowed so that they are instantly accessible after any use.

a landlubber might tie a granny knot (such as tying down the main on the boom). There is no worthwhile use for slip knots on a boat, except perhaps to booby-trap someone's hammock. The difference between the two is that a reef knot has both free ends on the same side.

The **sheet bend** is a close relative of the reef knot. Some books illustrate sheet bends as though they were related to slip knots, but I would not trust any of these half-breeds. A single sheet bend is actually rarely used, but a double sheet bend is extremely handy for joining two lines of differing diameters. I'm afraid I have only limited trust in even the double knot if it is subject to repeated variations in tension, unless each line is also secured with an extra half hitch. There is a simpler way of joining two lines: twin **bowlines**, looped through each other.

The bowline is the ultimate, the universal knot. No sailor can live without

it. Its unique trait is that the loop does not pull tight. American sailors and mountaineers have developed an idiot-proof method of tying a bowline. Depending on the size we want our loop to be, the rope end is passed round the marlin spike (as on p. 95, inset) and the looped end is pulled through to make a bowline. The major application of this universal knot is for the outboard end of a warp: it makes a good solid loop which can be thrown to a helpful landlubber. Surely nobody can make a hash of dropping a loop over a bollard . . .

A **clove hitch** should not be used to tie up a yacht. Some dinghy sailors use clove hitches to tie up, but on larger boats its main application is in tying the fenders on.

There is one thing which we must not forget about all the above knots. Knots weaken the rope. Most knots reduce a rope's breaking strain by about 40%, and a reef knot link is 60% weaker than straight rope. If you find

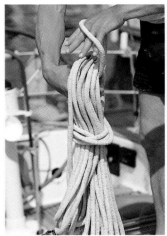

yourself in a storm, when these percentages might matter, tie up to a post or bollard with a round turn and two half hitches. This reduces the breaking strain by only 25%.

The easiest knot is left until last: the **figure of eight knot**. This is tied at the free end of every sheet to prevent it running through the block.

Blocks

Whenever a line changes direction under tension, it must be led through a block. Plastic blocks are usual for ropes. They are virtually maintenance-free; the only requirement is that they must be broad enough for the rope diameter. If a rope chafes on the sides, its life will be much reduced. Sheets or lines which are constantly running over blocks at the same place need to be protected, especially on long voyages. In our experience, beef tallow, carefully rubbed into the rope, is an excel-

lent lubricant. Any butcher will be able to give you some. We re-grease ropes every 2,000 miles. Lines which travel over sharp edges, such as mooring warps, should be led through simple plastic tubing.

Wires

Stainless steel has blessed the sailing fraternity over the last few decades. The price may be high, but the advantages of this material are substantial. In earlier times, wires and rigging needed galvanising, these days we can put up a stainless steel wire and almost forget about it. Admittedly one cannot repair stainless steel: it tends to be too brittle to splice.

Terminals can be fixed on using the on-board toolkit if you buy the screw-in, Norseman type. You will need a small screwdriver and a pair of pliers. If you follow the manufacturer's instructions, you can put an eye on the end of

Everything you need to know about knots.

1a: Making off a line on a halyard: wrong to start with!

1b: Correct beginning, just the last half hitch is wrong.

1c: Correct! Thin ropes will need one further figure of eight. Ensure that the finishing half hitch does not come under pressure.

2: Round turn and two half hitches.

3: Figure of eight.

4a–e: Clove hitch: handy for tying up the dinghy, but not for your precious yacht.

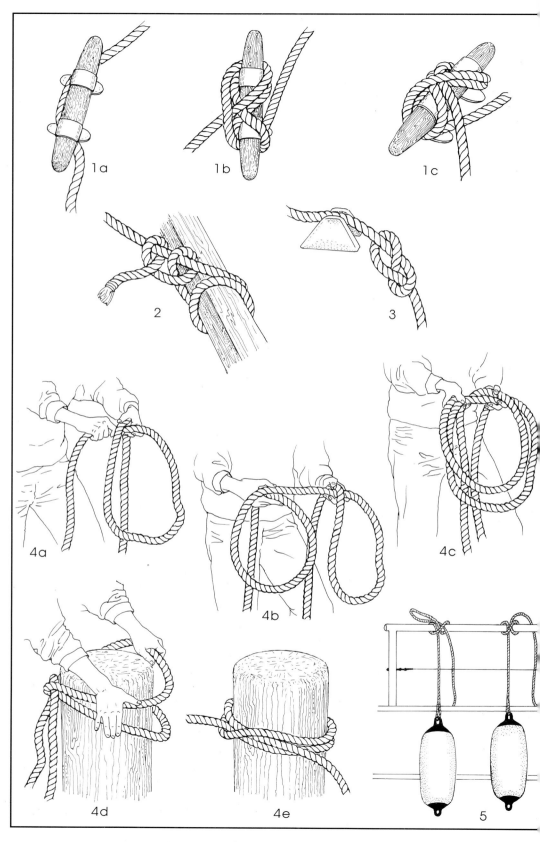

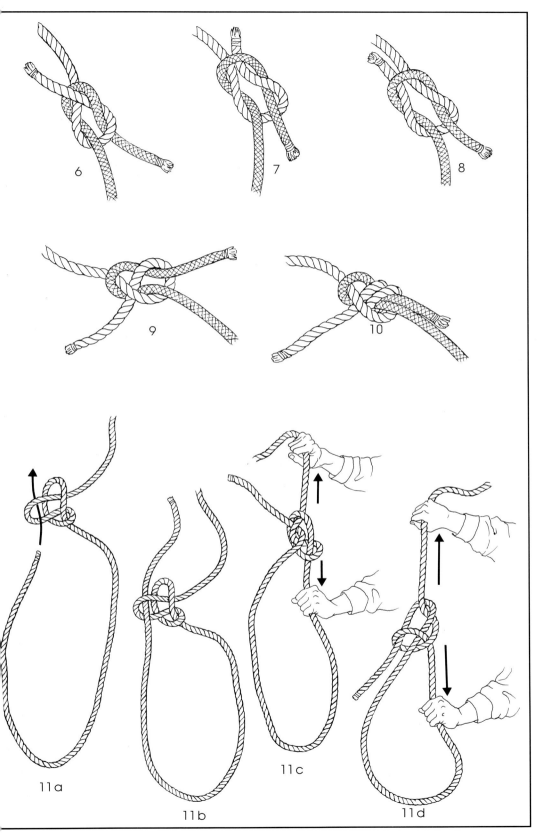

5: The correct application of a clove hitch, for fixing fenders. Note the slip clove hitch, left.

6: Granny knot.

7: A true reef knot.

8: A fool's reef knot, otherwise known as a slip knot (free ends on opposite sides).

9: Sheet bend, a relative of the true reef knot.

10: Double sheet bend.

11a–d: Bowline, tied the American way. Try it out: you can't go wrong.

When that squall strikes, you will need the mainsail down. Woe betide you if there is a kink in the wire halyard.

a wire halyard. The thread needs to be locked with an epoxy fixative to prevent the terminal coming undone. I have never been let down by one of these.

Stainless steel suffers badly when kinked. We are always careful when hoisting the genoa to make sure that there is space on the winch drum for the last few turns of halyard, so that the earlier turns are not squeezed.

There is one point to look out for when you buy new stainless wires: if individual strands start to detach themselves early in the wire's life, either the block is jamming or it is too small in diameter for the wire. Blocks which are bearing wire must be at least the following diameters:

wire diameter	block diameter
5mm	7cm
6mm	8cm
7mm	10cm
8mm	13cm

100

The skipper

The skipper is absolute master on board, old-fashioned though this may sound. Boats are not democracies, at least not in matters of boat handling. Anyone who still has their doubts on this would do well to consider the analogy with driving a car. A car driver has every instrument and control within reach; both hands and both feet are used to keep the vehicle on course. Cruising yachts are rather different, at least from a given size up.

All the controls are scattered about an area of 7m or more in length, and there is no way a single person can manage them all. The crew members are the hands and feet of the skipper. When you are driving a car, you increase the pressure of your right foot on the accelerator. The equivalent action on board a boat is probably hauling the mainsheet tighter; and if the skipper is not holding the sheet, then another member of the crew will have to take on the task, immediately, without questions or (worse still) alternative suggestions.

The skipper and crew can only work together well if the crew members listen properly to the skipper's instructions and have been trained to understand them. The skipper should insist that the language used on board for transmitting orders is clear and common to all the crew. Many of the orders used have been with us for centuries on boats. It is perfectly possible to invent your own orders, of course, but common sense indicates that you should use language as close as possible to that current on other yachts. One of your regular crew members might bring a friend along; and that friend will be a hindrance rather than a help unless they also speak your language. Similarly, if you ever need land-based help, use of a common language will greatly speed matters up.

Orders need to be given at a certain volume, dictated not by the requirements of courtesy but by those of the background noise. Orders must be at least loud enough for everyone on board to hear them correctly first time. Crew members show that they have understood a given order by repeating it back. If there is any chance that the skipper might not notice when the order has actually been carried out, the crew member must report back when the action has been completed.

If the skipper is in command, then there should be no possibility of a crew member taking the helpful suggestion of a land-based observer as an order; nor will it be possible for the skipper to hand over the captaincy to another crew member halfway through a manoeuvre. The following table lists the

The crew of the *Frabato*: the perfect team? The all-woman crew seems to think so; and the satisfied grin on the skipper's face tells the same tale.

commonest orders. You should be able to tell those which require a report when completed, such as 'stern warp away'.

Orders

Course commands
Rudder hard to starboard (boat turns to starboard)
Luff up
Sail course on the wind
Sail course wind abeam
Sail 220 degrees
Sail course for harbour, and so on

Line commands
Stern warp away
Make ready slip bow spring
Stern spring ready
Throw the bow warp
Make ready the springs
Make ready the tow rope
Make fast the stern warp

Sail commands
Ready to drop the main
Drop the jib
Tension the topping lift
Mainsheet hard in (only when sailing close hauled)
Hoist the jib
Slacken off the mainsheet
Trim the jib (The sheet is not pulled in completely, just enough to trim the jib for the course being sailed.)
Back the jib
Ready about (Some skippers use this to prepare the crew both for a tack and for a gybe; others prefer to reserve 'ready about' for tacking, and 'ready to gybe' as the alternative.)

Anchor commands
Ready to lower the anchor
Lower (or drop) the anchor
Ready to weigh anchor
Heave the anchor short
Up anchor

The skipper must prepare the boat and crew for the expected manoeuvre. It is better to start preparing much earlier than you think. It is always worth consulting the crew: no manoeuvre should be initiated until the skipper has got a clear plan in his mind's eye of every move and sequence involved.

The **strength of the crew** either in numbers or experience is seldom decisive for the success of a manoeuvre. The more experts there are on board, the smoother the operation will usually be; but almost any manoeuvre may be carried out with a minimal crew. Cruising yachts will often have only two people on board, charter yachts rather more.

Helpful but inexperienced guest crew are a problem. If you can handle the boat with the usual team, do not put everyone out to incorporate the novice. At best they will spoil the skipper's view; at worst they will actually get in the way. They are frankly better placed below deck. Under no circumstances should they be entrusted with a task which makes or breaks your tying-up or casting-off manoeuvre, however simple the task may appear.

Almost all the manoeuvres described on the following pages are easily carried out with a minimal crew consisting of skipper plus one. The skipper's task is to work things out so that the moves follow each other in order rather than all happening at once. It may look smart when the yacht comes into the harbour and the fenders are flipped over the side just as you approach the quay; but there is no shame in the one crew having tied the fenders onto the rail as you entered the harbour. The most important principle of any manoeuvre must be:

> Leave yourself time to think any manoeuvre through properly, plan the steps involved completely, and then carry it out firmly.

No manoeuvre should ever be carried it out under the banner of 'give it a try, it should work'.

Manoeuvres in harbour

The boat made fast

A cruiser must never be tied up to a jetty in the same way as you might tie up a sailing dinghy. If a cruiser of any weight is made fast with a bow painter alone, it will come crashing repeatedly into the jetty even in a slight offshore breeze.

Basically, whenever there is room, and assuming no onshore swell, a cruising yacht should be tied up alongside a jetty or quayside. Two warps, one forward at the bow and one at the stern, are insufficient for carrying this out properly: the boat would always swing about its widest point. You can prevent the boat swinging against the quay by using two additional warps, or springs, one forward and one aft.

The bow and stern warps should ideally be the strongest lines you have on board. Every warp should have its own deck cleat on the boat (as strong as you can make them). The warp is made fast on board by wrapping it several times round the cleat in a figure of eight, finishing off with a round turn. Assuming there are posts on the quay around which to tie it, always use a bowline at the land end of a warp. A bowline allows later arrivals to use the same post without trapping or undoing your line.

Any manoeuvre carried out with the help of warps (almost any manoeuvre) is subject to one inalienable law:

> All warp-handling must be done from the boat, not from the land.

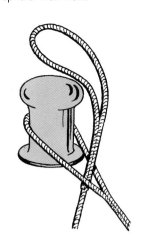

This is how not to upset the neighbours when you tie up later than them.

An everyday scene in Holland and Scandinavia: tied up alongside a raft of other vessels.

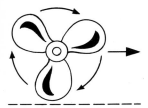
Right-hand screw: drives the stern to the right.

The warps should not be tied too tight. If you are in tidal waters, the tides will mean that the warps really need to be different lengths at different times of the day to avoid the boat hanging itself against the quay. The further fore and aft the warps are led, the less danger there is of this happening. If you know the tidal range is particularly large in a given harbour, you are better advised to tie up to floating pontoons or to commercial vessels which you know are not in use.

No cruising yacht should ever be tied up to a quay without fenders. The smallest movement of the water, including the wash from other boats, causes enough movement to turn your precious hull finish into something resembling a cheese-grater. You need enough fenders; and you need them where they are actually of some use, amidships. If you have made the boat fast correctly, with bow and stern warps as well as springs fore and aft, fenders will not be necessary at the bow and stern. Fenders distributed evenly along the length of a boat are a dead giveaway: spot the beginner!

Tying up alongside other boats is basically no different from making fast at the quay, except that you need to take into consideration the size of the boats: the largest ties up next to the quay. If the boat next to yours on the landward side is not substantially larger than yours, you should also tie your own bow and stern warps to the jetty. It should not need saying that any skipper must ask the permission of the boats next door before joining their raft. Similarly, you should not just use their decks as a bridge from your vessel to the mainland without checking first. When you do cross a neighbouring boat, always go across the foredeck, as this will cause them the least disturbance.

Manoeuvres in harbour under engine power

Once upon a time every sailor was proud of their ability to carry out all manoeuvres using sail alone. Harbours these days are so crowded that such pride is likely to cause upsets. Safety must take precedence. Manoeuvring under sail takes longer, is more difficult and less safe than under engine power. It is therefore more seamanlike to use the engine in crowded harbours. The only reason to use the sails is when the engine won't start.

> Whether under sail or engine power, your boat should have no more way on than is necessary for the manoeuvre you are carrying out.

The lowest speed required for any given manoeuvre is determined by your boat's handling characteristics: specifically, whether it will respond to the rudder. Assuming still water and still air, the average cruiser should be able to manoeuvre at 1 knot. When it is windy, you might need noticeably more

Boat correctly tied up: four warps, and fenders only where they are needed.

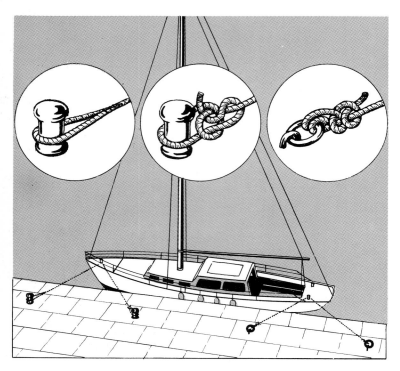

speed just to keep the bow up into the wind.

Before we carry out any manoeuvres in harbour under engine power, there are a few basics about propellers which need to be dealt with.

In the first instance, we are not concerned with the differences between outboard and inboard motors. A propeller turning in water not only propels the boat forward, but also exerts a turning moment dependent on its own screw direction, pushing the stern in one or other direction. This 'paddle-wheel' effect results from the fact that the water at the bottom of the screw's turn is under greater pressure than that at the top of the turn. You might find it easier to imagine this effect if you think of the propeller blades actually making contact with solid ground at the bottom of their turn.

A propeller with a right-hand screw (as seen from behind the boat) will tend to shove the stern to starboard; a left-hand screw will push the stern out to port. A right-hand screw turns left when in reverse, however; thus the same propeller which pushes the stern to starboard when you are travelling forward, pushes it to port when you are reversing. This effect is noticeable only at low speeds, and becomes negligible when you are moving normally. On most boats, you are no longer able to feel the paddle-wheel effect through the tiller or wheel above one and a half knots.

A basic rule: do not attempt a powered manoeuvre with a boat until you know whether the propeller has a right-hand or left-hand screw.

Manoeuvres under sail in a crowded Mediterranean harbour are not a good way of making friends.

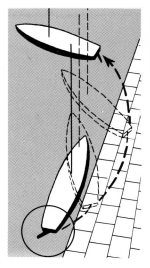

If you push the rudder hard to port, you will whack the quay with your stern.

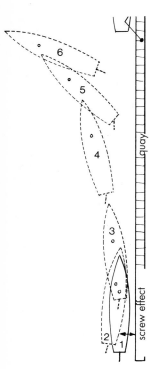

Casting off from the quay

Before we look at casting off under engine power, let us just revise the topic of how a vessel moves. Earlier, we compared the boat with a car. The comparison is no longer accurate in this context: the main difference is that a car steers through the front wheels, whereas a boat's steering (whether under engine or sail power) operates mainly on the stern. We shall examine the consequences of this in an example.

If the rudder is pushed hard to starboard, so that the boat should steer to starboard, then the first thing that happens is that the stern moves to port. If there is no room to port for the stern to move into (because the quay or another boat is in the way), the boat simply cannot turn. You need to take account of this in any manoeuvre involving tying up or casting off alongside.

If the boat has its starboard side to the quay, it will not be a simple job to cast off to port. The first task in casting off, in all cases, is to put enough water between boat and land to be able to turn in the desired direction. Once the turn is begun, the helm should continue to keep an eye on the stern.

Casting off is no great problem with small craft, since a shove with hand or foot (or better still, with a boathook) is sufficient to give you room to turn without scraping your rear end along the quayside. Pushing a larger vessel off from the pier will not work if you try it from amidships; you have a better chance if you push from either the foredeck or the aft deck.

Casting off boats of over 6 tonnes, or casting off into the wind, is extremely difficult if done by hand. We need the engine. The propeller's paddle-wheel effect is strongest and most useful when the boat is not moving through the water. We shall assume our vessel has a left-hand screw (as almost all modern yachts have) and we are lying with

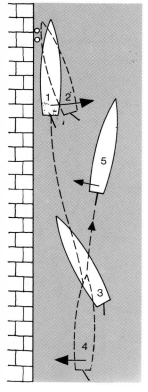

Left-hand screw, quay to port.

our starboard side on to the quay.

If the wind is offshore, it helps: it will help push the bow round and off the wind. Large yachts which are virtually impossible to cast off normally can still use an offshore wind. An onshore wind makes life much harder; in fact, a strong onshore wind can frustrate even the following technique.

> A basic rule: always take the wind into account, whether you are manoeuvring under sail or engine.

Once the boat and crew are ready to cast off but while the normal warps are still in place and under tension, loop extra warps around a post on the jetty and back to the boat. These become your slip warps. You then take in the normal warps so that the boat is now held only by the looped slip warps.

The purpose of this swap is that the slip warps can be handled exclusively from on board the boat, and we are not dependent on some kind passer-by. Passers-by always let the warp go at exactly the wrong moment anyway. The slip warps must be free of knots and kinks, so there is no danger of them catching on anything: the success of the manoeuvre frequently depends on the lines being hauled in speedily.

The skipper starts the engine and gives the order 'ready to cast off'. All surplus lines are brought inboard. Now you need to get the stern away from the quay. In the current situation (left-hand screw, starboard side to the quay) this will happen of its own accord. You cast off and go slow ahead, and the stern swings out from the quay well before the boat actually starts moving forward. If there is enough water between the boat and the quay the skipper can give a touch more throttle and the boat can start moving slowly forward.

It would be a mistake to throw the

rudder hard to port at this stage, because there is almost certainly not enough room, and the stern would scrape along the wall. Boats need a surprisingly large turning circle when casting off. You should also ensure you have some distance free ahead of you, so that you do not crash into some broad-beamed yacht up front! Do not shift into 'full ahead' until you are certain that the yacht is clear of the quay and any other obstacles.

In this situation the paddle-wheel effect assisted casting off. With a left-hand screw, the starboard side to the quay (or with a right-hand screw, port to the quay) is the most comfortable starting point for casting off. Casting off in this manner is not possible when you have a left-hand screw but the quay to port. You could have a crew member permanently pushing you away from the side but you would never make enough room to put the rudder hard to starboard. You would succeed merely in sanding down your rear quarter.

The way to leave the quay in this situation is to use the right-hand paddle-wheel effect of the screw in reverse, thus dragging the stern out to starboard. When you do this, you must take care to place fenders strategically by the bow to prevent damage through contact with the quayside. The boat's centre of resistance, around which it turns, is approximately at the mast

step, so that when we move the stern away, the bow comes towards us and vice versa. The boat needs to be about two or three times its own length from the jetty before we dare push the rudder to starboard and the engine ahead, and begin chugging slowly off.

This manoeuvre is so slow that we need a lot of space fore or aft of our boat in order to carry it out. One rarely comes across this ideal situation in a real harbour. More usually our boat will be right between two others. The next simple and effective example will show how to escape from this position.

Casting off using engine and spring

First, the bow spring is replaced by a slip bow spring. Be sure to pad the bow well with fenders, and make the slip fast as far forward as you can. Once all other warps are taken in, we motor slowly (as ever, in harbour) into the spring. Since the spring is tied at the bow, the thrust of the boat pushes the bow gently in towards the quay. If the quay is to port, the rudder should also be hard to port, as though our aim were to drive up onto the quay.

Once the bow spring is tight and the bow (nicely padded) firm against the side, we can increase the revs to half power ahead. The stern will drift out really quite fast. Even with a strong headwind, this manoeuvre will allow the boat to reach an angle of 45° to the quay. The engine is then put into neu-

Left: Slip bow warp. Before you cast off, your slip warp should be the top one on the post.

Right: Slip stern warp. Note that the slips can be handled exclusively from on board.

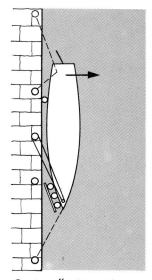

Casting off using engine and spring requires you to drop fenders all along the bow quarter. With the quay to starboard, the rudder should be hard to starboard.

107

Casting off using slip bow spring.

tral, and finally slow astern. The stern is free by this stage, and the vessel will move slowly astern. Once the bow is clear of the quay, haul in the spring. We have acquired enough room to drive backwards out of the berth, then slowly ahead and out of the harbour once we are entirely clear of other boats.

> A basic rule: never change gear in one move from 'full ahead' to 'full astern' or vice versa.

You should always ensure that you engage neutral for a few seconds between a forward and a reverse gear. A quick change will stress the gears and shafts in the engine and may end up breaking something. (Breakages are less likely with a hydraulic clutch.)

Untying warps which are under tension is a two-person job. One crew member is positioned on land to remove the bowline from the post, and the on-board crew member allows a little slack into the line. In this way the loop may be removed from the post with no danger of trapping a finger. All the skipper needs to say is 'warps in', and a well trained crew will know that one of them is to let slack into the lines.

Those crew members who are following an order from the skipper must be sure to report what they are doing or

have done. Thus the order 'stern warp in' will be followed by the report 'stern warp inboard'. This is just as true for a small boat: the skipper's job is much easier with a precise running report on the state of the boat's readiness. The skipper should not have to check everything with his or her own eyes.

When you are handling warps, be sure to lead them once around a deck cleat. If a warp comes under tension while you are trying to feed slack into it, it can be virtually impossible to regain enough slack to cleat it. And if a warp is led once round a cleat, even a weak member of the crew will have enough strength effectively to brake the warp and stop a heavy yacht from drifting, singlehanded.

Tying up under engine power
The first commandment of harbour manoeuvres is:

> Never carry out a manoeuvre in haste!

The skipper must calmly choose a spot for tying up. The local topography needs to be considered. There is nothing wrong with chugging past the apparently free spot by the quay once or twice just to check that it really is free and that you will not have to leave again in half an hour when the local fishing fleet returns. There is nothing impolite about asking people on other yachts about the harbour, the local conditions and the proposed mooring or tying-up spot. This is not to imply that the skipper can miss out on the relevant homework: harbour pilots, charts and other documents on board should all have been checked thoroughly before you enter the harbour. You should be suspicious of that ideally sited spot just the right size for your boat in a crowded harbour. And the crew should be helping as you cruise around the harbour, by sitting somewhere where they do not spoil the skipper's view: they should certainly not be standing around or doing their hair to prepare for the evening's excursions ashore. All sails should have been neatly stowed by this stage.

Once you have identified a suitable spot by the quay, a moment's reflection on the manoeuvre is in order. Do not forget every boat has a preferred side for casting off from. The preferred side is the one opposite the screw direction, thus starboard for a left-hand screw.

If you do decide to tie up starboard side to land because of the left-hand screw, then let the crew know. A well trained crew will then set the warps (fore and aft, plus bow and stern springs) without being told, and put the fenders in position. The warps are correctly set when their outboard end, with bowline already tied, is on top of the flaked pile of rope and ready to be handed overboard. The bowline should always err on the large side: to be certain, look at the size of the posts on the jetty!

A practised crew will carry out their tasks when told to prepare warps and fenders to starboard. The skipper's job is made much easier if the reports come back in order: stern warp ready, bow warp ready and so on. With a smaller crew, if the boat is being sailed two-handed, for instance, it is enough for the crew to report: 'warps and fend-

ers ready to starboard'. When you are tying up on the preferred side (that is, starboard if you have a left-hand screw), you also need a bow fender right forward.

At the very beginning of the manoeuvre, the skipper throttles back so as just to retain steerage way. In a wind, the skipper can tell the boat is travelling too slowly because it becomes difficult to keep the bow up as the wind overpowers the rudder. If your log is an electronic one which measures even small variations in speed, you may find it easier after a little practice to moderate your speed according to the display.

The yacht should approach the intended berth at an angle of about 30°. Ideally, a crew member will be positioned at the bow and will sing out the estimated distance to the quay (in multiples or fractions of a boat's length).

Depending on the weight of the boat (and this is something you will learn after a very short apprenticeship) you will choose a moment to put the engine in neutral. Ideally, the bow should come up to the quay as the boat has almost completely lost momentum. In practice, this ideal is seldom attainable. You will usually need to engage reverse at some point. This has a double effect: it slows the boat and ultimately stops it; and the paddle-wheel effect brings the stern in towards the quayside just at the point when this is needed.

If you are going to make mistakes, it is far better to approach the quay too gingerly, so that you need to go through the procedure again, than to crash into the wall. Even the best fenders will not stop you scratching that precious gel coat then!

A 30° approach to tying up. The rudder is turned (in this case to port) when you are half to a quarter of a length away. The amount of rudder depends on the boat's turning circle. The stern warp is first out, then the bow warp, followed by the springs.

Left to right: To tighten warps once the boat is attached to the shore, use a friend's weight, not your biceps. With one turn on the deck cleat, a friend stands on the warp and then removes their weight allowing you to heave the line in further.

Left to right: Throwing a line: one third in the throwing hand, two thirds in the other. No figures of eight. Practice makes perfect.

If the manoeuvre is carried out well, it is easy for a crew member to hop off the boat onto the quay, or even to step off. The best spot to leave the boat is amidships: the quay is closest, and the shrouds are a convenient, if temporary, handhold.

Important: the warps must be brought on land as fast as possible, especially in wind, waves or current.

The securing warps are thrown onto the quay. Every crew member needs to have practised this: it is not so easy as one might think. Few people can throw a line further than 20m, and into the wind throwing distances are much shorter. Getting a line ashore can save a yacht's (and its crew's) hide in some conditions.

Throwing a line This must become part of your regular practice procedures. First, the line is coiled overhand in about ten fairly large loops. The first two loops must under no circumstances be larger than the others, as this would prevent the line snaking out in flight. About one third of the coil is held in the

throwing hand, and the other two thirds on the open fingers of the other hand. Make sure the inboard end is tied, or at least that you are standing on it. The only other problem to look out for is catching the warp on a shroud or the safety wires.

The massive warps of large vessels cannot really be thrown. You need to use a throwing line, a fairly light line with a weight (a hefty knot, or a small sandbag is ideal) tied to one end. Throwing lines can be thrown for much greater distances. Even on smaller boats, it is worth keeping a suitably coiled throwing line readily to hand. (The Panama Canal workers reckon to be able to throw such lines 40m, with considerable precision.)

Once you have the weighted end of the throwing line ashore, the inboard end may be attached to the warp itself. The best way of doing this is by two bowlines looped through each other, or a double sheet bend. The double sheet bend is quicker, but the bowlines will never let you down (assuming they are correctly tied) and the main warp has probably got a bowline in the end already.

Manoeuvres in harbour under sail power

For some reason one is always meeting sailors who have not noticed that sailing boats, unlike motor boats, do not have a reverse gear. Reverse gear is seldom used for going backwards anyway: it is more a question of braking a boat which is drifting forwards. Sails are less effective at this job: a backed jib or mainsail will certainly slow you down, but its effect is so tiny that you should not rely on this to get you through a manoeuvre.

> Do not attempt to berth a yacht at a jetty or quay by luffing up and 'shooting' the last few metres.

Small boats and dinghies quite correctly approach the jetty by sailing dead to windward, relying on the wind to slow their approach. Heavier yachts cannot do this. The difference is that a light boat slows down appreciably after a short distance; and if it slows too much, it can be relied on to accelerate quickly and recover.

With a heavy keelboat, you can neither slow down nor accelerate quickly. Most textbooks will tell you how to work out the 'braking distance' required for your boat, but if this distance is to be any use at all, you need to be able to estimate it to within at most one metre. You might just manage this with a 7m or even a 10m yacht; but it is impossible with a heavier boat which might take 50m or so to stop. Once a keelboat has come to rest, you will not be able to get it going again by pumping the mainsail: it is too heavy. Instead it will begin to make leeway.

If you have the jib up at this point, the boat will also bear away. If you calculate the stopping distance too generously (even just by a metre or two) no arm or leg will be able to prevent several tons of boat colliding with the

Opposite: one of the charms of cruising is that massive ships and tiny sailing boats need to get along together. They cannot always avoid sailing the same stretches of water, especially at moorings or in marinas.

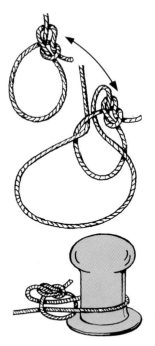

A handy way of reducing the size of your bowline loop if it is too large for the post.

quay. It will have the same momentum as a slow truck. A slight over-estimation of the stopping distance will cause considerable damage to your bow.

Approaching the quay under sail is possible, but the sails need to be taken down in plenty of time. The final part of the approach is made using warps which are taken on land earlier in the manoeuvre.

All the approaches described (except the last one) are possible even with a small crew, so long as the preparation is done adequately.

> **A basic rule:** A heavy cruising yacht must never reach the quay with its sails up. A flapping mainsail or jib can still push you forward uncomfortably fast. If the wind is abaft the beam, it will in any case not be possible to get the sails let out far enough.
>
> **A further basic rule:** The mainsail must not be pulled up during any manoeuvre, whether tying up or leaving the quay, unless the boat is head to wind or virtually head to wind. The jib may be raised or pulled down no matter where the wind is coming from.

Any skipper who is thinking about approaching the quay under sail must know the quay well, and must know what the wind is doing close to the quay. You should certainly take a quiet lap or two of the harbour to familiarise yourself with the conditions at the quayside. Take a look particularly at the posts and check their size. Will you be able to tie the fenders so that they do their job and prevent you scraping the sides? If not, do not attempt to tie up there: tying up under sail always requires the use of fenders! The final thing to check is whether you will be able to get a line onto the quay: is it low enough for a crew member to hop off onto? Is there a trustworthy-looking

character there whom you might ask to catch your line? If you have enough bodies on board, it is worth sending one out in advance in the dinghy, or dropping them off as you pass by, so that you are certain they will catch your line.

> Preparation is everything when approaching the quay under sail. Ropes and fenders must be ready for use, and the manoeuvre must be minutely planned.

There is no harm in the skipper telling the crew half an hour before landfall is expected, to get lines and fenders ready for tying up to starboard. The manoeuvre actually sailed will depend on the direction of the wind relative to the quay.

Tying up under sail in offshore wind
If there is space by the quay, this is a straightforward move. If you fail with the first attempt to get a line ashore, you can always wait for the boat to drift out, set the sails again and come back for a second try.

Important: You cannot haul the mainsail down except when you are head to wind or thereabouts. Tying up in an offshore wind therefore requires you to approach parallel to the quay on a beam reach, about four boat lengths away depending on the size of your boat.

The boat should be made to luff up into the wind once the skipper has ordered 'ready to drop the main' and has received the reply 'main ready'. The skipper must be certain that the main will actually come down the moment the order to drop it is given. The main should be hauled down the moment the bow comes into the wind. The jib must come down smartly, too, so that there is no danger of bearing away or maintaining excessive speed. At this stage, the boat should have no more way on than is absolutely necessary to steer. In light airs, you should aim to be approaching the quay under bare poles at no more than 1 knot.

The manoeuvre can be made easier still, especially for a small crew, by dropping the jib before you start. This depends in part on how well your boat sails under main alone. In this case, you can approach the quay at an angle of about 30°, as if under engine power. This must only be attempted if there are at least two boat-lengths of gap at the quayside.

Any remaining momentum in the boat needs to be dealt with not by putting the engine astern, but using the stern warp. The fenders should be placed amidships and at the stern. The stern warp is the only one which can be used for this manoeuvre, so it needs to be prepared with particular care.

If you are sailing two-handed, one of you jumps on land as early as possible and runs aft with the stern warp, dropping it over the bollard. Assuming the boat is already pretty much parallel to the quay, you need not worry any longer about the rudder: the warp is the only important control left. Both hands to the warp, then, which must be turned once around a strong deck cleat. Then the person remaining on board brakes the boat firmly. This will press the stern quarter against the quay wall, which is why you put the fender there. Once the boat has come to rest, we cleat the stern warp and hand over the other three lines to our friend on land.

> **A basic rule:** always brake the boat using the warp which is opposite to the direction of travel.

Trying to brake a boat with the bow warp when it is still travelling forward will simply end up with the bow crashing into the wall. If you have a deck hand dedicated to handling the stern warp, then the rudder should be used to steer against the tension on the warp as soon as it goes tight. If you are tying up to starboard, put the rudder hard to starboard as though you were trying to drive up onto the quay.

Tying up under sail in an onshore wind

The same basic rule as last time: the mainsail may not be taken down except when you are head to wind. It is perfectly possible to steer under jib alone, except on a close-hauled course. So the main needs to come down early, and the jetty is approached under jib alone. Remember, the jib can be taken down on *all* points of sailing.

The skipper should check that the boat is ready for the manoeuvre and under control, with a hearty 'ready to drop the jib'. The response is 'jib ready'. Approach the jetty at the usual 20°–30° angle. You will certainly need at least two boat-lengths this time to stop the boat with a progressive pull on the stern warp. If you feel you are nearing the jetty too fast, kill the jib early and take it down as soon as required.

Take care: this is not an easy manoeuvre to interrupt and start again. The slower you sail, the stronger will be the effect of the wind even on bare poles and hull, pushing you onto the jetty. You must not try to carry the manoeuvre out too slowly. Any mistake in throwing the line or using it to brake the boat could be critical. Do not forget to hang the fender out at the stern quarter: as soon as the stern warp comes under tension, the stern will be pulled in towards the quay.

Tying up with the wind parallel to the quay

This should follow the same procedure as with an offshore wind. If you can, aim to finish the manoeuvre sailing into the wind. A strong following

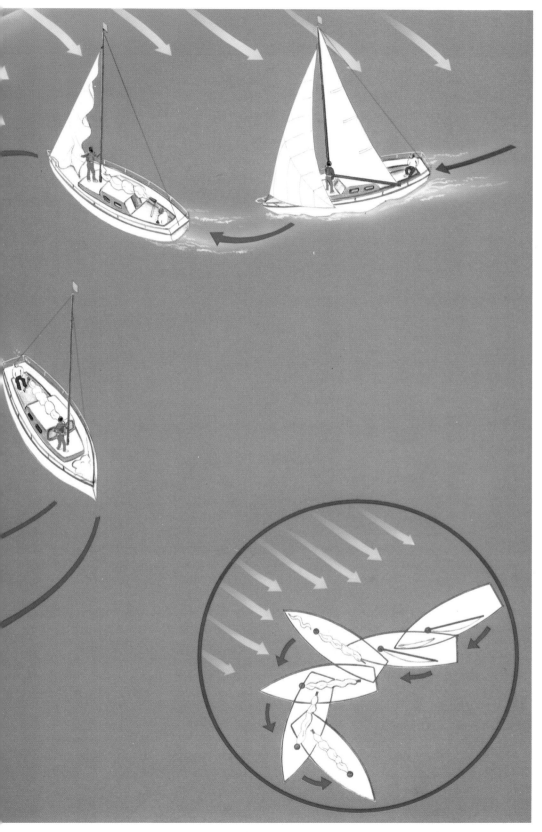

Approaching the jetty under sail. The main must be taken down while you are head to wind, and must be properly stowed as you near the jetty. The first step is: head to wind, and drop the main. With the wind on or behind the beam, the jib is adequate for you to steer by. You can drop the jib at any time. If you already have enough way on, take it down. Any remaining speed is taken out by the stern warp . . . and only the stern warp!

breeze can push a yacht forward at 3–4 knots even under bare poles . . . and 3 knots is much too fast for you to stop the boat and tie up. The manoeuvres we have just described may be carried out two-handed or even single-handed, so long as the skipper has worked out all the steps in advance, and they are followed in order, rather than all at the same time.

> The larger the yacht, the more difficult it is to tie up under sail. Above a certain size, sail should only be used if all else fails.

Tying-up manoeuvres under sail should only be carried out in a crowded harbour if:

(a) there is no alternative, because the engine has broken down; or
(b) no other vessel or person will be inconvenienced and the skipper is quite certain the manoeuvre will succeed.

One of a sailor's worst nightmares is a boat drifting around in a crowded harbour, unable to manoeuvre, sails up. The skipper needs to take every eventuality into account. That kindly character on the jetty might catch your line but then hang on to it, not knowing that the line is to be slipped over a nearby bollard. So much for your plan of slowing down!

If your engine has conked out and you doubt your ability to tie up safely under sail, you still have an option available which will allow you to tie up without damaging your boat or crew. You anchor temporarily in the harbour, then bring the boat to its planned resting place using either your tender or the assistance of neighbours. For single-handed sailors this will often be the only realistic option.

Getting under way using the sails

Just as you might need to use the anchor and then tow the yacht using the tender in order to tie up, when you have only sails as your source of power, the anchor and the tender can also come in handy for leaving a berth. The tender is used to take the anchor out into uncrowded or safe water, the boat hauled along away from the quay, and then the usual method of weighing anchor (p. 130) may be followed.

There are cases, however, when even the smallest crew can get under way using the sails in complete safety. In order to leave the quay under sail in an offshore wind, you first raise the jib, then take in, in order, the springs, the bow warp and the stern warp. The wind will take the boat downwind of its own accord. Once you are well clear of the quay, a brief luff should suffice to enable the mainsail to be raised; you then have the boat completely ready to go.

With the wind parallel to the quay and behind the beam, you can use the same approach. You do need to be careful not to scrape the stern quarter along the quayside: this implies leaving the quay at only a slight angle, rather than steering away too early. If the wind is parallel to the quay but forward of the beam, you need to start by turning the yacht round: easy enough if you use the wind to work for you rather than against you.

The first step is to attach a warp to the bow on the side away from the quay. This warp is led aft, outside the rails and shrouds. The existing bow warp is loosened progressively, and the wind turns the boat round. Be sure to keep good hold of the original bow warp, however, as this is what controls the speed of the turn, at least until it is at too acute an angle to be of any further help. For this turn, you need a lot of fenders at the stern and rudder, with one crew member looking after the stern full time.

The only move a small crew cannot make unaided is getting under way into the wind under sail. This involves setting a slip warp well ahead of the boat (at least two boat-lengths) with one end tied at the stern and the other end pulled by as many crew as you can muster, all on the foredeck. This pull should be used to give the boat enough speed to turn it head to wind, some distance away from the quay, so that the main can be raised. If you try this before the vessel is far enough from the quayside, it will be blown back to the quay. It should not need pointing out that this manoeuvre is impossible with boats any larger than about 6 tonnes or in a strong wind. The alternative to this manoeuvre is to send the dinghy out with an anchor, haul the boat out to the anchor and then set out safely from there.

Don't forget: a cruising yacht under sail has neither brakes nor a reverse gear. The mainsail can only be raised and lowered on the wind, or head to wind. The jib can be raised or lowered any time. Any approach manoeuvres need a trial run, or a practice session. Practise by tying the dinghy to a buoy with a long floating line, and sail up to the line as though it was the jetty.

Surely one of the world's loveliest natural harbours, and a cruising paradise: Antigua, in the British West Indies.

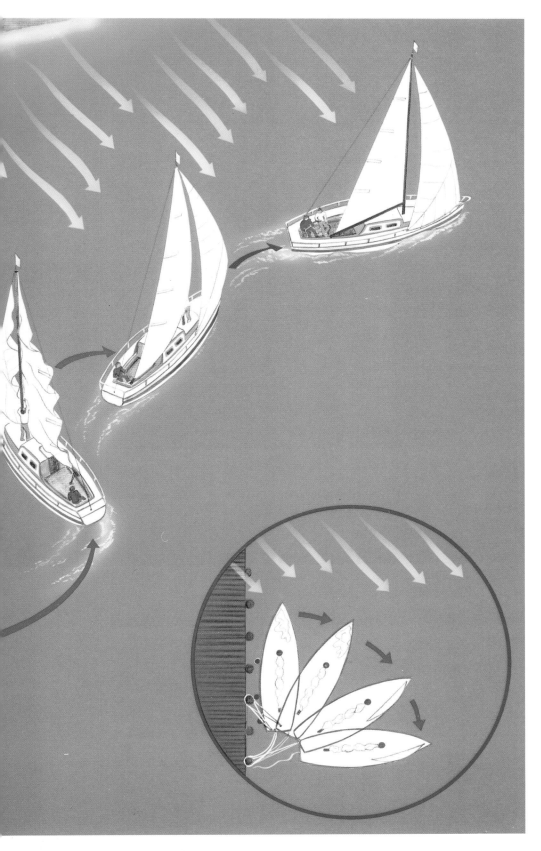

Getting under way using the sails. A slip stern spring is the last warp to be released. Note the fenders over the aft quarter. Once the yacht is free of the jetty, the slip warp and spring are brought inboard and the jib is raised. Pick up enough way under jib alone to luff up and set the mainsail, then bear away on the correct tack.

Anchoring correctly

Equipment

Adequate anchor equipment rarely receives the attention it merits. After all, the boat's (and thus the crew's) safety depends upon the anchor gear, to say nothing of the anchor's role in protecting your financial investment. A cruising yacht needs more than just an anchor and warp. For a start, you never know whether you will be anchoring on a sandy bottom, gravel, mud or rock.

There is no such thing as a universal anchor which works equally well in all applications. This explains some of the variety to be found today, and types such as:

- the fisherman or stock anchor
- the CQR or plough anchor
- the Danforth anchor
- the Bruce anchor

The Fisherman anchor

Any stock anchor needs to be heavy to hold properly. For this reason, fisherman anchors are losing popularity. Its weight and sharp fluke points mean that the fisherman tends to dig in quickly, a major advantage for any anchor: after all, the best and most secure anchor is no use until it has bitten. However, the fisherman anchor, although it bites well, does not hold particularly strongly relative to its weight. If you use an anchor of this type, you must choose one much heavier than the equivalent in any other design if it is to hold you and your vessel in a storm.

There is of course no such thing as an anchor which is too heavy, as far as stopping power is concerned. The limits are set by the strength of the crew or the anchor winch.

Opposite page: the loneliest anchorage in the world: Isla de los Estados, off Tierra del Fuego. The ketch *Ksar* has led two strong cables to the rocks either side of her, knowing that this secure-seeming harbour can be turned into a frothing trap by sudden force 12 gusts coming down off those cliffs.

A museum piece: the heavy Fisherman anchor.

Left: plough anchor; right: Danforth.

Bruce anchor.

A Danforth stowed on the stern for instant access.

Recommended weights for a Fisherman anchor:	
yacht weight (tonnes)	anchor weight (kg approx.)
up to 2	20
up to 4	25
up to 7	30
up to 10	45
up to 20	60

The CQR or plough anchor

British sailors, led by Eric Hiscock, have sworn by the CQR for years. Their enthusiasm is quieter nowadays, as it has become clear that CQR anchors have one unlovely habit: only relatively large and heavy ones tend to bite reliably. Many a table relating yacht tonnage to anchor size fails to take account of one factor which does not change as the boat gets bigger: the sea floor. I am convinced that a 3kg anchor would hold a dinghy in a storm, but the anchor needs first to bite into the bottom, which is not necessarily going to be the case if the mud is at all hard.

That same broad blade which gives the CQR anchor its phenomenal holding power once it has bitten actually works initially to make it harder to get it into the mud. On my first circumnavigation I had a 35kg CQR which held beautifully once it had actually buried its flukes; unfortunately, just as often, it slithered across the floor. American sailors grew wise to the shortcomings of the CQR some time ago, and took to filling the hollows on the underside of the flukes with lead to weigh it down. I would not recommend a CQR lighter than 23kg.

Once a CQR has buried itself, it holds amazingly well. The 13 metre yacht *Shebessa* was caught in Hurricane Bébé and had to ride out the 150 knot wind with two 32kg CQRs. Not only did the anchors hold, but once the storm was over it took a team of divers

and a high-pressure hose to un-bury the anchors, 4m into the mud.

The Danforth anchor

This is an extremely popular anchor because it weighs so little. Danforths hold far better than any other anchor. Above a certain weight, say 30kg, it is actually difficult to break a Danforth out. I always recommend a tripping line and anchor buoy for this reason.

Recommended weights for Danforths are:	
yacht weight (tonnes)	anchor weight (kg approx.)
2	10
4	13
7	15
10	20
20	30

Danforths have one major disadvantage, unfortunately. They might be unbeatable on sand, but on a rocky bottom you will be forced back on your old fisherman anchor.

I have now tried out all three of these anchor types on round-the-world voyages, and I would recommend only the fisherman and Danforth anchors for use on cruising yachts.

The Bruce anchor

The Bruce anchor has become popular only in the last ten years on cruising yachts, so there is less collective experience to go on than for other types. My guess is that the Bruce anchor will behave similarly to the plough anchor, though without the problems associated with the hinged flukes of the CQR. On some bows you will find that a Bruce fits more easily than a CQR, and if you are choosing between them, ease of stowage should be the deciding factor. The relationship between weight and hold is about the same for a Bruce as for a CQR.

Warp or chain?

Both, is the answer. Warps are best for those frequent occasions when the skipper needs to bring out a second anchor in the dinghy, and chain is much too heavy to be taken more than five to eight metres away with the dinghy. A warp, on the other hand, can be taken out to windward even in a gale with a light Danforth in the dinghy. (It can even be swum out by a strong crew member plus buoyancy aid).

Chain is nevertheless the obvious choice for most occasions, and must be seen as standard equipment. Recommended strengths are:

yacht weight up to (tonnes)	anchor chain (diameter)
4	6mm
8	8mm
10	10mm
20	12mm

The major drawback of chain, of course, is weight. This is particularly problematic on light yachts. The minimum length you should have on board is 50m; 50 metres of 8mm chain weigh about 100kg. Obviously you do not want this weight concentrated where it will cause you problems, ie at the bow. Nevertheless, this is precisely where many boat designers place the chain locker.

If your yacht is made of fibreglass you also need the chain locker to be wood lined, so a couple of hundredweight of chain are not slamming into the hull every time you hit a wave. This would be like dropping the chain from a height of two or three metres. On the other hand, there are those who move the chain locker aft, then try to feed the chain down into it at less than 70°. This guarantees that it will stick and fail to stow itself. It will stow itself only if it is fed into a roomy locker, vertically.

The major advantage of chain over rope warps is that it does not rag or fray on rocks. A sharp rock can go through an anchor warp under tension in a few minutes. One common ploy to get the best of both worlds is to shackle 5 or 10m of chain on to the anchor, and then the warp above that. If you then buoy the warp to keep it from rubbing on the sea bed, you can be virtually certain it will not wear through.

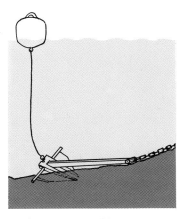

Danforth anchors hold so well that a buoyed tripping line will come in handy.

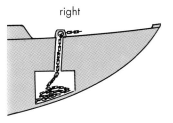

right

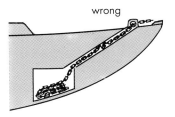

wrong

125

This ratchet cleat stops the chain slipping back.

Hand-powered anchor winches are a good toy for tiring out the younger crew members.

Electric capstan. This one has a vertical shaft which might make it difficult to keep the deck watertight.

This ploy is a compromise, of course. It loses the other major advantage of chain, which is its weight. The weight causes the anchor line to sag, so it springs the anchor against any sudden pulls as waves hit the boat. Modern synthetic warps are less of a problem in this regard than old ropes were, as they are more elastic anyway. The warp must be at least as strong as your mooring warps. I recommend the following diameters:

yacht weight up to (tonnes)	anchor warp (diameter)
4	c. 12mm
8	c. 16mm
20	c. 22mm

The anchor winch

Yachts of up to 6 tonnes do not need an anchor winch. Anchors of up to 25kg can readily be dealt with by hand, even by your less muscular crew members. Hand-powered anchor winches, if they are any good, are extremely slow. Your mechanical advantage arises from moving the hand drum many times more than the chain drum.

You should not haul the boat to the anchor, but motor up to the anchor spot to reduce the length of line to be brought in. The warp or chain is brought in by hand, as the winch would be too slow; you only need the winch for the moment in which the anchor breaks out. At that moment, the boat becomes uncontrollable: it has no way on. You therefore need to get the chain in fast, and the winch is once again useless where speed is of the essence.

The anchor can be broken out without using a winch by using the following technique. Pull the anchor line so it is up-and-down (or as near as you can manage). Wait for a small wave to lift the bow, and it will lift the anchor very firmly, for the few centimetres that count. If this does not work, bring the whole crew onto the foredeck to sink

the bow, then send all but the anchor hands back to the cockpit. If this does not work (very rare indeed) the anchor must be caught on an obstruction.

For small yachts, then, a good strong bow fitting with a cleat is more use than a winch. The ratchet cleat illustrated above is ideal: it allows chain to pass in one direction only.

If your anchor weighs over 30kg, all the advice given above is not for you. You need an electric or hydraulic anchor capstan. These are phenomenally powerful, so you should avoid having to use them manually, as they are also phenomenally slow. If your yacht is sensibly equipped, you will be using the capstan only in conjunction with the engine, drawing current direct from the alternator, so power is no problem.

Anchoring

Anchoring is like any harbour manoeuvre, in that it needs to be prepared and carried out with care. Read your cruising pilot carefully. An anchor on the chart does not mean that it is a suitable spot for your 8m boat: it is probably better for an oil tanker which is less sensitive to wind and swell.

The first step is for the skipper to check the chart and see what sort of bottom you have to deal with. Avoid rocks if possible. There are two basic sorts of anchorage for cruising yachts: those which are 100% safe, even in storms; and those which may be considered safe only when the wind blows from a given direction.

With the latter type, the skipper should have a plan prepared for when the wind comes round into the 'wrong' direction: will you have to leave that anchorage? If the anchorage cannot be left safely with the wind coming from that direction, do not use it for an overnight stay. There is no harm making a few circuits around the bay before deciding on the precise spot, asking advice of other yachts if there are any around. In any case, you must ensure that you check the depth of water in your proposed anchorage with the echo sounder, so as to have the right length of warp or chain ready.

Beware of the old rule: 'three times as much anchor line as the depth of water'. This rule might be valid for still conditions but a responsible skipper thinks through all eventualities before anchoring . . . and these eventualities must include the weather turning nasty. In general, the longer the line, the safer you will lie. If the yacht has enough room to swing at the end of the line, there is no reason not to have a line five or even ten times the depth of water. Whatever, the depth of water, you should never anchor on less than 25m of chain or warp, because the longer line reduces the jerkiness with which the boat tugs on the anchor gear.

You should always approach the anchorage head to wind, even under engine power. Drop the anchor when the bow has headed slightly off the wind, with the engine in neutral; let the chain out just fast enough to prevent it from coming under tension, but no faster. Once you have drifted back downwind to the chosen spot, you should feel the anchor line tug the bow back up into the wind. Then you know it has bitten.

Your engine is still running, so be seamanlike about it, and drive the anchor in. Run the engine slow astern, then half, then full astern, to fix the anchor. I am forever seeing people miss this part out because they are worried they might pull the anchor out. This is plain stupid. If the anchor cannot hold the boat with the engine full astern, how long do they think it will survive in strong wind and swell? Even when I drop anchor under sail power, I use the engine in reverse to settle the anchor.

Under sail power, the preparation for anchoring is the same: a few turns round the bay to check the depth and surroundings. The jib is put away to leave the foredeck clear. We then approach our precise spot in the way I describe on pages 149–51 for practising 'buoy overboard' drill. I was shown this manoeuvre by fishermen who used it in the days before trawlers were equipped with engines. It is not taught in sailing schools, because if it is attempted in a dinghy it tends to lead to a capsize.

The trick is to approach the manoeuvre downwind, with no jib, and as slowly as you can. The boat's way is cut to zero by a last-minute luff. If you follow the instructions exactly, it usually works even on an unfamiliar boat. You pass one to one-and-a-half boat lengths to one side of the target spot or buoy; at the moment the stern aligns with the spot, luff through 180°. This should bring your boat to a standstill with the bow over the spot. I have tried this move under a huge variety of conditions and with many different boats. It is amazing: even the heaviest cruisers come to rest at exactly the required spot. It even works in waves!

The anchor is dropped once the wind has pushed the bow slightly off. Wait until you are certain the anchor has bitten before dropping the mainsail, as this would leave you with no power if the anchor dragged.

> One more time: it is good seamanlike practice to run the engine in reverse to dig the anchor in.

Cruising yachts rarely anchor except very close to land. Bearings to landmarks cannot help to tell you whether the anchor is dragging, since the bearings would also vary depending on the boat's natural swinging at anchor; hence I strongly recommend,

The fisherman's anchoring manoeuvre described on page 127. The boat loses all way as it luffs.

that you hop into the dinghy and drop a second anchor. It only takes a few minutes to shackle the second anchor on and row it out the moment you have arrived. You do not want to have to do this in the middle of the night, in pouring rain and heavy seas. I always use two anchors for my yachts. It adds five minutes to the day's work, but improves the quality of your sleep, however much the wind howls in the shrouds. A second anchor also helps limit the swing circle, in cases where this is an issue.

If we are putting out a second anchor for safety reasons in the expectation of heavy weather, ensure that both anchor lines are in the direction of the expected storm, and at an angle of 30°–45° to the bow. There is no point trying to calculate things so that both lines take the same tension: in heavy weather the boat will pull on each line in turn. The point of putting out two anchors is not to halve the tension on each, but to put up a second defence in case the first one does not hold. If the anchors do drag in a storm, leave the anchorage, and come back tomorrow for your anchor tackle which you can leave tied to a floating fender.

Backed anchors

This technique is described in virtually every manual, but I have never once seen it, in all my time at sea. This is because it is much easier described than done. It is far easier to let out a second anchor in the manner just described than to fix and use two anchors on the same chain.

We were in Suva (Fiji) once when a hurricane warning was received, and I was interested to see what precautions were taken by our neighbours in the harbour, who were all highly experienced cruising yachtspeople. Not one of them used backed anchors; nor did any of them use a sliding weight on the chain (another method beloved of handbook authors). Every one of them simply let out as much anchor chain or warp on as many anchors as they could find. *Bebinka*, for instance, was on 100m of chain attached to her most reliable anchor (a Danforth) in a mere 4m of water. In the entire large bay, not one yacht had fewer than three anchors out. *Skylark* used four.

Once the hurricane had swept away, carrying its 150 knot winds, we found that very few anchors or warps had let

One of the world's most famous anchorages: Marigot Bay in St Lucia, in the West Indies.

129

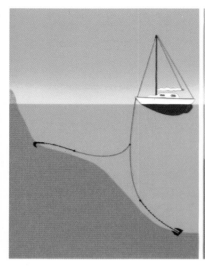 

Left: backed anchors on a
split line.
Right: backed anchors on a
single line.

The usual method of
mooring in mediterranean
marinas.

to the deck. Nevertheless, even some well known boatbuilders appear to think this is adequate. An obvious point for you to check on any boat you are skippering.

Weighing anchor

This can be a simple manoeuvre under engine power; under sail power, though, your success can depend on a few unpredictable factors. It will only be problem-free if you have plenty of water to sail away in, and this is rarely the case these days. Your escape route is normally decided for you by the position of other boats.

their owners down. The weakest points on board tended to be the deck cleats. One boat was destroyed, having lost all its cleats. The deck cleats were the weakest link in almost all our chains. Of course, they are a vital part of the boat, and should not be simply screwed

If you weigh anchor correctly and if the anchor has bitten properly in the first place, you can be confident it will work, which is one more reason to settle it with the engine. The mainsail is raised. (A raised jib would clutter up the foredeck, but for safety's sake we

do shackle the tack and head on, and tie it to the rail.) Leave enough slack in the mainsheet to ensure the yacht does not start to sail off. You should only need to sail over the anchor if you have serious problems breaking it out; and this can be highly risky in a crowded anchorage with only one exit, since the anchor can be guaranteed to break out when you least want it to, ie when it has just turned the bow in the wrong direction.

If there is only one way out, you must haul the boat up to the anchor slowly, keeping a close eye on it. You want the anchor to break out only at the opportune moment, which is when the boat is heading in the correct direction. This is achieved by backing the mainsail to bring the stern round. The boat pivots more or less about the bow, which is another reason why the jib is unhelpful at this stage. In a light wind, the boat can take a while to reach the desired start position. When you are certain the mainsail would fill if the sheet were trimmed, the skipper gives the order to haul the anchor in.

At this stage, the helm cannot see what is happening to the anchor, so coordinated action between the skipper and the foredeck hands is vital. The anchor line hand must report the moment the anchor is free. The boat will be moving slowly aft under the backed mainsail, and the helm must assist the boat's turning moment using the rudder. If we are planning to head off to port, the rudder needs to be hard to starboard while the boat is moving aft. The helm needs to be reversed the moment the mainsail is trimmed and the boat moves forward. Of course the anchor needs to be hauled inboard as fast as possible to give the boat full manoeuvrability. Safety is more important than a tidy foredeck in this instance.

The major risk in this move is that the anchor breaks out when you do not want it to. If there is a danger spot

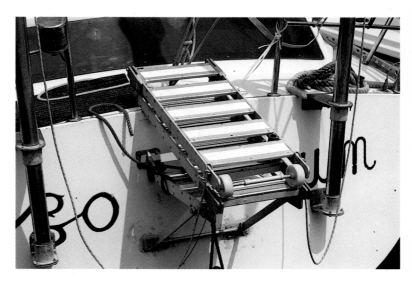

close to your anchorage, it is worth taking a further anchor out with the dinghy. You can then haul the yacht to this second anchor before setting off, with more freedom to choose your course. Another case for that unsung hero, the inflatable!

Mooring in the Mediterranean fashion is problematic in a number of ways. You need to keep a fair distance from the quayside to prevent the rudder smashing into the wall. This makes it hard to get onto the quayside without using a gangplank. You really do need the anchor to grip well in such circumstances. If it slips in an onshore wind, you will damage your stern and rudder. You need to use the engine hard astern for several minutes to drive the anchor into the bottom.

Mooring Mediterranean-style can be pretty difficult (and entertaining for onlookers) as few yachts are at their most manoeuvrable when motoring in reverse. It will often be better to drop anchor calmly in the correct spot and use the dinghy to bring a line onto the quay. You then manoeuvre back along the line, and use the sheet winches to dig the anchor in.

Leaving this type of mooring requires considerable skill to keep the boat under control and weigh anchor. The stern warps are replaced by a long slip

If you moor with your stern to the quay, you need to keep your distance, to protect the gel coat on your stern, and to look after your rudder. Your gangway is almost certainly too short; but look at this smart folding model!

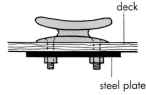

A correctly installed deck cleat.

warp, which is slowly let out as the anchor line is hauled in. If the wind is abeam, you need to keep some tension on both lines, or the yacht will hit your neighbour's yacht.

If you are unfortunate enough to pull up someone else's anchor chain with your own, use the boat hook to keep their chain out of the way while you deal with yours. It is far worse if you actually dislodge their anchor. Of course, you must not then just throw their anchor back in. The skipper of the other boat needs to be told what has happened, and you should then give the other boat all possible assistance to put matters right again.

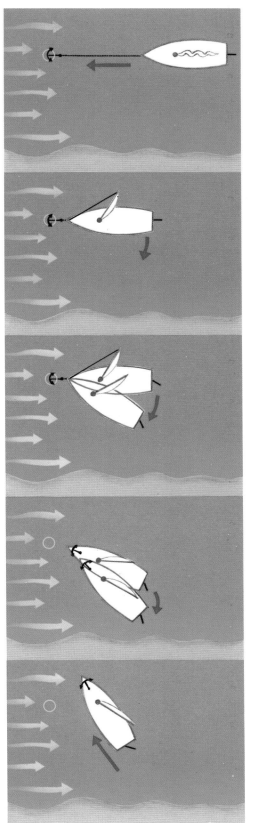

Weighing anchor under sail in a pre-chosen direction: pull in the chain to the up-and-down position.

The wind in the backed mainsail takes the stern to port.

The boat is far enough off the wind to fill the main, and the skipper orders the anchor to be brought in.

The rudder is hard to port while the boat is still moving astern, aiding the turn.

The rudder goes hard to starboard as soon as you pick up forward way.

Opposite page: the kelp forests in Patagonia are a menace: they prevent the anchor reaching the bottom, then hang onto the anchor on the way up.

After the storm in the Le Maire straits. Ahead of us, the most densely populated ship's cemetery in the world.

Underway

Using the engine

The engine should not be needed too often on a cruise in open water. Motoring along is an uncomfortable way of travelling, unless there is dead calm or you are also using the sails.

Any well set-up boat will sail faster in a decent wind than it can comfortably motor. What do we mean by 'comfortable' motoring anyway? The criteria are not the same as for commercial vessels, obviously: range and economy are not our chief concerns. We shall seldom run our diesel tanks dry. A cruising speed for motor boats is the speed at which maximum range is achieved. We are not going to bother finding this out by subjecting ourselves and our crew to long test voyages under engine alone.

We shall use the engine in whatever rev range gives us reasonable performance, with a little diesel in reserve for emergencies. Assuming the engine power is about right for the boat, we should be able to run it at 70%–80% of its red-line speed. If 'full ahead' is 2,500 rpm, say, then the cruising speed will be 1,750–2,000 rpm. If you try it out on any boat with at least 3PS per tonne, you will quickly notice that there is precious little difference in speed anyway between 2,000 and 2,500 revs.

Our second criterion is noise. Marine diesel engines tend to be very loud compared to petrol engines. Single-cylinder engines are the worst sinners in this respect; four- or six-cylinder engines are relatively meek. Unfortunately, modest-sized cruising yachts (up to 11m LOA) tend to be equipped with one- or two-cylinder diesel engines. Flexible rubber mountings have solved a lot of problems since they were introduced, but even so there are rev ranges in which the engine's normally quiet vibration can become uncomfortable. The precise point around three-quarters of maximum revs at which you pitch your cruising speed should be the quietest point in the range.

Motoring at sea is rarely pleasant, since the sea usually has some swell remaining from earlier wind. The consequent pitch and roll affects not only the crew's nerves but also the engine's efficiency. Any muck in the bottom of the diesel tank, or even just water condensation, can get swirled around and clog the fuel line filters. The engine mountings are designed normally for bearing vertical weight, and any horizontal load can add to the vibration.

Setting the mainsail and hauling it fairly close will reduce the roll. Even then, the main will tend to flap and get on your nerves, so you might take in a reef to reduce the belly in the sail. Alternatively setting the storm mainsail has the same effect, for a bit more work. The jib or genoa, of course, cannot be set amidships, so they would back and slow you down.

If there is enough wind to sail by, you cannot justify using the engine except under one condition: if you would otherwise fail to make enough ground to windward. The engine can be used to improve your pointing angle slightly, though it cannot help if you try to point so high that the sails no longer fill. You should use the speedometer to tell you which is the most favourable course that can be sailed with full sails.

You must not motor-sail if the wind is strong and the boat heeling noticeably. If the engine is run on a constant slant of 20° or more, the lubricating oil cannot get round properly. You might expect that designers of marine diesels would apply themselves to this problem, but it appears not. A short roll such as might be caused by a wave is not going to cause difficulties, but continuous operation at this angle will wreck your engine. Only large diesels, such as a MAN or the Caterpillar six-cylinder with twin oil pumps, have overcome this inadequacy.

If the engine has been installed correctly, it should be able to run all day without a break. You simply need to keep an eye on the oil pressure and temperature gauges.

Engines which are water-cooled, especially those which use seawater in the cooling system, need to have the temperature checked every ten minutes. If seawater exceeds 60°C, salt crystals start to form and block the narrow water jets. If this is allowed to happen, the temperature rises very suddenly. The inlet valve can get blocked from time to time. Plastic bags and other flotsam are the commonest cause of this. If the outlet of the (water-cooled) exhaust is above the waterline, the helm will quickly notice the exhaust note change to a dull thud. This means something is wrong. A quick look at the temperature gauge will show a sudden rise. You need to throt-

tle back and switch the engine off immediately afterwards. Do not switch the engine off direct from full throttle. If the cooling water inlet is blocked, the engine may not be used, even in an emergency.

If the engine is used continuously over long periods, you should remember that some engines need fairly frequent oil changes, every 50 hours for some models.

As you motor, be sure to keep the vessel well aired. As far as possible, hatches should be open. If any crew member is sleeping while the engine is running, they should sleep under the foredeck, with an open hatch. Engines must of course be mounted so that no exhaust gases escape into the accommodation areas, but you cannot be too careful in this regard.

A slight case of carbon monoxide poisoning will probably not even be recognised, but it can ruin the crew's effectiveness through a combination

There is insufficient wind to keep the boat moving, so the engine is running, and the sails keep the boat stable.

of headaches, tiredness and loss of appetite. If you have a following wind, it can blow exhaust fumes into the cockpit and down the main hatch. Although this is not dangerous, because it will be well mixed with fresh air, it can still cause considerable discomfort after a while.

> If the helm hears a sudden change in the engine note or any strange sound, the engine should be put into neutral and turned off immediately.

Offshore under sail power

To windward

Opposite page: long keeled yacht sailing to windward.

The saying has it that only idiots and regatta-sailors choose to sail to windward. The reasons are obvious: the relative wind is much stronger, and the waves are working against you. If there is a true force 4 wind and you are making 6 knots, your anemometer will be showing force 5; with the same wind and speed, but downwind, the anemometer shows force 3. This is also one of the reasons one tends to underestimate the strength of the wind when sailing downwind.

The boat heels much more when beating; this in turn leaves the crew feeling less comfortable. The rig and hull are subject to far greater stress when sailing close-hauled than when sailing any other course under the same conditions. The shape of the waves exaggerates this, as the vessel climbs up the steep lee slope of the waves.

Offshore sailors generally prefer to wait for the wind to change rather than bash through a stiff breeze to windward. On long passages it is often worth heaving to for a while to give the crew a rest in the hope that a wind shift will allow you to sail straight for your destination.

It is rare to find that the wind is blowing straight from your target harbour. Usually there will be a clear choice between port and starboard tacks. You simply need to check the compass heading on each close-hauled tack, then take any current into account.

In my experience, many people carry too much sail to windward. If the yacht develops strong weather helm when close-hauled, take a reef in the main. You will lose very little speed, but the boat will respond better to the helm, heel less and feel generally more comfortable. Since the relative wind is stronger to windward, you will need, once you have reefed the main, to swap the genoa for a jib earlier than on a reach or downwind. Do reef the main first, however; exchanging the genoa for a jib while keeping a full mainsail will increase the weather helm.

The foresail should be hauled as close as possible when beating. You are no longer steering a compass course, but trying to make as much ground as possible to windward. As the wind fluctuates around its general direction, we aim to take advantage of these slight shifts. Feathering into the shifts was once the preserve of the skilled helm, but now we can all try our luck with the aid of modern electronic wind direction indicators. At a price, there are waterproof instruments which give the optimum course to windward.

A few metres more or less to windward makes the difference between victory and defeat for regatta sailors, but the cruising skipper survives well enough without these gadgets. The helm simply sits to leeward to watch the jib luff, which is the boat's early warning system when it pinches or is sailing too free. The luff generally begins to collapse about half way up the forestay when it is time to bear away a little. You then need to feel your way back into the wind until the same flutter at the luff betrays that you have gone a touch too far. The leech of a correctly set sail should not flutter (unless the sail is shot and stretched!), but

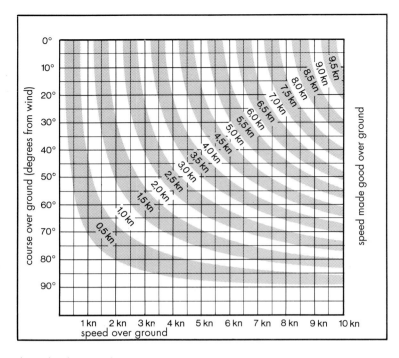

This polar diagram shows (in the curves) the speed over the distance made good by any combination of course and sailing speed to windward. Thus, if you are making 50° to the wind, at 7 knots, your speed made good to windward is 4.5 knots.

The lee side of a wave is steeper than the windward side. For this reason, beating into a swell is harder work than running with it.

if the leech does collapse, you should haul it in harder.

Courses to windward are the ideal circumstances for self-steering gear. Some claim that self-steering gear is better than a human being at the helm. This is incorrect. Human beings can react immediately they see a lift at the jib luff, whereas the self-steering gear does not bear away until rather later.

If the yacht is making way against a severe sea, it will occasionally smash into the back of a wave and come almost to a complete standstill. If this happens, make sure you bear away to help the boat pick up speed quickly. If it happens frequently, it is probably a sign that you are sailing too high. This is self-defeating anyway in high waves,

and you should bear away onto a course which does not bring you into such direct conflict with the swell.

> The rougher the sea, the freer you must sail.

Pinching into the wind is not much help even in gentler seas, actually. If you look at the speed polar diagram, you can tell that a course of 50° to the wind at 6 knots will actually make you more ground than sailing at 5 knots at 45°. It is also much more comfortable.

Reaching

Never forget that you should be sailing to avoid accidents. Safety is the first commandment. A swinging main boom is highly unsafe. The boom is unlikely to swing anywhere to windward, as it will be close hauled, with plenty of air pressure to hold it in position. Even if you sail into a hole in the wind, the boom will not swing far. On any other point of sailing, though, you should rig a boom preventer. A boom preventer is a simple line attached as close as possible to the bow and led to the outboard end of the boom.

When you are sailing any reaching course, you should let the mainsheet out slightly further than you need, attach the boom preventer, then trim the mainsheet. The preventer fulfils two functions. Firstly, it stops the boom swinging in the swell if the wind drops: the sheet is of course kept too tight for the boom to damage the shrouds, but it could easily bend your mainsheet traveller if allowed to slam to and fro. Its second purpose is to prevent the boom rising up and putting twist in the main. Keeping the sail in shape is very important. It can also be accomplished by using a boom downhaul, though these are rarely found in cruising yachts, as they are tricky to construct so that they can be used with roller reefing gear.

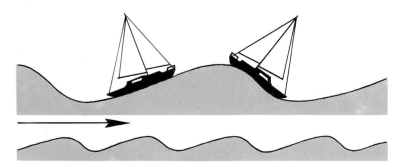

If we follow our safety first principle, we shall spend only as much time as necessary on the foredeck, since this is the location from which people are most easily lost overboard. There is a simple method of rigging a boom preventer so we do not have to send anyone onto the foredeck. A long line is set up from the end of the boom and led through a block at the bow back (on the other side of the boat from the boom) into the cockpit. The boom preventer is then led round the unused windward sheet winch and can be adjusted from the cockpit.

You still need to send someone out on the foredeck when you first rig it, but any later adjustments are then much safer and easier using the winch. It is a good idea to set two standing boom preventers through a twin block at the bow; you then change them over on the boom end when it comes across during the tack.

When reaching in strong winds, the helm needs to ensure that the boat does not luff up and broach in the gusts. Pre-emptive action is needed, with the helm bearing away as the gust arrives. If the pressure on the tiller becomes too great, take in a reef. A decent yacht will almost never suffer from lee helm; and reefing the main is the best remedy for excessive weather helm.

Obviously one cannot sail a windward course under jib alone, because the boat cannot be made to point; but if the wind gets too strong for even a reefed main, there is no harm sailing a reach under foresail only.

> Always reef the mainsail, or even take it down entirely, before reducing the size of the jib.

Downwind

If you bear away further from the reach, say, to 30° off the true wind direction, the mainsail will begin to smother the jib. This has two further effects:

- the jib is useless, as it is no longer drawing, so you might as well take it down
- the yacht is sailing almost straight downwind, so extra attention is needed to avoid any accidental gybes, which might cost you your mast in a strong wind.

A rigid metal kicking strap prevents the boom lifting on a reach. You need a large-section boom to use this type of kicker.

141

Left: shackles like this one catch the sheet when you want it released. Centre and right: only this type of snapshackle works when a sheet is carrying a lot of load.

Logically, you then take the jib down. At this point you discover a weakness in conventional rigs: downwind, you want as much sail area as possible, yet you have just begun by halving yours. You might be better advised instead to set the jib on the other side. It will set if you boom it out with a whisker pole, even though it might not pull so strongly as you would like.

It will pull harder if you sail direct downwind, in that narrow angle where the airflow from each sail does not disturb the other. The angle is so narrow, in fact, that self-steering gear, with its sudden and significant changes of course, cannot cope. The gear is driven by the wind, and it is not unusual to have changes of 30° in the apparent wind direction.

If we are not satisfied with halving the sail area, by taking down either the jib or the main, and reducing our speed accordingly, then we must come up with an alternative rig for downwind courses. There are two options.

Spinnakers were invented by racing sailors who wanted a speed advantage over other boats downwind. The spinnaker is never carried upwind, only on the reach or the run, where the apparent wind is lighter. For this reason, it can have a relatively enormous area. Spinnakers are not easy to set. You should practise raising and lowering the spinnaker lots of times in light wind, because a twisted spinnaker can cause unimaginable problems once the wind gets up and you cannot bring it inboard.

If you are sailing with a spinnaker, the helm must keep it under constant observation. If it starts to fold at the luff, the sheet must be trimmed or the boat must bear away. Only the smallest spinnakers are so stable that they can be cleated and left to their own devices. If the spinnaker collapses completely, you react by bearing away, not luffing up. Since spinnakers need such constant care, the self-steering gear is inappropriate for a spinnaker run: it

This boom preventer can be controlled from the cockpit.

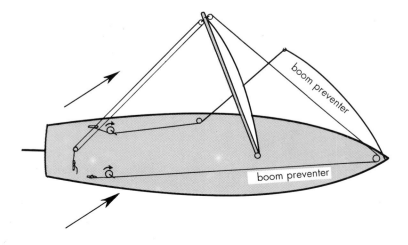

can change course well enough, but it cannot trim the sheets for you!

Spinnakers are not particularly useful on long voyages. On a reach, the spinnaker pole will rub on the forestay. The pole can be protected with a cuff, but this does not help the forestay. On a run, the foot of the spinnaker will rub through on the forestay, unless your kind sailmaker has sewn you a double or treble thickness at this sensitive spot.

Twin staysails are becoming more popular among cruising sailors. They arose to satisfy the skipper's desire not to have to steer so hard downwind; nowadays they are part of the standard wardrobe for long downwind stretches. Twin staysails are set identically either side of the forestay, each with its own whisker pole.

The wish to find a downwind sail which would permit the use of the self-steering gear was what led to the development of these sails. In the years

before the windvane-driven autopilot, the staysail sheets were simply tied to the tiller, and the boat was steered by the sails. At that time, the tack of each staysail was placed not at the bow but just in front of the mast, the two tacks a quarter of the foot length apart. This, it was said, improved their steering characteristics and the airflow over the sails. There was also a debate about whether to set them flying or on a pole which needed to be set before the sails were hoisted; and a further debate about how far forward to leave the sheet fairleads to get the best self-steering response.

These days the autopilot is controlled by a windvane, so these debates are purely theoretical. Our only concern is that the twin staysails should be effective over the widest range of courses. I am content with using the same stem fittings as for the genoa or conventional jib. They are much easier to raise and lower as a result of being set on the normal fittings rather than flying.

The most beautiful sail, and the hardest to master: the spinnaker. These are 500m² in area.

Under twin staysails, especially when sailing dead downwind, a yacht will tend to roll. On this occasion, we put up the storm main specifically to counter this tendency . . . but without much success.

If your yacht has only a single forestay, this need not be a problem. The heads of the sails can be attached to each other then hoisted with a single halyard. This means that you will need a strong halyard winch, because the two sails together will be too heavy to hoist by hand.

If you are steering by hand, twin sails can be used up to 30° from true downwind; this is not possible with the autopilot, which steers in jerks, so is quite likely to end up backing one or other of the sails if it is sailing at the limit of the sail's ability.

The main disadvantage of twin staysails is the amount of time it takes to hoist them and drop them. You need to take this into account when you are making a night passage and need to take avoiding action to clear an unexpected merchant ship which leads you more than 30° from downwind. Oceangoing cruisers, which may follow the same course for a week at a time, have

Left: this is how to rig the spinnaker so it can be hoisted without trouble. Right: as soon as you release the snapshackle, the sail collapses and you can take it down easily.

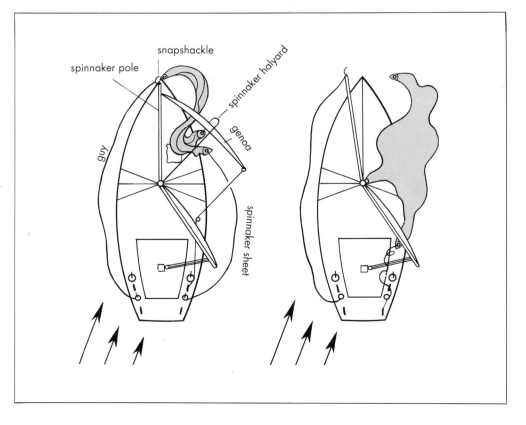

adopted twin staysails for this reason to a much greater extent than have their shore-hugging cousins.

Changing sail

You can drop one foresail and hoist another on any point of sailing. For some reason, any number of people heave to, head to wind to change jibs. The boat stops, loses steerage way, and plunges up and down in the swell. The foredeck is awash and the crew slip around. The mainsail then starts to flap and the boom becomes a deadly weapon.

If we change jibs downwind, the apparent wind is lighter, and the jib might even flap a little if it is in the shadow of the main. We can grab the clew with one hand as we release the halyard winch with the other. The jib might fall partly into the water at this stage, but this need not worry us: the foredeck is nice and dry, and the yacht reasonably level, so we can still unhook the head

of the sail at our leisure and take the jib inboard.

Similarly, setting the new sail is easy, provided you have a decent halyard winch. If your winch is not quite up to this, you can go head to wind for a moment so that the luff slides are not stuck against the forestay as you pull the sail up.

There must be a way to exploit the advantages of a downwind leg (level boat, relatively calm wind) when changing the mainsail, too. The only things stopping us are the battens in the sail. On a cruising yacht, these are often more trouble than they are worth. Before we centre the main boom to stop it hitting anything, of course we have to tighten the topping lift. With the wind from behind, the mainsail is pressed against the mast, so it is unlikely to come down of its own accord, but one person can easily pull down a mainsail of anything up to 30m² , so long as the luff groove is smooth. If

If you leave yourself plenty of time, sail change can be simple. Here the mizzen staysail is coming down.

not, you should spray on some WD40 or similar lubricant every time you pull the main up. It works wonders.

There is no particular problem in hoisting the mainsail, using the halyard winch. Again, it may be necessary to get the last centimetre or so of tightness in by heading up into the wind. You can even hoist a battened mainsail off the wind so long as you ensure the battens do not catch in the spreaders. This is done by getting a crew member to keep the leech amidships as the sail is being hoisted. In harbour, however, it is safer to hoist and drop the mainsail while sailing to windward or even head to wind.

Setting the spinnaker need not be difficult; it only turns nasty when the enormous sail starts to fill before you have got it all the way up. I have seen one technique for hoisting and dropping the kite used successfully on cruising yachts with minimal crew, ever since it was first shown to me by Berend Beilken on his one-tonner *Optimist*.

The sail is stowed in its bag with head and both clews poking out at the top. The bag is attached to the foot of a rail stanchion beside the genoa. The halyard is fed behind the genoa and attached to the head; the sheet comes around outside and under the genoa, and the guy is fed round the outside of the forestay up to the spinnaker pole which is set before you start to hoist the sail. The pole may touch the forestay at this stage without causing damage. The tack is attached with a snapshackle that can be opened at a distance even under tension. Hoist the spinnaker behind the genoa, so that it will not fill until the genoa is dropped.

To take the kite down, we simply open the guy snapshackle. The sail flies out like a flag. One lets the halyard down, while the sheet is used to pull the sail into the cockpit under the main boom. The spinnaker can then be neatly packed away for its next use.

Reefing

Almost all yachts these days have a roller reefing system. Not so long ago, cruising skippers were suspicious of these gadgets, because we had all been let down by one once. Those were the days before synthetic bearings, which are virtually maintenance-free. I went round the world with roller reefing gear which was still working perfectly on the last day of the trip. I admit that I had greased the bearings regularly, even though they were synthetic; and I had had slab reefing points put into the sail before leaving home, just in case.

The main advantage of a roller reef is that it allows you to reef on any point of sailing. You can take in as many as six or seven turns before the aft end of the boom starts to reach the cabin roof, because of the cut of the sail. You can delay this moment by rolling the sail onto the boom with the battens still in it, or by inserting wooden wedges at the leech as it is rolled in. There is no point holding the boom up with the topping lift: this just puts twist in the sail and stops it drawing.

Tied reefs do not present such problems. They present different ones, particularly the problem that the boom has to be brought amidships and the sail must not be drawing when you reef. You cannot avoid a short period head to wind, with the boat plunging into the waves, but you can reduce this period with good planning. Once you have secured the luff and leech reefing points, you can bear away again and tie the rest up, while the boom is secured with the boom preventer.

Tied reefs, of course, are unbeatable for reliability. My personal choice for the future is to have both a roller reef and tied reef points on my boats.

Opposite page: Wolfgang Hausner controls these enormous sails on his own, aided by the gentleness of the catamaran's motion.

Thalassa's roller reefing lasted over 50,000 miles. The boom preventer is rigged here, on the reach, to stop the boom rising.

Safety at sea

Even the best designed small cruising yacht is prey to all manner of hazards at sea:

- losing someone overboard
- collision with another vessel
- going aground
- an accident or illness on board
- sinking by taking in water
- fire
- capsized by a large wave
- collision with a whale.

The collision with a whale is at the end of our list, but there are experienced yachtsmen who fear this above all other hazards. I know of twelve yachts which have fallen victim to these mild creatures. A yacht is unlikely to be attacked by a whale: the whale is no keener on a collision than we are. Collisions between whales and motor boats are virtually unheard of. In the whaling grounds off the New Hebrides, the whaling boats head out every morning, but no-one has ever heard of a boat being rammed by a whale. As far as I am concerned, this proves that loud engine noises keep whales at a distance.

I am less convinced by another widely recommended recipe, namely using the echo sounder. I tried it out once in a school of dolphins. The poor creatures were so confused they ended up crashing into the hull. There was one ecologically sound method which I used successfully for 15,000 miles, and I never once saw a whale: I attached a length of flag cord between the rail and a hook below the waterline. As the boat sailed along, the cord vibrated, making a permanent hum. This noise may well have woken a sleeping whale or two in my path. It certainly took me a while to get used to.

Dramatic photographs of the *Tjisje* going down in the North Atlantic. In the first picture, the yacht appears to be safe, but its fate is already sealed. Henk van de Weg, her skipper, was losing the battle with the water pouring in, and had to abandon the boat for his liferaft. His last act on board was to close the cabin hatch. Then he sat and watched his uninsured boat sink . . .

Man overboard

Man overboard means immediate danger, whether you are near the coast or not. Depending on the state of the sea, the visibility and the water temperature the prospects of rescue are poor to hopeless. You will have practised your man overboard drill (or preferably buoy overboard drill) many times, but in an emergency you should use the drill only if the engine is out of action. And this in itself is bad seamanship: the engine should always be ready for use.

There are two errors possible in the following procedure. Sheets or ropes might be dangling and catch in the propeller. And experience has shown that in real emergencies the manoeuvre can also be ruined by a lack of orders (if the skipper is the man overboard) or by the orders being too vague to be carried out.

If you have a large crew, there is no sense in shouting 'get the main down!' Either no-one will do it or everyone will. A better command is: 'Julie, get the main down!' If the skipper goes overboard, then someone must deputise. It makes sense for this to be whoever is helming. Either way, there must be a plan.

The man overboard drill needs to be practised at least once, without warning, on any new crew:

1 The tiller is put hard down to bring the boat's bow into the wind. This should be an automatic reflex.
2 The lifebelt is thrown to your person in the water. Better still, throw a dan buoy which will mark the spot. Further floating objects are then thrown overboard at short intervals to mark the route back to the accident spot.
3 As the boat tacks through the wind, the helm starts the engine.
4 The jib is backed and the boat is more or less under control. As soon

Bottom photo: Henk van de Weg owes his life to one of these four-man inflatables made by the Deutsche Schlauchboot-Fabrik.

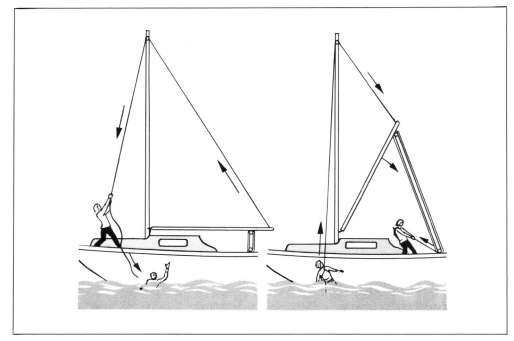

If the halyards or the topping lift are run outside the mast, even a weak crew can pull a heavy person out of the water this way.

as the engine is running, the sails are dropped. There are no prizes for elegance in this. Do not forget the topping lift as the main comes down, and then pull the mainsheet tight.

5 Approach the victim. If the water is colder than 16°C, there is a risk that the victim might lose consciousness very quickly, so you need to get a line out immediately. He might be able to help himself only for a very short time. Do not waste this time by expecting him to climb the emergency ladder. He has little hope of succeeding, with frozen fingers and sodden clothing. Once he runs out of strength, he will no longer be able to tie a bowline round his chest.

When someone falls overboard, the spot needs to be marked. This Kadematic dan buoy can be released in seconds, and does not cause storage problems, unlike conventional models.

If the water is 20°C or warmer, your main concern is to get the victim to windward of the boat, at its widest point. If he is in the lee of the boat or at the stern there is every chance that a wave will bring the boat crashing down on the person you are trying to help. The emergency ladder over the stern is the best solution only if the sea is calm. Be careful of the propeller, which can cause serious injury.

6 If you have got a line to the victim, you are already past the greatest danger. It is rare, though, for the victim to be able to climb back on board unaided; and there is no single best way of pulling a person out of the water. Under no circumstances should a further crew member jump overboard to help, however well equipped the helper may be. We need as many able hands on deck as possible.

If you have good deck winches, I recommend you use the jib or main halyard as a rescue line. The best solution of all is often to yank the boom up with the topping lift and tie the free end to the victim. The mainsheet, with its multiple purchase, can then be used to haul your mate back on board. This method only works if the halyard block is outside the mast. If the safety rail is in the way, cut it with wire cutters. We are saving a life.

One further method which can be used with a strong, practised crew, involves a small sail. The storm jib is attached at the tack and clew to the deck. The halyard is then shackled on and the sail allowed to float on the water. You use the boathook to manoeuvre the swimmer onto the sail, then you simply hoist the head of the sail. If the victim is too weak to tie a line to himself, this method may be the only one which works.

If you lose visual contact with the accident victim, then I agree with Berend Beilken, who says you should also definitely throw the liferaft overboard. Even in a force 5 or 6, the wave crests are large enough for us to lose sight of a person in the water who might be only a few hundred metres away. That person, however, can almost certainly see us. Throwing the liferaft overboard gives the person a further small chance of safety. They might not be able to swim as fast as the liferaft drifts in the wind, but their location is at least roughly marked.

Another occasion on which I would use the liferaft is if the sea was so rough that we might injure the accident victim while pulling them aboard. The liferaft is easy to clamber into, and we can attach it to a long warp, say, 100m long, and tow it until the weather improves. If we are not close to a lee shore, the liferaft can provide warmth and shelter for hours or even a day or two, giving time for the weather to

This Kademic life-jacket with integral harness is ideal from a safety point of view. It is comfortable to wear when deflated: it even fits under a pullover if required. It is easy to check the inflation mechanism.

The lifejacket inflates automatically a few seconds after immersion, and turns the accident victim onto their back in case they lose consciousness.

improve or for another vessel to come along and help us.

Advice for the victim
● Don't panic. Panicking will halve your chance of survival.
● If there is a float (lifebelt or similar) nearby, try to reach it and keep hold of it.
● Do not take off any clothing, under any circumstances.
● Do not wave or shout or splash. Lie on your back, with your face away from the wind.
● If your lifejacket has a whistle attached, blow it every 30 seconds.
● Pray!

This rescue line is ready to unroll. You let it out then sail a circle around the accident spot. It should guarantee that the man overboard can pick up the line.

Kademativ lifejacket with built-in hand-held radiotelephone.

Photos right: Self-inflating liferaft. In an emergency you can jump onto the liferaft. This is the model I entrusted with my life when I sailed round the world.

Clipping on

The only way to be certain of avoiding a man overboard situation is to use a harness and safety line. This is certainly to be recommended on a day's cruise, though it is less practical on a long journey. You must get used to wearing your safety gear when you go onto the most dangerous part of the boat, however, and that is the fore-deck. This should be as automatic as putting your seatbelt on in the car.

In bad weather, no-one leaves the cockpit without being hooked on. If there is the slightest danger of waves coming into the cockpit, then you hook on even there. Much has been talked and written about what sort of safety line is the best. Individual lines with no crotch strap are a good compromise: the crotch strap is not really necessary, and the lack of it makes the harness more comfortable. This in turn means you are more likely to wear it.

Sailors have been washed overboard on occasion despite wearing a harness. No, the line did not break. They were on their way forward, looking for a new spot to clip on to, when they slipped. It is actually impossible to get right from the cockpit to the bow without unclipping momentarily. The jib sheet always gets in the way. It even gets in the way when you rig up a special running harness line from the cockpit to the bow. There is no alternative to unclipping for an instant, while you keep an eye out for particularly nasty waves.

The best spots to clip on to are those in the centreline of the boat. The rail is pointless. That will never stop you falling over: the best it will do is tow you alongside the boat in the water. I am not impressed by carabiner-type hooks, as there are circumstances under which they will fail to open when you want them to under tension. I am aware of one death in a Fastnet race, where the sailor had climbed into the liferaft and could not unclip from the

sinking boat. A tug-opening snap-shackle could have avoided this tragedy. Safety harnesses incorporated in oilskins are an excellent invention, in my view. The belt is built in, so no further straps are required. One swipe and you are hooked on.

Safety equipment

A dan buoy needs to be standard equipment on any cruising vessel. In an emergency, a floating torch would do a similar job. You should always check the batteries at the beginning of a voyage, and ensure that the item is working. This cheap piece of equipment is the only thing that might save the life of someone lost overboard at night. To be effective, it needs to be released as soon as the accident is noticed.

Actually, a dan buoy can save lives in the daytime, too. If someone falls out of the boat in heavy weather (and let's face it, it probably will be heavy weather) it is all too easy to lose sight of them. In a force 5 wind, with the swell that accompanies it, you will not be able to see a head in the water at a distance of 100m. A yacht under full sail travels 100m very quickly. If the spot is not marked, you have little chance of finding it: the sea is not littered with easy landmarks . . . unless you have jettisoned the dan buoy.

If the buoy is to be visible it must be fairly large. If it is not to get in the way of people and lines on board, it must be small. One solution is to keep it in easy reach tied to the backstay. This is not ideal. The Kadematic patented inflatable dan buoy overcomes both problems. It sits in a small container at the stern, and inflates itself in seconds to a 1.50m long floating pole the moment it is released into the water.

The light is turned on automatically. In a strong wind, it can be blown flat, but bobs up at frequent intervals, fluttering and drawing even more attention to itself. Just like a lifejacket, you

need to check it regularly to ensure it is in working order. Fortunately, like automatically inflating lifejackets, it can be used to practise drill without needing to be sent back to the factory for reloading.

Lifejackets should keep your head above water, even if you are unconscious. Most modern ones turn the wearer onto their back, holding the chin up and the breathing passages unobstructed. One can buy solid lifejackets as well as the inflatable sort.

Inflatables are easier to store, and are replacing solid lifejackets. Some inflate entirely automatically, and some are semi-automatic. On the semi-automatic jackets, you need to tug a cord in order for the compressed carbon dioxide cylinder to inflate the jacket; fully automatic jackets inflate on immersion. They are sufficiently reliable that a rain storm or even a once-off large wave will not trigger inflation. Obviously there is not much point having a lifejacket which needs to be blown up by mouth if you are lying unconscious in the water. I recommend either a solid lifejacket or an automatically inflating one.

Lifejackets are like safety harnesses: you should wear yours all the time, but nobody really does so. Of course the crew should pull on lifejackets when there is some danger around, such as fog which might cause a collision with another vessel. In an emergency which might result in you having to abandon ship, you should always be wearing your lifejacket.

Kadematic makes a small radio-telephone, which is rather expensive, unfortunately, but it is like an extra life insurance policy: it comes built into a lifejacket. The radio is waterproof, but can easily be operated by someone in the water. It may be used to communicate with the boat on VHF Channel 16.

When the current model was undergoing trials in the North Sea, they found that a person in the water could

Not quite child's play: a liferaft weighs 20 to 30 kilos.

All three skippers will be able to get the liferaft out in seconds. The stowage on the stern probably allows the fastest release: one hand to release it, then a push.

contact a yacht 5 miles away. They also found in these trials that the radio works best if used by the person in the water to direct the yacht helmsman, along the lines of: 'flash your masthead light a couple of times . . . yes, I've spotted you, you need to head further left'. A further use for this particular bit of kit is as a walkie talkie between the boat and the tender, since it operates just like the boat's radio. These advantages somewhat offset the high price of the combined radio-lifejacket.

Every lifejacket needs a light and a whistle. The light is powered by a saltwater activated battery. Lifejackets, especially the fully automatic kind, need to be checked annually. If the cylinder has any rust spots on it, change it. Frankly, the cylinders are not expensive, and it might be as well to change them annually without looking for rust flecks.

Emergency flares must be carried on board, and need to be changed regularly. They have an expiry date stamped on the side. Do not rely on a flare which is past this date. Rocket flares with a parachute are the best, and also of course the dearest. They stay visible for much longer than any other type, as they float down from a height of 70m, increasing the chances of someone spotting you. Of course you should not shoot off your flares as soon as the emergency strikes: wait until you think there is a reasonable chance of someone seeing them. In any case, save a couple to lead your would-be rescuer precisely to you.

Flare pistols should be easily to hand on the aft cabin wall. They must be used precisely in accordance with the law. Beware: a loaded pistol is a deadly weapon, so be careful with it. You can fire flares in an emergency, or you can use a red or white flare to draw the attention of the crew on the bridge of that tanker which is just about to run you down.

Flare pistol. Use with care! And follow the regulations.

The **liferaft** is an essential on any cruising craft. It must be stored in reach of the cockpit, not below deck. On small yachts, the liferaft can be hung on the stern. On larger boats, it can be stowed in the cockpit. Liferafts do not open in the water of their own accord. They open when you pull the rip-cord. This is a long line, which needs to be tugged with a jerk to activate the CO_2 cylinder.

> Take care. Liferafts need to be opened before use!

The cylinder inflates and unfolds the raft in one go. This is one reason why you must never activate the cylinder while the raft is on deck: it can catch in the shrouds and prevent you launching it. The valves on the liferaft will hiss at you for a while after it is inflated, signalling that the pressure release system is functioning.

The liferaft will have a folding knife as part of its equipment, which is used to cut the umbilical painter attaching the liferaft to the yacht. Do not worry, though, if there is no time to cut the painter. The liferaft has a designed weak spot where the painter will tear out if the yacht sinks first. Liferafts come from the manufacturer equipped with very little water, maybe enough for a day, and next to no food. Clearly they cannot be used for crossing an ocean in this state. A healthy human being can survive for up to a month without food, but only 40 hours without water. Water takes up a lot of room, however, so you will not be able to pack much extra in the liferaft itself. You can carry an emergency canister with you.

What you can do is ask the manufacturer to pack:
● a plastic bag or a solar distilling kit (for instance a Mark 3 Solar Still)

This photo of the *Ksar* after a Mistral storm is dedicated to those of you who would like to find out what it's like to sail in really bad conditions. This is all the work of freak waves, which engulfed the (ex-) ketch repeatedly, almost tearing off the entire superstructure. Take a look at the bow fittings to see the effect waves can have even on small surfaces. The yacht and crew survived, but both were badly injured . . .

- aluminium foil sleeping bags or space blankets
- a small, very fine mesh net
- fishing line, hooks, etc
- a mirror

They will certainly be happy to do so.

Plastic sheeting is used to make drinking water out of sea water, when the sun shines: you spread the bag or sheet over sea-water-soaked clothes, and collect the condensation. The foil blanket is a protection against the sun, and lowers the rate at which your body dehydrates. The mirror is for signalling. The fine mesh net is for catching plankton, which is good nourishment. All you need as fishing gear is 20m of line, a few hooks and a spoon or mirror lure for the fish. These few items fit easily in the liferaft and improve your survival chances considerably, especially if you are sailing far afield. You can banish care entirely if you can fit a large drinking water container in as well. For this reason, ensure that you store a large container of drinking water right next to the liferaft.

Bilge pumps are of course part of a boat's safety equipment. The hoses leading to and from the pump should be reinforced with steel ribbing. Normal plastic tubes work well and last a long time in the cold waters of the North Sea, but they get soft in the heat, and tend then to collapse, especially at the suction end. These days, cruising

Hard to believe, but this pretty boat cruising off Tierra del Fuego is the *Ksar*, the steel-hulled ketch you last saw after the Mediterranean storm. It took half a year to sort out the damage from that episode.

yachts should be built so watertight that the bilge pumps are rarely used: all the more reason to check them regularly.

A well equipped yacht should have two powerful independent bilge pumps. One of them should be capable of operation from the cockpit without opening a locker or chest. Ideally, you should be able to steer and pump at the same time in an emergency. When you are fighting for survival, a simple bucket is your best hope.

Fire on board is a peril which you should not underestimate. Fires can start even if there is no gas or petrol on board. Remember, though, that fires need oxygen to burn. For this reason, if there is a fire in the engine compartment, keep the compartment lid closed and starve it of air. If fire breaks out, make sure the yacht is pointing so that the fire is downwind.

You need two fire extinguishers on board, one in the cabin and one in the cockpit locker. They should be maintained regularly. Ordinary fire extinguishers are not designed for use at sea, so you need to protect them from spray. If the paint peels off one of your fire extinguishers, and you see rust underneath, get rid of that item of equipment. It is under pressure, and could be dangerous if it is rusty.

**Countless accidents at sea have shown:
do not leave the boat, so long as it is afloat.**

Avoiding collisions

Dr Gerhard
Meyer-Uhl

The greatest danger for a small yacht at sea is other, larger vessels. There are international regulations for the avoidance of collisions at sea (COLREG) which became part of international law on 15 July 1977, aimed at improving safety for all vessels. These regulations are valid at sea and on any contiguous navigable stretches of water, unless local regulations exist which take precedence.

Every skipper who takes a vessel out of harbour needs to know the rules, especially those concerning right of way and collision avoidance. Uncertainty or errors in following the rules can mean death, or damages claims running into seven figures. Imagine if you force a vessel with right of way into taking avoiding action, and it goes aground as a result.

Constant bearing means collision course

Our starting point has to be the combined speed of the vessels which are approaching each other. If a tanker is doing 15 to 30 knots, and you are doing 5 to 10, you probably have some 5 to 15 minutes after sighting the tanker to take a bearing on it, check the bearing and decide whether to take avoiding action. By day, it is not too hard to work out what course another ship is sailing. You can see its bow wave and superstructure, and make a guess at its size, speed and direction.

At night, though, if the position of the approaching monster's white lights (of which the further aft is always the higher) or its side lights does not clearly indicate that it is sailing away from you, then you need to do a careful check on its course, using a watch and an illuminated hand bearing compass.

If the bearing does not alter over time, there is a danger of collision.

Opposite page: both white lights lined up, one above the other: too late for evasive action.

You need to write down the measurements to the nearest minute.

Who makes way for whom?

These days, there is not much point in sailing craft skippers relying on Rule 18 which states that powered vessels give way to sailing boats. Tankers and other large boats are often physically not able to get out of the way, given their size and speed. A 100,000 tonne tanker has a 'braking distance' of three nautical miles, with all engines full astern. To turn 20° off its original course takes one nautical mile and two minutes with the rudder hard a-starboard.

Furthermore, if merchant shipping is not expecting to come across pleasure craft in the waters you are sailing, you will probably not have been seen in the first place. The bridge is often left empty for short periods: after all, they have autopilots and radar! If you consider all this, you will conclude that it is better simply to avoid all large ships, however much the law may say that the other ship has a duty of care and we have a duty to continue our course and speed.

In any case, you are well advised to phone big brother up on Channel 16 and let the bridge know your intentions. You can check whether you have been spotted and (crucially) identified on the radar. Once they have identified you, they can use the radar to check whether you are on a collision course.

Right of way and collision avoidance rules
two sail vessels
● the vessel on port tack gives way to the vessel on starboard. The position of the mainsail determines what tack you are on.
● if both are on the same tack, the vessel to windward must keep clear. In cases where doubt exists or damage may be caused, a right-of-way vessel must take avoiding action.

Two powered vessels

● vessels approaching on opposite courses avoid each other by keeping to the right.
● vessels approaching on intersecting courses: you must keep clear of a vessel approaching your starboard bow.

Powered vessel and sail vessel

● the powered vessel must keep clear, but in restricted waters the sail vessel should not cause an obstruction.

Right-of-way vessels

● if you have right of way, you should maintain your course and speed.
● if a collision nevertheless appears likely, you may alter course or speed at the last moment to avoid the other vessel.

Overtaking

● the overtaking vessel must keep clear until the overtaking manoeuvre is complete. This applies also in cases of doubt.

Duty of care

vessels higher up the list must avoid those lower down:

    overtaking vessel
    powered vessel under way
    sail vessel under way
    fishing vessel
    vessels restricted by draught
    disabled vessels or those restricted in their ability to manoeuvre.

Rule 34 (warning signals) is closely connected with the above list. The rule actually applies to powered vessels only, and they tend to use sound signals infrequently, especially in crowded waters, so as not to confuse other skippers. However, these signals should be used simultaneously with a change of course if there is danger of collision. They may be accompanied by a light signal, which should be visible at a distance of 5 nautical miles, in all sectors.

Warning signals for visible powered vessels changing course

When taking avoiding action

●	I am changing course to starboard
●●	I am changing course to port
●●●	I am reversing
●●●●	alert signal if in doubt

In restricted waters or channels

‒‒●	I am overtaking to starboard
‒‒●●	I am overtaking to port agreed
‒	at blind bends

All this makes it hard for the sailing fraternity on the sea. On the one hand we have right of way and should maintain our course; on the other hand, we are never certain if we have been seen by the other vessel and they are actually avoiding us as they should. For this reason, I recommend that you steer well clear of other vessels, especially where there is little traffic. That way, questions of right of way should not arise.

Advice for the sailing skipper

- make sure you keep a good lookout
- use the binoculars early: white navigation lights can be seen at a great distance
- check regularly that your lights are working and your battery is charged
- carefully check the course and speed of the merchant ship
- always assume that the merchant ship has not seen you
- keep a flare pistol to hand on the aft cabin wall, loaded with white flares to draw attention to your right of way in an emergency
- if you need to alter course, do so early and by at least 45°: avoiding action should be taken towards the other vessel's stern, not towards its bow
- Cross shipping lanes by the most direct route
- if your green navigation light is on the same side as the other boat's green light, or if both red lights are on the same side, there is no danger of a collision
- if you can see a powered vessel's white lights to starboard, and the lower light is to the right of the higher light, there is no danger; the same is true if the lights are to port, and the lower light is to the left

Two Maxi-Racers about to collide. Who has right of way?

Distinguishing between vessels

Between dusk and dawn, vessels must carry lights which aid identification. Any other lights carried must not obstruct identification or the vessel's own lookout; nor should it be possible to mistake them for the required lights. A diagram on page 167 summarises the lights to be carried and their range. You can see that a powered vessel needs to carry top lights and a stern light which together cover a sector of 360°. The stern light, like a tugboat's towing light, has a sector of 135°, within which it should not be possible to see either of the side lights. Any vessel following in this sector must be regarded as the overtaking vessel. The only vessel which has both side lights visible at the same time is one which is coming straight at you.

Small boats in particular often fail to attain the prescribed range for their lights: a sailing vessel heeling over is especially hard to spot. White lights are generally much easier to see than the red and green ones. Small vessels under 20m long may combine red and green lights in one. In practice they are almost always combined, because every skipper is concerned about electricity consumption, and this is an opportunity to save 20W. We are also seeing three-sector combined lamps these days, which include the white stern light and are permitted on sailing vessels up to 12m in length. If such a vessel is motoring, however, it also needs a white top light.

Even in harbour, sculling around with the tender at night, you come under the category of oar-powered craft and must have a white light available. Of course, self-preservation indicates you will have a torch with you anyway!

You will only ever see the special fishing-boat lights if you are crossing fishing grounds. When a trawler is travelling, it carries the normal navigation lights for its size.

Any vessel over 7m long is required to show anchor lights. This is particularly recommended for cruising yachts in unfamiliar harbours, even when moored at the quayside, where you are not only obeying regulations but quite likely saving your boat from nasty midnight scrapes.

Relatively few shapes are used as signals in daylight. The commonest is the inverted cone which shows that a sailing vessel is motoring and no longer enjoys a sailing vessel's right of way. If you see an upright cone combined with a basket or hourglass shape, you are dealing with a fishing vessel whose nets extend over 150m! A lozenge must be hoisted by any vessel towing or being towed, if the combined length of the 'train' exceeds 200m. A black cylinder indicates a vessel with exceptionally deep draught. Black balls with a diameter of 60cm have the following meanings:

Radar makes it easier to avoid others and to be avoided. Every yacht should have a radar reflector; but even the best reflector will only make you 'visible' at a range of three to five miles.

> 1 black ball = at anchor
> 2 black balls vertically = unable to manoeuvre
> 3 black balls vertically = grounded
> 3 black balls horizontally (at the yardarm) = minesweeper
> ball–lozenge–ball = restricted ability to manoeuvre
> 2 black balls to one side and 2 lozenges to the other = dredger: pass to the side of the lozenges

In fog: sound signals and what to do

Just as any enthusiastic sailor will one day encounter a strong wind, we all sooner or later come up against fog. The weather forecasters do their best, and no-one in their right mind leaves harbour when fog is expected. Nevertheless fog banks sometimes emerge suddenly and unexpectedly.

Reduced visibility means that there is a substantially increased probabil-

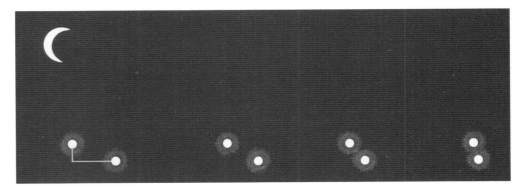

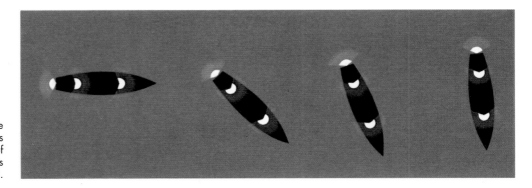

ity of collisions at sea, particularly for small craft. It may sound unlikely, but the availability of radar has actually added to the likelihood of accidents in some respects. There are three hidden risks exacerbated by fog:

● modern merchant ships travel very fast
● the echo from small craft's radar reflectors can easily be suppressed on a screen when the navigation officer is trying to cut out interference from wave reflections
● it is hard to tell where a sound is coming from

According to the regulations, in reduced visibility every vessel should stick to a safe speed and should cut its engine and manoeuvre with care if a fog signal is heard ahead (Rule 19). These regulations apply equally to vessels equipped with radar. They are more honoured in the breach than the observance. Large vessels have timetables to stick to.

Time and again, it has been shown in court that a ship was travelling at 18 knots through a fog bank. It is no technical problem for a large ship to keep steaming full ahead in a force 8 gale with only moderate visibility. For this reason, sound signals and rules of the road take on added importance when you cannot see very well.

It is easy to tell the difference between the bass foghorn of a large ship and the higher note of a small boat's signals. It is worth pointing out, though, that most commercially available fog warning equipment for small boats is not up to the job. Very few can be heard in fog more than a few metres off, especially over the throb of a large ship's engines. You can pick up really useful foghorns second hand: ones which were once used on large sailing boats.

It is easy to get the direction wrong.

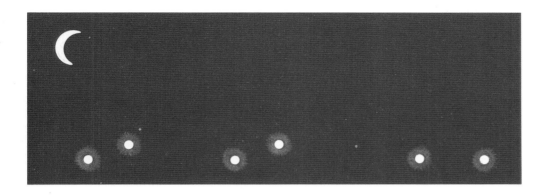

Fog banks tend to distort sounds and echo unpredictably. Our eyes and ears, straining, are easily misled. The best we can do is to follow the basic rules sensibly. We start by assuming that you know the boat's true position, or can ready-reckon one pretty precisely. From the time you hit fog, you will have to navigate more painstakingly, using compass, log, speedometer, chart and atlas of currents.

The deeper the note, the further the sound travels.

Further precautions are as follows:
● give regular sound signals
● check the radar reflector
● mount a listening watch on the fore-deck
● sail out of any shipping lanes
● put your lifejackets on

One piece of advice: stay well out of the path of big ships. That way, you will not have to worry about who has right of way.

Sound signals in reduced visibility

at least every 2 minutes	at least every minute

at least every 2 minutes

—   power vessel under way

—   power vessel engines off

—•• vessel unable to manoeuvre,
      limited in its ability to manoeuvre,
      restricted because of draught,
      sailing vessel,
      fishing vessel,
      tug

—•••vessel being towed
      rigid tow group as for power vessel
      loud sound signals vessels <12m

•••• additional sound signal for
      pilot vessel in service

at least every minute

vessel at anchor <100m LOA

vessel at anchor >100m LOA

vessel grounded <100m LOA

vessel grounded >100m LOA

• short tone, up to 1 second   bell = 5 sec quick rings   = single ring
— long tone, 4–6 seconds   gong

Distress signal at sea: flags N and C flown together.

Distress signals

Every skipper must know these. There are 14 of them, listed in appendix IV of the collision avoidance rules. They may only be used when there is immediate danger requiring immediate assistance. A broken mast or running out of fuel, when there is no immediate danger to life, may not be considered sufficient grounds for sending a distress signal. At short range, the accepted sign is to raise and lower both arms to the side of the body. Apart from that, you must know the following:

Sound signals
• cannon or other shots at intervals of about one minute (not really appropriate for small craft)
• continuous use of fog signal

Flares
• red rocket flares
• red parachute flares or red hand flares. These are the most useful emergency light signals for small craft. They can be seen at 5 miles by day and up to 20 miles by night, under favourable conditions. Keep them in a dry place and watch the expiry date.

Radio
• Morse SOS ••• ––– •••
• Morse alarm call: 12 dashes of 4 seconds within a minute

• radiotelephone: Mayday on 2182 KHz
• alarm call two alternating tones maintained for 30 seconds in every minute
• automatic emergency transmissions from radio buoy
Most yachts these days do have radiotelephones, so the use of this medium is increasing.

Flags
• flags N and C flown one above the other
• rectangular flag flown above or below a shape (ball or fender)

Fire
• flame (burning oil drum)
• orange smoke signal (useful for small craft).

Vessel LOA	>50m	12–50m	<12m	<7m
Lights	range in nautical miles			
top light	6	5; 3 if <20m	2	–
side light	3	2 combined if <20m	1	–
stern light	3	2	2	–
tug light	3	2	2	–
360° light white/red/ green/yellow	3	2	2	–
	power vessel <7m LOA and maximum speed <7 knots			side lights if possible, otherwise white light 360°
	sail vessels must carry side and stern lights according to size		may use 3-colour combined light	side lights if possible or hand-held lamp
	oar-powered vessel may carry lights as for sail vessel, otherwise hand-help lamp			

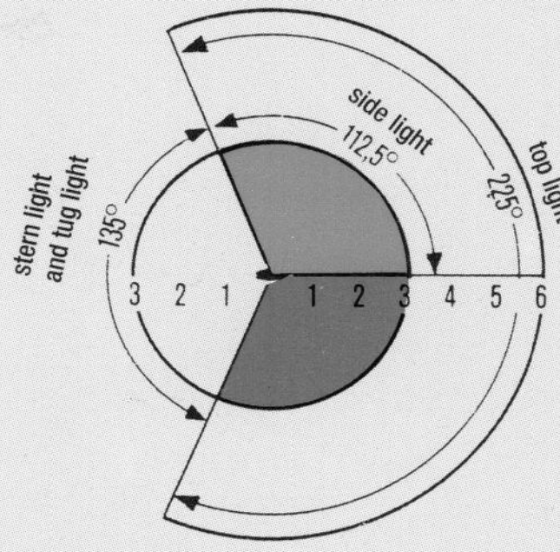

side light 112,5°
top light 225°
stern light and tug light 135°
3 2 1   1 2 3 4 5 6

symbol for 360° light

symbol for top light

symbol for flashing light

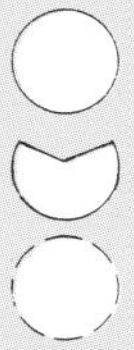

powered vessel under way; * <50 m can carry 1 top light	hovercraft under way; * <50m can carry 1 top light	tug <200m under way */***	tug >200m under way */***	sail vessel* may carry	pilot in 1. at anchor appropriate light; 2. under way*	trawler under way*	fishing vessel under way*
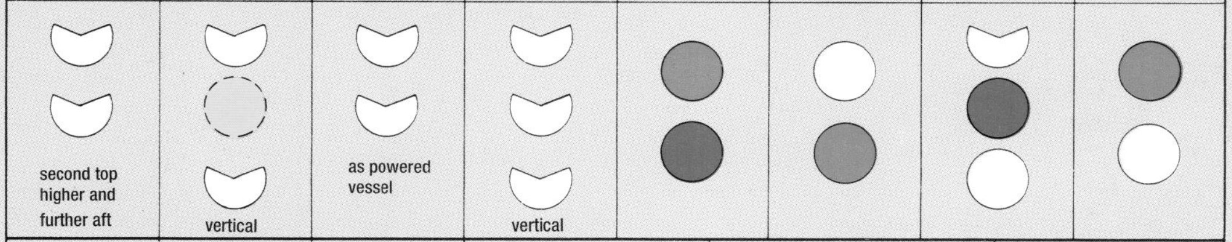 second top higher and further aft	vertical	as powered vessel	vertical				

unable to manoeuvre; under way*	restricted ability to manoeuvre; under way**	restricted by draught **	tug which cannot deviate from course while towing >200m	vessel restricted in ability to manoeuvre carrying out dredging or other underwater work**		vessel under tow
						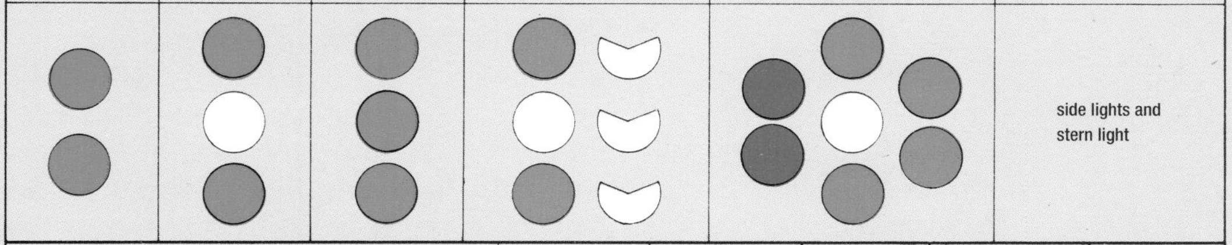 side lights and stern light

minesweeper***		vessel at anchor >50m; deck lights if >100m	vessel at anchor <50m	vessel aground plus anchor lights according to size	sail vessel <12m may use combined light	sail vessel <7m using lamp in place of side, top or combined light	motor vessel <7m, max 7 knots
			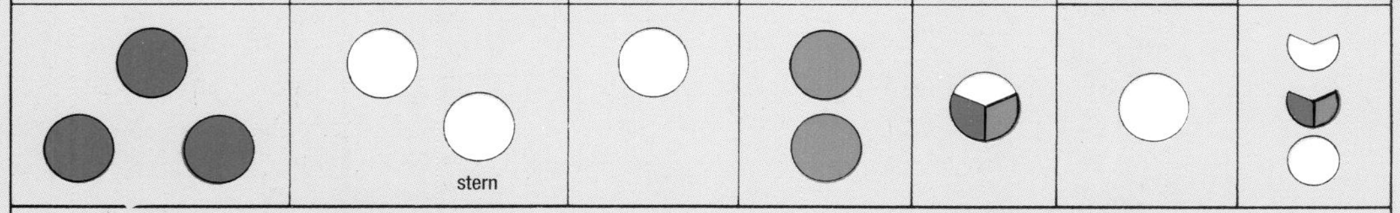 stern				

* plus side and stern lights corresponding to length   *** plus yellow tug light above stern light
** plus top and stern lights; plus side lights corresponding to length when under way

What to do in a storm

Let us say it now: storms are rare in Europe in the season in which we normally sail. A sailing yacht is not designed to withstand a Force 12 hurricane with accompanying waves. My guru Eric Hiscock correctly points out that anything from Force 9 upwards is a fight for survival. In this context, though, note that your anemometer indicating a constant Force 6 with gusts of Force 8 does not mean that there is a Force 8 gale blowing. This is a Force 6, a strong wind.

Our major problem in a storm is the lee shore. We avoid finding ourselves on a lee shore in a storm if we can. You might have no serious problems in a Force 8 out at sea, but if you are a few miles upwind of the coast you are in danger of wrecking your boat. Let us never forget this: you cannot sail (and you can certainly not motor) into a Force 8 gale. Even if the boat could still carry sail, you would make no headway to windward against the waves. For this reason, listen to all available weather forecasts the moment you get close to shore.

There are no particular problems if a storm strikes out at sea. If the wind is stronger than Force 8 you will not be able to heave to; but you should be able to run before the wind, if necessary under bare poles. Do not underestimate the speeds you can reach this way: 4 to 5 knots are easily achieved in a Force 8. This makes 100 nautical miles or so in 24 hours.

Above Force 8 the waves get really enormous and your yacht begins to surf down the lee slopes of them. At this stage you actually have to slow it down. In the old days, sea anchors or drogues were recommended, but these days sailing experts agree that sea anchors do not actually help. If you attach it at the bow, like a normal anchor, it will bring your bow up into the wind; the wind resistance of the boat's side is much greater at the front, so you will be blown back round, and end up just where you do not want to be: beam on to the wind and the breaking waves.

The sea anchor is not even much use for keeping the stern to the wind. In order to have any effect, it would have to be so large that you could barely handle it in a storm; and a sea anchor large enough to brake you would hold the stern so tight you could not steer at all. It is easier and more effective to tow some warps along behind you. If they do not slow you down enough, tie a few knots in them. Your target should be to achieve a compromise speed of somewhere around 20% under the hull's maximum.

There were once some wise men who advised sailors to hoist as much as possible up top when running before the storm, but I shudder to think what would become of my mast and boat if I followed their advice. Cases of yachts 'tripping up' over themselves down the lee of a large wave have been known. I stood on the deck of the *Sandefjord* and could not believe that this solid vessel, 15m long and 5m wide, once somersaulted down a wave in the Roaring Forties. That somersault cost a man his life.

Years ago, Bernard Moitessier maintained that it was best to run at an angle of 20° before the following waves, towing nothing behind. His was something of a lone voice, and he did admit to me subsequently that when he sailed round the world the second time he did not use this technique. I have to admit that some of the storms he survived between Tahiti and Alicante were notably severe; but this does not prove that his technique is the Holy Grail.

Gale warning

All objects which are not riveted in place need to be tied down. This is

If an onshore storm blows up now, you are in the wrong place. Look at that reef a couple of miles offshore.

You cannot really photo-
graph a storm, but this was
one of those hurricane-
powered waves that did
the damage you saw on
page 155.

particularly true for the tender. If you are just waiting for the gale to arrive, take the mainsail off the boom straight away. Check all hatches are tightly closed (including the anchor locker).

If anyone suffers even slightly from seasickness, they should take a tablet a couple of hours before the storm is expected. You may not be feeling hungry, but remember that survival in heavy weather takes energy, and you should therefore eat something. A large vacuum flask is extremely handy for this purpose, for drinks and even pre-warmed solid food.

If possible, you must establish the boat's true position. If there is anyone not currently doing a useful job, they should go down below and catch up on their sleep. Obviously, everyone should be wearing their harness and lifejacket, and be clipped on. If the wind is already sufficiently strong to make you worry about the possibility of a broach, take the autopilot down. However weak the crew in numbers or strength, one person is needed at the helm all the time, clipped on and ensuring the boat does not get beam on.

No sailor really enjoys bad weather. You always hear some idiot at the clubhouse bar saying 'I'd like to experience a really bad storm, just once.' If we are honest with ourselves, fear is a major part of any storm. We hide our fear, as much as we can. We overestimate the severity of the storm when the sky is dark and threatening, or at night. I lived through a Mistral storm in the Mediterranean which frightened me at the time far less than a laughable force 6 off the Azores with the rain driving into my face.

One final point: yachts rarely succumb to storm. There are many more cases of crews deserting their boat in a panic, and the boat being found a couple of days later floating calmly about with no-one on board. There is basically nothing to fear, unless you are being driven onto a lee shore.

A personal comment at this stage. I have sailed almost every sailable sea, about one hundred thousand nautical miles. I have spent weeks in the Roaring Forties and gone round Cape Horn through the fearsome Le Maire straight, where gales are three times as frequent as in the Bay of Biscay. I have to conclude that there are very few storms worth being frightened of.

Severe gales may not be that rare in temperate regions, but they seldom last long enough for life-threatening sea conditions to arise. The wind is less of a problem. You (along with 95% of sailors) don't know what a force 12 feels like? If you drive along the motorway at 70 miles per hour and stick your hand out of the window, you can feel a force 11. (Force 12 is 74 mph, not permitted on our roads!) The wind is not dangerous: the waves out at sea can be.

There is little point getting too precise about the right response to a gale. Every boat and every wave is different, even within one sea area. One storm can create a hell of a problem, because it coincides with some left-over large waves from the last storm; the next storm might come after a calm period, and make long, gentle waves which simply make the boat bob up and down more than usual. Whatever the wind, your response to it will be determined by the overall weather and the proximity of that lee shore.

If you are still trying to decide whether to sail upwind or downwind, you are in no danger. Each of the few times I have been hit by a really severe storm, I always had the decision made for me by the wind. I simply did what the sea demanded to survive. All the plans I might have made on land were irrelevant. The most important point is:

Your boat is stronger than you are. It is the safest place to be in a storm.

171

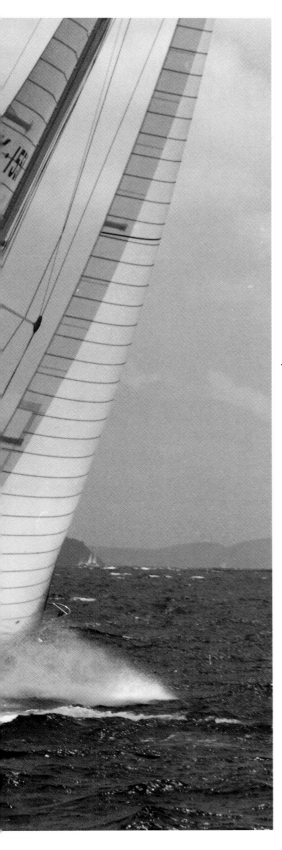

Wind, Weather and Waves

Many sailors wrongly think it pointless to bother about the weather because even professional weathermen often get it wrong. Unlike landlubbers we aren't bothered about whether it's going to rain or if the sun will shine, but for the safety of our ship it's important to know how strong the wind will be and from which direction it will be blowing.

Wind

Almost everything can be explained easily by the relation between different air pressures. As we know, the world is surrounded by a mantle of air, which is only about 20km high. Air also weighs something, however little. Through its height it exerts a pressure on the earth's surface of about 1 kilopond per square centimetre.

This air pressure is obviously not the same everywhere, and depends generally on the temperature. If two areas next to each other have different air pressures, the air will endeavour to flow from the area of high pressure into the area of low pressure, thus balancing out the difference in pressure. It is just this air flow which powers our boat – the wind. The greater the difference in pressure, the faster the air will move from an area of high pressure into an area of low pressure.

Wind strength

These days, wind speed is measured in the speed of air masses, given in knots. The traditional Beaufort Scale is practical for sailors: these wind forces (from 1 to 12) correspond to a particular band of speed, in knots.

173

Stormy sea near Cape Horn.

The sailor can establish the wind force either with a wind speed indicator or by estimating it. Of course, measuring it on board will only give the apparent wind speed. So, if we are sailing downwind at 5 knots, to establish the force of the real wind we must add 5 knots to the measured speed. If we want to measure the wind force according to the Beaufort Scale using an anemometer, we should not take the peaks but the mean, which all measurements revolve around.

In a 40-knot wind, an anemometer can show a reading of 60 knots in a gust of wind, without it being anywhere near wind force 11. This is why

The Beaufort Scale

force	knots	sea conditions
0	0	Sea like a mirror.
1	1 – 3	Sea ripples slightly.
2	4 – 6	Waves appear, small but distinct.
3	7 – 10	Crests begin to break.
4	11 – 15	White horses appear fairly frequently; continuous rustling from breaking waves.
5	16 – 21	White horses everywhere; breaking waves sound like murmuring.
6	22 – 27	Breaking crests leave behind white foam, probably some spray.
7	28 – 33	White foam begins to be blown in streaks along the direction of the wind.
8	34 – 40	Foam lies in distinct streaks along the direction of the wind.
9	41 – 47	High waves with crests of considerable length; the seas begin to roll over and break up.
10	48 – 55	Spray affects visibility, the whole surface of the sea begins to look white because of the streaks of foam.
11	56 – 63	No longer possible to guess the wind force.
12	64 +	Severe hurricane, no chance of survival for a yacht.

you should take what weekend sailors say with a pinch of salt. An experienced elderly ship's officer once told me that the strongest storm he had experienced was a force 10 wind. When I think of all my friends who experience storms almost every year of force 10 or 11 wind, I am inclined not to trust them. A sailor can estimate the wind force from what the sea looks like as well, which needs some experience. The table below left gives a rough guide to guessing the wind force.

The wind force can also be felt in the handling of the boat. In force 6 wind you can still sail close hauled, but in force 7 wind this becomes hard going if at all possible. In force 8 wind you can only just heave to, and in winds of force 9 and over you aren't 'sailing' any more as the crew and the boat are struggling to survive.

One of the most important measuring instruments which you should have on board is a barometer. All it does is indicate the current air pressure, which is measured nowadays in 'hectopascals'. Before using the barometer, turn the screw on the back to adjust the indicator to real current air pressure, which can be obtained by telephoning the weather station. If you want to read the pressure, knock the barometer gently and the needle will return to the right position. You can tell from this short jump if the air pressure is rising or falling. It is important to realise that you can't do anything on board with just an air pressure reading. Only weather forecasts or a weather chart will give you a clear picture of the current weather and its development.

Pressure patterns It is much easier to read a weather chart than most sailors think. If you know the three basic elements – pressure patterns, isobars, and fronts – you can say a lot about the different winds in their respective areas. A pressure pattern simply shows

the area of lowest or highest pressure in the surrounding area – a low or a high. Therefore, an area of low pressure must be surrounded entirely by areas of higher pressure, and the other way round for an area of high pressure.

If you were to take as many air pressure readings as possible around an area of low pressure, you would be able to tell that the air pressure rises fairly fast further away from the low. You can illustrate this by joining together the points with the same air pressure, giving you isobars. You obviously don't draw an isobar for every hectopascal of difference, but only for every fifth or tenth isobar – 995 hPa, 1000 hPa, 1005 hPa, 1010 hPa etc. On a weather chart you don't write '1005' but '05' to keep it simple. If you imagine that isobars are just a line of the same pressure, it is reasonable that isobars never cross, because if they did cross there would have to be two different pressures, which simply isn't possible.

So what is the practical use of isobars? They tell us a lot, but specifically

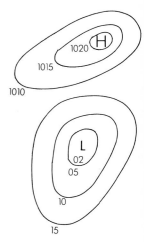

High and low with isobars.

Actual wind strength at 10 am (upper portion of graph) was 30 kn (force 7) while gusts (lower portion) reached as high as 50 knots.

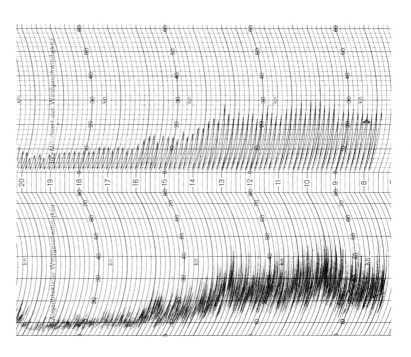

175

Cape Horn at dusk. It looks peaceful, but of all sea-lanes it has the highest storm frequency.

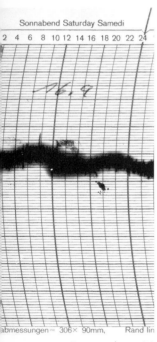

Sonnabend Saturday Samedi

2 4 6 8 10 12 14 16 18 20 22 24

abmessungen = 306× 90mm,   Rand lin

Barograph: on 16 September there was a force 4 wind. The oil damper isn't functioning properly.

The distance between the isobars gives the approximate wind force on the Beaufort scale.

the direction and strength of the wind which is exactly what a sailor wants to know. As we said before, the greater the difference in pressure, the stronger the wind, which in isobars means the nearer the isobars lie together, the stronger the wind.

If the isobars are in relatively straight lines, you can estimate the wind force at your ship's position if you measure the distance in latitude between two isobars which show a diference in pressure of 10 hPa. If the isobars curve strongly, you can subtract about 1 wind force.

Estimating winds from isobars		
distance in latitude (isobars 10hPa apart)	Baltic & North Sea	Medi- terranean
	wind force	wind force
1°	12	12
2°	8	10
4°	5	6
8°	3	4
15°	2	3

Wind direction

So how does the pattern of isobars tell you the wind direction? It is very easy if you consider (as earlier) that air masses always flow from areas of high pressure into areas of low pressure, and that they blow clockwise out of the area of high pressure and anti-clockwise into the area of low pressure. Circulation is the opposite way round in the southern hemisphere. The diagram on p. 179 shows how the isobars are always at an angle of about 15° to the wind direction.

A weather chart is only accurate at the time of observation. But you can easily calculate the conditions which will affect your ship's position from the direction and speed of the wind on the chart. A forecast is more exact the less time has passed since the last information has been collected.

A barometer is invaluable for observing developments in the weather. As mentioned earlier, the air pressure on board at a particular time means very little if you don't take into account the developments over the past hours or

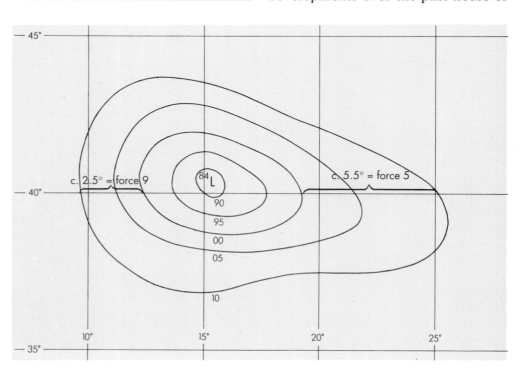

178

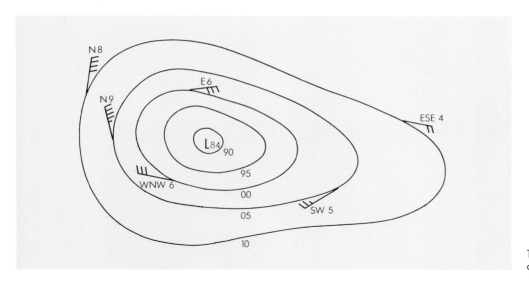

The wind is blowing anticlockwise into a low.

days at your ship's position. You should enter the air pressure in your log book at short intervals. A barograph is therefore useful to have on board, as it records the air pressure. From this, you can easily see developments in the weather, eg a low moving away.

A barograph is unfortunately very sensitive to the vibrations on a small yacht, so you must make sure you deaden the vibrations as much as possible when you install it. It helps to have rubber supports under each corner, and a special 'oil damper' on the indicator, but they don't always have the desired effect. Even if you have a barograph on board, a barometer is not in any way redundant as it is generally much more exact.

Recently, electronic barometers and barographs have come onto the market which are completely immune to violent movements of the boat. You can also instal an alarm in it for either a drop or a rise in pressure. Compared with conventional barographs, the electronic device has the advantage that it doesn't need any paper.

Weather forecast

You should always try to get the latest weather chart before you set off on a trip. The harbour master will often be

able to help you. When you are under way you will have to rely on the weather forecast from your radio receiver. When you are abroad you should always find out in good time which radio stations broadcast weather forecasts at what times, and you should have enough knowledge of the language. The times and frequencies of weather forecasts are in the nautical radio communication service all over the world, wavelength III, which everyone should have on board their yacht like wavelength II.

If you don't speak a particular language, record the weather forecast on a cassette, so that you can then go through it using a dictionary. The relevant meteorological expressions are

An electronic pressure gauge. Like a barograph, the device 'draws' the pressure pattern over a long period with no disturbance. You can see the wavy movement typical of trade wind areas.

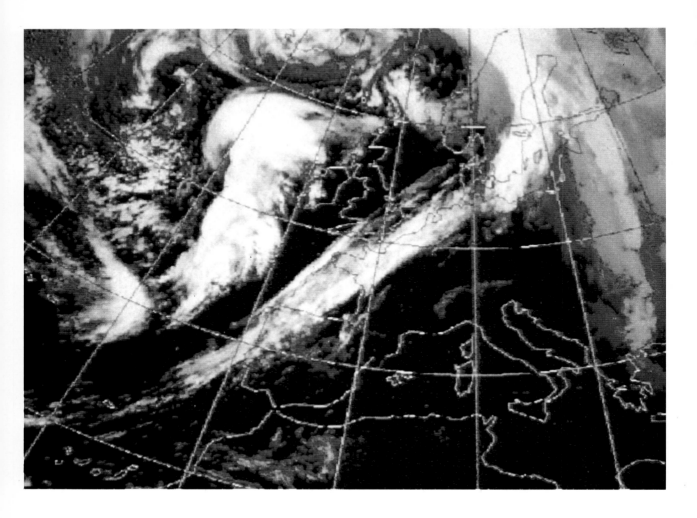

A satellite photograph received by the simplest of methods. All you need is a PC, the relevant software and a radio receiver.

compiled for a lot of different languages in the nautical radio communications service. If you have a mini TV on board, you can see the weather chart on the news in harbour.

Weather chart

If you are on the open sea, you can try to draw a weather chart yourself, on the basis of the details which are given for stations in the Baltic, the North Sea and the Mediterranean. It is not an easy task to get it right straight away, as it needs practice and some experience. You will find an excellent introduction to working out weather charts, particularly constructing isobars, in the nautical radio communications service on wavelength II, section D.

Onboard weather fax

Satellite photographs and the latest weather charts would have been imaginable only on luxury yachts even a few years ago. Today it is almost the meteorological norm to record these kinds of radio messages and analyse them yourself. The basic equipment needed for this is already there on most yachts – a good radio receiver suitable for single side band and a battery-driven computer. All that is left is to get the software. A demodulator is delivered with it, which you attach to the headphones outlet on the radio receiver. At first it might be difficult to tune in the software and radio correctly, or to find the right stations. The Guide to Facsimile Stations helps on the last count, and is

Equipment for receiving weather charts and satellite photos on board: a battery-driven PC (DOS computer), the ship's radio receiver and the software together with the connection between radio and computer.

Satellite photos can even be printed on board if you have an independent printer like the Canon BJ 10e. The Sharp PC-3000 computer feeding the printer here will work for 30 hours with three walkman batteries.

A weather chart received with a computer, radio and weather fax on long wave. Using what was said on pages 173 to 179 you can estimate the expected wind forces and directions.

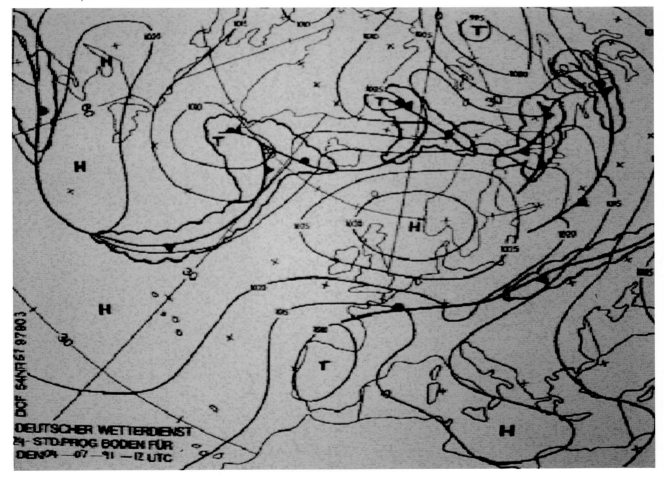

Antarctica: a harsh area for offshore cruising.

available in English from Klingenfuss Publications, Hagenloher Strasse 14, D-74000 Tübingen, Germany. Once you have got the right wavelength, it is not difficult to receive good quality weather charts and satellite photos.

The main advantage of a weather chart and a good weather forecast is that you can predict a change in the wind direction early enough, and you can choose the right tack when beating. You will naturally have a better chance of avoiding bad weather too.

Weather charts will convey only the general weather situation. Even if you find only wind force three on the chart for your area, you might find yourself having to weather considerably stronger gusts or even stormy squalls. The 'normal' weather you have read from the chart can change when a front is passing through. You should reckon with heavy showers and strong gusts particularly when there is a cold front (usually on the back of a low), which is air masses colder than their surrounding areas. It is when these are passing through that jumps in the wind can occur, recognisable on a weather chart as dents in the isobars.

The wind can be influenced all the same by localised currents of air. Near to land in particular you will have to deal with so-called sea breezes and land breezes. These arise from the different rates of cooling or warming of the layer of air over the land mass and the layer of air over the sea. Generally speaking, the air over the coast which is still cold from the night will warm up during the morning in the heat of the sun and rise accordingly. This brings about localised lower pressure, which is balanced out by a cooler sea breeze blowing onshore. It can be so strong that the prevailing wind can be completely shrouded by it, so that you have to account for a different wind direction completely if you are sailing in coastal waters.

At night, completely the opposite course of events can occur, when the air masses above the land cool down and the cooler air sinks, to flow out to sea eventually. A land breeze is generally considerably weaker than a sea breeze. Especially in the Mediterranean you can make good headway with the sea breeze even though summer calms are extremely common, whilst another yacht a few miles further out can be becalmed on a leaden sea just out of reach of the breeze.

Of course it can always happen that you won't have a weather chart or receive any other weather reports, above all abroad. You then have to try to predict the weather as well as you can by using any means you have on board. There aren't many possible routes you can take, but you should always be clear in which direction an area of high or low pressure is to be found. With the barometer, or better a barograph, you can at least establish whether you are approaching a low or a high. The following rule of thumb helps: if you are standing with your back to the wind (in the Northern hemisphere), the high is to your right and the low to your left.

It is comforting to think of the captains of proud square-sailed ships who completed their journeys without weather reports in the roughest waters, having to rely on what they could see from their ship. Many of the fol-

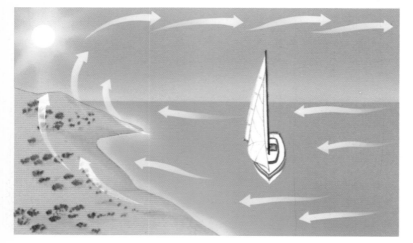

Sea breeze by day.

184

lowing tips come, not coincidentally, from a modern textbook for professional sailors.

Weather maxims

● Except in the tropics, if the barograph rises slowly and steadily it indicates an approaching high

● Except in the tropics, if it falls slowly it means an imminent low. It can also mean a weakening of a high

● If the sun rises brightly or with a slightly red glimmer and then disappears behind clouds, it means wind and rain are coming

● If the sun goes down in the evening shining and clear over the horizon or behind cumulus clouds with brightly shining edges, you can look forward to good weather

● If the sun is particularly big and gleaming white before it sets, you had better reef the sails

● Black clouds at sunset or a yellowy-green light mean bad weather

● If the moon is only pale at night you can expect rain. If it's red and there is a wind or if it rises bright and silvery you can expect good weather

● If the sky is clear and starry but only the brightest stars show, be prepared for rain

● A red morning sky and fiery colours mean a rainy windy day

● If the evening sky remains red after sunset you can expect good weather, but only if there is no red glow in the East. A yellowy- or coppery-red evening sky means wind and rain

● Little cumulus clouds around midday mean good, dry sailing weather, if the morning sky was cloudless

● Bad weather follows heavy clouds in the morning or evening skies

● Unusual cloud formations or colours are always a warning sign

● If the wind freshens in the morning, you will get good weather, and if it freshens in the evening, bad weather

● If the wind suddenly changes direction after a long time it indicates a general change in the weather

● Wind then rain is a blessing; rain followed by wind means you will need a reef

● If there is crackling or other atmospheric disturbance on your radio, especially in daytime, you can count on stormy showers

In the *Tropics*, and so usually in trade winds, these rules only apply within limits. From time to time I would watch clouds form there which would put the fear of God into a sailor in somewhere like the North Sea, but it rarely led to a deterioration in the weather. In the trade wind regions you should be especially attentive to changes in air pressure. A steady rise and fall of the barograph where the difference in pressure is not higher than 3mb over the day is typical. However, if the barograph deviates more than 3mb from this steady line, you should prepare for the worst, a tropical hurricane.

Land breeze at night.

Swell

Swell also has a considerable influence on the speed of your boat or the course you are able to take. The wind and its strength dictate the swell. Waves are not the water itself moving forward but parts of the water moving up and down in the rhythm of waves. Sailing against the swell will cause great difficulties for your boat. This is mainly because your boat will always have to scale the giant wave on the steeper lee side.

The swell depends on the wind, meaning the stronger it blows, the higher the individual waves. Waves as high as a house have actually been seen. In the North Atlantic 16m high waves have been measured scientifically. Even 20m is within the bounds of the imagination. However this doesn't mean that these 'white giants' are always going to put a yacht in great danger. The waves are usually of a corresponding length (200m and more). Swell only spells real danger when the sea breaks, not like a crest toppling over but when it bursts like a breaker. Luckily this happens only extremely rarely. A yacht would have no chance of survival when you consider that with a giant wave like that you would be looking at 30,000 tons of water.

Swell begins to be unpleasant when the wind blows against the current, and the waves become considerably higher. In unlucky circumstances it can happen that a sea really does break. The Agulhas current on the east coast of South Africa sets in occasionally at a speed of 4 knots. Good sea charts will have the following advice printed on them at this point: 'Danger – giant waves over 20m high possible'.

Force 8 wind, luckily from astern so the yacht remains dry.

Portsmouth 1974

Lat. 50°48'N Long. 1°07'W

September						October						November						December					
Time	**Height**		**Time**	**Height**		**Time**	**Height**		**Time**	**Height**		**Time**	**Height**		**Time**	**Height**		**Time**	**Height**		**Time**	**Height**	
h m	m		h m	m		h m	.m		h m	m		h m	m		h m	m		h m	m		h m	m	
1 0515	1.0	**16** 0511	0.4			**1** 0515	0.9	**16** 0008	4.8			**1** 0031	4.6	**16** 0120	4.7			**1** 0054	4.7	**16** 0144	4.5		
1218	4.5	1216	5.0			1215	4.6	0533	0.5			0553	0.9	0629	1.0			0610	0.9	0644	1.1		
Sun 1730	1.0	Mon 1733	0.6			Tue 1732	1.0	Wed 1236	4.9			Fri 1252	4.7	Sat 1332	4.7			Sun 1311	4.7	Mon 1347	4.5		
								1753	0.6			1812	0.8	1849	0.9			1833	0.7	1904	0.9		
2 0024	4.4	**17** 0030	4.8			**2** 0024	4.5	**17** 0053	4.8			**2** 0112	4.6	**17** 0202	4.6			**2** 0140	4.7	**17** 0221	4.5		
0545	0.9	0556	0.4			0548	0.9	0616	0.6			0631	0.9	0704	1.1			0653	0.9	0718	1.1		
Mon 1247	4.5	Tue 1301	5.0			Wed 1246	4.6	Thu 1318	4.9			Sat 1330	4.7	Sun 1408	4.6			Mon 1355	4.7	Tue 1421	4.4		
1802	1.0	1817	0.5			1804	0.9	1834	0.7			1850	0.8	1925	1.0			1917	0.7	1938	1.1		
3 0054	4.4	**18** 0115	4.9			**3** 0057	4.5	**18** 0139	4.8			**3** 0155	4.6	**18** 0242	4.5			**3** 0229	4.7	**18** 0257	4.4		
0616	0.9	0639	0.5			0621	0.8	0654	0.8			0710	0.9	0739	1.3			0737	0.9	0753	1.3		
Tue 1318	4.5	Wed 1345	5.0			Thu 1319	4.6	Fri 1357	4.8			Sun 1411	4.6	Mon 1443	4.5			Tue 1441	4.6	Wed 1457	4.3		
1834	0.9	1859	0.6			1838	0.8	1913	0.8			1931	0.8	2002	1.2			2004	0.8	2013	1.2		
4 0125	4.4	**19** 0159	4.9			**4** 0133	4.5	**19** 0222	4.7			**4** 0240	4.5	**19** 0320	4.4			**4** 0318	4.6	**19** 0333	4.3		
0648	0.8	0720	0.6			0656	0.8	0731	1.0			0750	1.0	0817	1.6			0825	1.1	0832	1.5		
Wed 1351	4.5	Thu 1426	4.9			Fri 1356	4.6	Sat 1434	4.7			Mon 1455	4.5	Tue 1521	4.3			Wed 1531	4.5	Thu 1534	4.2		
1906	0.9	1939	0.7			1913	0.8	1950	1.0			2014	0.9	2042	1.4			2052	0.9	2052	1.4		

Example of using a nomogram. On September 1st 1974 at Portsmouth there was a low tide of 1m at 5.15 am, and a high tide of 4.50m at 12.18 pm. This means that if you read a depth of 2m on the chart for your anchorage, at high tide it will amount to 6.50m. If you have the times and heights of high and low tide, it is easy to establish the depth of the water at all times if you use Rudolph Braren's nomogram, using the entries in the table on the opposite page.

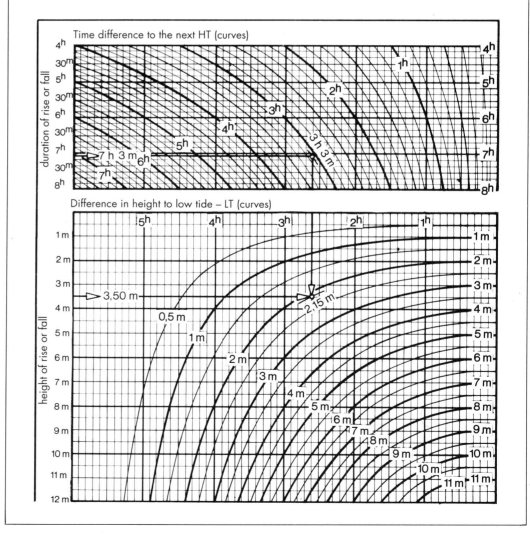

The tides

Knowledge of the tides, that is the times and heights of high and low tides, can be extremely important for a sailor:

● Inshore waters are often so shallow that they are only navigable at high tide. Particularly in the North Sea, your knowledge of the tides will determine whether or not a day trip can be carried out at all safely.

● Currents along the coast usually depend on the tides. In pilots you will find the details of direction and strength of current referring to high or low tide. Local currents can also occur in otherwise current-free inshore waters, which you should then make use of, or avoid if they are opposing.

● In tidal waters you can make use of the variable depths of the water for repairs or overhauls on the underside of your boat. There are so few ship-yards in many areas around the world that you will be glad to come across tidal variations which just about match the depth of your yacht. You can then wait until your yacht is 'high and dry' and paint the underside between the tides.

In order to predict the tides you will need the tide tables. Every year the Admiralty publishes new tide tables. The details they give make it extremely easy to read the height and time for high and low tide from them.

Naturally the tables don't have exact details for every little place on the coast, but they choose certain prominent places which are the points of reference. If you are in one of the few places referred to on the chart, it is all straightforward. One look for the relevant date and there you have the details you want.

So what is the depth of the water at your anchorage on September 1st 1974 at 9.15 am GMT in Portsmouth?

Using a nomogram to find the depth

1 Duration of rising tide		12h 18min −05h 15min
		7h 03min
2 Time difference until the next high tide		12h 18min −9h 15min
		3h 03min
3 Rise in tide		4.50m −1.00m
		3.50m
Answer:		
difference in height to low tide		2.15 m
low tide		+ 1.00m
depth on chart		+ 2.00m
		5.15m

In a few cases the tidal curves are atypical so that you can't use this nomogram which refers to a regular curve. If a case like this occurs, you will find a curve in the tide tables with which you will be able to establish the depth of the water at any time.

Of course you won't always be lucky enough to be in one of the places referred to in the tide tables with all the details. In this case you look up the list of places which gives details of how much they differ from the points of reference. If you are on the coast in a place where there are no details given in the tide tables, just take the nearest place.

The details given in the tide tables refer to 'normal' conditions. In stormy weather the results can be quite different. Calculations which are exact to the centimetre are not advisable, and you should always allow 20cm leeway for safety.

Tidal waters in Guernsey, where the tidal range is over 8 metres.

Sailing to the edge of the world.

Navigation

Coastal navigation

The art of navigation lies in finding out the course you should take in order to reach your destination safely by the quickest route. To do this you must be as exact as possible about your ship's position.

The position is always given first in latitude then in longitude. To facilitate this the earth is covered by a grid of co-

marked in the circle, and read the latitude to the left or right on the edge of the chart. The longitude is read in the same way, from the top or bottom edge of the chart.

Never use school dividers because it is easy to hurt yourself with them, and they can damage the sea chart. There are special chart dividers, and from my own experience I would advise using the sort which can be used with one hand on a rolling boat. However, you should never leave them on the chart table. If the boat heels, this dangerous instrument will fly across the boat.

Incidentally, each degree of latitude is exactly 60 nautical miles long and so

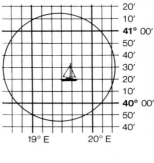

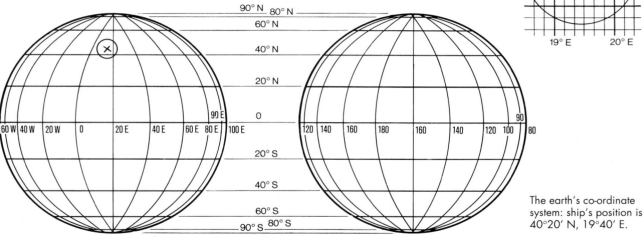

The earth's co-ordinate system: ship's position is 40°20' N, 19°40' E.

ordinates. The degrees of latitude are counted from the equator (0°) to the north or south, for example 44°N or 56°S. Each of the poles therefore stands at 90°. The degrees of longitude are counted to the west or east of the meridian which runs through Greenwich from the North Pole to the South Pole. Unlike latitude, longitude goes up to 180°, and the 180° line runs from north to south near Fiji. Longitude is given as, for example, '44°W' or '166°E'.

Ships' positions are measured on the chart with chart dividers, where you quite simply take the distance from the ship's position to the next latitude

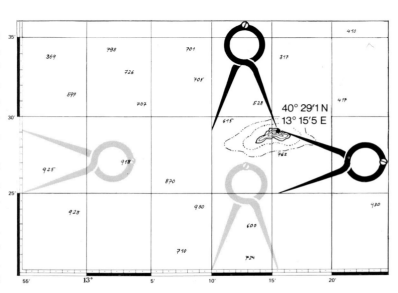

40° 29'1 N
13° 15'5 E

English dividers can be adjusted with one hand, leaving the other one free.

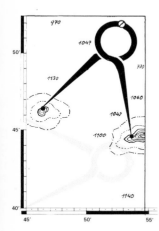

Measuring distance is easy. Remove the dividers and read the distance off the edge of the chart.

Right: the compass needle doesn't point to magnetic north but aligns itself parallel to the magnetic lines of force.

Question 1
What are the co-ordinates of the following five points on the enclosed test chart?
● navigational light visible at 17 sea miles' range on Cape Circeo;
● air radio beacon on Ponza island;
● the top of Vesuvius;
● flashing light visible at a range of 9 nautical miles from the mouth of the Volturno;
● red flash visible at 7 sea miles' range from Amalfi.
(Solutions to test questions, all of which are set in 1975, are on pp. 276–8.)

every minute of latitude is exactly one nautical mile. If a boat covers 1 nautical mile per hour, you are talking about a speed of 1 knot. This is the reason why this natural unit of measurement is the only one used at sea. If you want to measure distances on a sea chart, you therefore don't need to look for a scale on the chart, you just measure the distance with your compasses and lay these on the right or left edge of the chart over the latitude scale, and so directly establish the distances.

Important! Only the minutes of *latitude* are one nautical mile long. Distances should therefore never be measured off the top or bottom edge of the chart where longitudes are marked.

A little invention was needed to transfer the earth's sphere on to a flat surface (the sea chart), so the distance between the degrees latitude on the sea chart (but not in reality) becomes greater as you move towards the poles. You should therefore measure off distances on the left or right of the chart as near as possible to the height of your position. On standard sea charts the differences are hardly noticeable, but on transoceanic charts which cover a larger area you can see a few irregularities.

Question 2
How many miles is it from the top of the Terracina mole to Punta Imperatore on the most westerly point of Ischia?

Compass

At least one should be to hand on every yacht. The compass scale where the degrees are marked from 0 to 360 is just a free-moving magnetic needle. Everyone knows from physics lessons that this always points north. It is important on yachts that the compass card moves as freely as possible so that it can always level off at north during the boat's movements. The best way to achieve this is with a spherical casing which is filled with liquid to deaden the vibrations, or by freely suspending the compass.

Magnetic variation

It is not strictly true that the compass needle aligns with north, as we said earlier. The earth's magnetic field has its own magnetic North and South Poles which are not identical to the geographical poles. Between these magnetic poles run the magnetic lines of force, though not in a straight line. The compass needle or the north-south

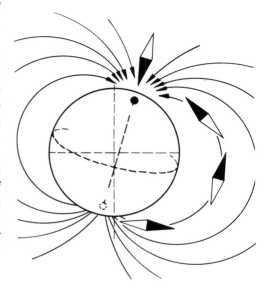

Question 3
How big is the magnetic variation
in 1975 for the Gulf of Naples, if
you also allow for the annual
change?

axis of the compass rose will always
align itself parallel to these. It doesn't
necessarily point to magnetic north.
The nautical term for the compass's
deviation from geographical north is
magnetic variation. The magnetic variation is given on every sea chart with
West (minus) or East (plus).

Map course

To find out which course the helmsman should steer from one point to
another, first you measure the map
course, or real course, from the sea
chart. You need a set square to do this.
Lay the long edge between the point of
departure and place of arrival, so that
the right angled corner points as far as
possible towards you. Lay a second set
square along one of the short sides of
the first, moving the first so that the
zero on its long edge lies on any meridian (these are the degrees of longitude
which have been drawn in). Where the
meridian runs through the degrees
marked on the set square, this is the
chart course. Depending on the direction in which you are travelling, two
values are given.

If you have to draw in a particular
course on the chart, follow the procedure the other way round: lay the set
square with its zero point and the desired course on the meridian, and then
move it with a second set square so
that the long edge of the first set square
runs through the point from which you
will be sailing. At first it is tempting to
read or to draw in the course with one
set square. It is possible, but it leads to
inaccuracies and it takes longer.

As well as set squares, there are a lot
of other aids for reading or setting
courses, most importantly the Cras

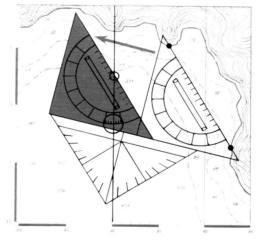

Measuring the real course
1 Lay the long edge of the
set square along both
points
2 Using another set
square, move the first until
the zero on its long edge
lies on a meridian
(longitude) (small circle)
3 Read the course (large
circle).

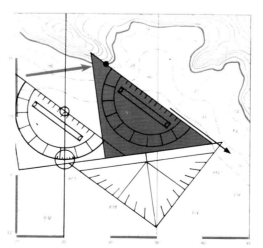

Drawing in a course
1 Lay the set square on the
chart so that the course
you want and the zero lie
on a meridian
2 Push the set square with
another one so that the
long edge runs through the
point of departure
3 Draw it in.

ruler, which you can buy from any good chandler. You have now measured the map course from the points of departure and arrival. But because of magnetic variation you should not steer this course from the compass. First you must alter it according to the amount of variation. I would highly recommend here that you don't worry too much about how you calculate this, but follow mechanically an easy navigational rule.

> **Principle:** Calculate from the right course (chart course) to the wrong course (compass course), then use the opposite sign.
> Or the other way round if you want to draw in the course you have covered on the chart: from the wrong (compass course) to the right (chart course) = right sign.

This simple rule comes up time and again in navigation, and should be memorised by every navigator. Eg: if the map course or right course is 261° and the variation is minus 11.2°, then the compass course is:

RC	261°
var	+ 11.2° (wrong sign, because we are calculating the wrong course)
compass course	272.2°

Question 4
Which compass course should you steer in 1975 from Cape Tiberio to Cape Miseno?

Question 5
What are the coordinates at 9 am of our position if we sailed from Punta Madonna at 8 am at a speed of 5 knots (= 5 mph) with a compass course of 74°?

Top: a ball compass at eye level.

Centre: Sestrel Moore – popular with offshore sailors.

Bottom: a precision ball compass in the steering column.

Deviation

'From wrong to right course with the right sign' or 'From right to wrong course with the wrong sign' is the rule always used in navigation when you have to change course due to other influences. It is also used in what is called deviation.

The compass won't just point to the earth's strong magnetic field, but it will also be influenced by any metal nearby. This deflection is deviation, which is naturally far greater on a steel boat than on a synthetic boat. However, on the latter you can also get considerable deviation values if the compass is situated too near the engine or the electronic instruments. Metal objects in the helmsman's pocket can also cause magnetic deviation. Buying an expensive compass is not the answer, even if some firms have made blatant claims that it is. Even if the compass were shielded from metal parts or magnetic fields, the needle would not align in a certain direction according to the earth's magnetic field either.

You should not use a compass if you haven't already established the exact deviation, so that you can take it into consideration in the same way as the variation when calculating the compass course from the map course (or the other way round). The deviation will never be the same, as it changes depending on the boat's direction. For this reason it should be established for every course direction the boat will take, and should be written down on a navigation chart. To do this you need a calm anchorage, a dinghy with which you can turn the yacht, a sounder (not near the compass), and a bearing attachment on the compass, with which you can take the bearing. With a ball compass you will have to use a bearing disc (illustrated on page 198).

Navigation table If you draw one of these up, you will need to turn your boat full circle with the aid of a dinghy attached to the stern. One person watches the compass course and gives the signal 'now' every 10°. A second person establishes the compass bearing to a landmark with the help of the bearing attachment. It doesn't matter too much if one or other of the plottings fails because the mast or something else is in the way. First of all you draw up a deviation curve which will make it possible for us to establish the missing values later. For each bearing, the corresponding deviation is calculated from a simple formula:

Map course to the bearing object
– variation
– compass bearing

= deviation

Now you only need to enter the calculated deviation values as a curve in the table above right. You will be able to recalculate the missing values and notice at once if one of the values is wrong.

If you aren't able to take a bearing with your compass on board, if you have a ball compass or a bad position for it, you will have to use a bearing disc. This is just a branch of the compass. You should therefore note down the compass course the moment you take the sounding. To reach the compass bearing, the following formula works:

Bearing + compass course =
compass bearing.
(Over 360° subtract 360°).

If the deviation values are under 15°, you can use your ship's compass with the navigation table. The compass must be compensated for it, especially on a steel boat, which should be left to an expert.

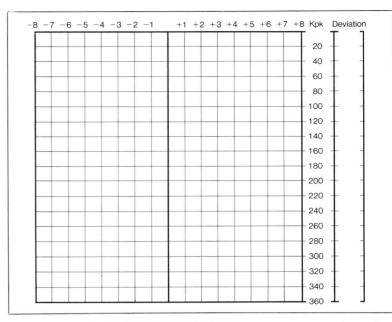

Drawing a curve above all serves to recognise wrong measurements or to add in missing bearings.

Question 6
Our boat is lying at a buoy near the entrance to the harbour at Castellamare at 40° 42.4' N, 14° 28.6' E. After we have turned it once, using the peak of Vesuvius as our sounding object every 10°, we have:

compass course bearing	compass course bearing
10:351	190:355
20:350	200:350
30:350	210:349
40:349	220:348
50:349	230:347
60:353	240:348
70: missing	250:349
80:351	260:350
90:352	270:353
100:353	280:354
110:354	290:355
120:354	300:355
130:355	310:356
140:355	320:356
150:354	360:356
160:354	340:355
170:353	350: missing
180:352	360:352

What do the deviation curve and the navigation chart look like, if you use the above figures?

A good position for the compass: no bearing disc is necessary.

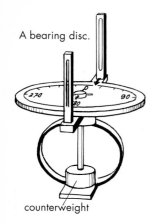

A bearing disc.

counterweight

A modern bearing compass with digital display and memory.

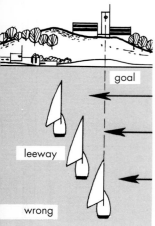

goal

leeway

wrong

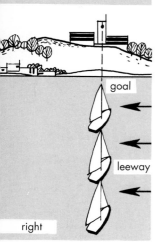

goal

leeway

right

Compensate for leeway as you go.

If the compass is installed in a good position in a synthetic ship, for instance, the deviation should not be much more than 5°. Deviation changes from time to time and should therefore be checked at the beginning of every season. So if you charter a boat you should only set off once you have established the deviation.

> When calculating map or compass course, deviation should be taken into consideration just as much as variation, using the following formula:
> 'From wrong to right = right sign. From right to wrong = wrong sign.'

On a synthetic boat, to establish your position you can always use a hand-bearing compass on deck, without considering deviation because when you hold the compass up it is far enough away from distracting objects. Watch out if you wear glasses! Some frames can cause deviation. Don't take a bearing near the steering compass as it is a strong magnet itself.

Question 7
Once we have set up the steering chart, we want to go under engine from Castellamare di Stabia to Punta San Pancrazio, near the southern tip of Ischia. Which compass course do we give the helmsman?

Leeway
Particularly when sailing close-hauled it is obvious that your boat does not go exactly on course, but is driven to leeward. This movement is called leeway. When calculating your course this also has to be taken into account, as you want to steer a course which really will take you to your destination. You can't measure leeway, but only estimate it

by comparing your course through the water with the wake.

From experience, values for this are:

	moderate sea	heavy sea
close-hauled	10°	20° and above
free wind	5°	10°
downwind	0°	0°

In order to include leeway when we alter course, we need to add a sign.

Leeway moving us to starboard: +
Leeway moving us to port: –

There is therefore no such thing as a leeway of 5° but a leeway of +5° or –5°. As with deviation and variation, the following rule has to be included when calculating leeway: From right to wrong = wrong sign etc.

The ship's position

This is determined by the point where two or more position lines cross.

Question 8
We want to sail from Punta Imperatore to Punta dell Arco on the southern tip of Ventotene in Bft 2 from the Northeast. Which compass course should be sailed taking into account variation, deviation and drift?

Position lines
A position line is quite simply a line on which you find yourself to be. For instance, if you take a bearing from a lighthouse at 270° (actual), you will find yourself somewhere on the line which runs at 270° to the lighthouse on the map. This is a position line. If you have a second position line crossing your course of 270°, your boat is at exactly this crossing point, because

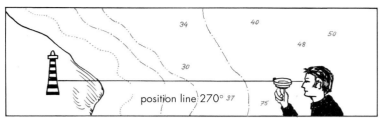

The skipper takes a bearing of 270° from the lighthouse, and is therefore on a line at 270° through the lighthouse.

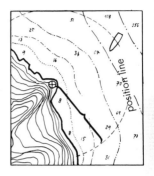

you are only on both position lines at once in that place.

The skill of navigation lies in maintaining as good position lines as possible. You can combine one with another only if they cross at an angle of more than 20°. Position lines don't necessarily have to be straight lines. If you know that you are 6 miles from an object, your position line is a circle around the object of your bearing with a radius of 6 miles. If you are approaching a coast and the echo sounder shows exactly 20m, your position line is curved quite unevenly, following the 20m contour on the chart.

As conscientious navigators, we

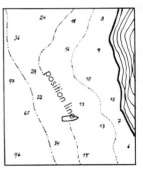

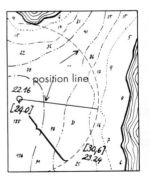

A nearby lighthouse confirms our position. Check the light sequence on the chart or in the Pilot.

should always try to establish our boat's position as exactly as possible. Two position lines are therefore not satisfactory, and we will look for a third or even a fourth. A polygon will result when you do this. The bigger it is, the more sceptical you should be of your position. Not every possible position line is as good as others. Some of them are full of such uncertainties (estimated distances) that it would be stupid to use them if you are able to use better position lines.

You usually work with the following position lines on board a yacht:

Course covered This is a straight line and a good one to use in waters with no current. But if other factors such as drift, current or inaccurate steering come into play, you will have to look for better position lines. If you use it nevertheless, only do so with sufficient margin for error.

Distance covered This is a circle around the ship's last position. I don't like using this position line either, because it is usually affected by inaccuracies of measurement or changing currents. A mechanical log (propeller towed on a rope, which drives a measuring instrument) is inaccurate by 5%. Electronic logs measure to within 1% and better (if they are adjusted), but only the course through the water. There is no log which can measure the 'ground course' on yachts. You should therefore be careful in currents!

Deck bearing This is a straight line

Top: If you know the distance, the position line is a circle.
Centre: A 20m depth contour, only good as a position line if the sea bed rises up steeply.
Bottom: The most common position lines, course covered and distance covered; the crossing point is usually a very inaccurate position.

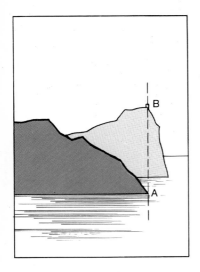

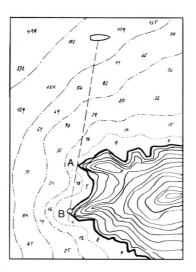

You don't need any instruments, you just need to wait until two landmarks coincide.

follow the course to the bearing object and use the steering course as compass bearing.

Measuring distance This is a circle around the bearing object. You need a sextant for this exact position line, and you need to know the height of the object above the surface of the water, which you will have on the chart, handbook or table of navigational lights.

and the most exact position line at our disposal, because there are hardly any measuring errors or other factors which can affect the accuracy.

Calculate the distance in nautical miles with the formula:

$$\frac{13 \times \text{height in metres of light above surface of water}}{7 \times \text{minutes of the angle}}$$

Compass bearing This is also a straight line and very useful in good weather after taking into account deviation (not with bearing compasses on a synthetic boat) and variation. If the boat is affected by heavy movements, inaccurate measurement up to 10° and above can occur. In this case

If you are further than 2.5 miles from the bearing object, you can't use this method, because the foot of the object will be covered by the apparent horizon in between. In practice if you are in any doubt take a measurement and only use it if the calculated distance is under 2.5 miles.

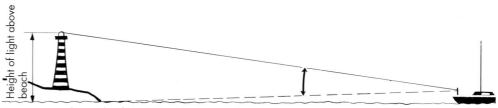

Distance given by angle of height to object nearer than the horizon.

Distance given by angle of height to object beyond the horizon.

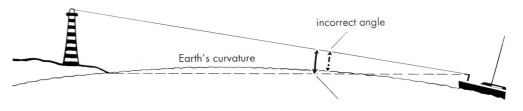

Horizontal angle This is a circle round the bearing object and likewise a very exact position line. Measure the angle between two bearing objects with a sextant (a cheap plastic one will do here) and using the complementary angle (90° minus the measured angle) construct the mid-point of the circle which runs through both objects.

Plumbing This gives an irregular line. Beware! Only use this to establish where the sea bed changes. It is only worth using with an echo sounder. Take the tide level and position of the transmitter on the keel into consideration.

Radio direction finding This gives a straight line. Beware! This is usually full of inaccuracies which can be got round with modern direction-finding such as Decca or Loran C (see pages 231–2).

Consol radio direction finding Another straight line, relatively accurate in high seas, but less so the greater the distance from the consol transmitter. Unfortunately there is only one consol navigation light left in Europe.

Astronomic position line This is a straight line. You cannot rely on this being accurate to within two nautical miles even in favourable conditions. On the open sea it is more than satis-

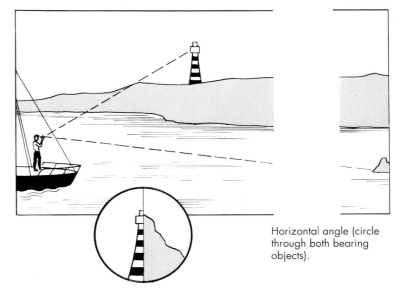

Horizontal angle (circle through both bearing objects).

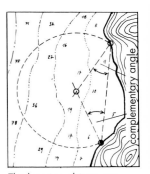

factory, but in coastal waters you should use a 'terrestrial' position line.

Position lines already passed If you have only one bearing object and sail past it, you can take a bearing from it twice. Transfer the position line from the first measurement onto the actual course on the course covered. The inaccuracy of the log, steering error, drift or an unknown influence of the current will affect the calculated position. This sort of position line is hardly used in terrestrial navigation because of the room for error. They are often used in astronavigation.

The bearing objects are joined and the complementary angle from the bearing object to the ship's position drawn in (minus complementary angle away from the ship's position).

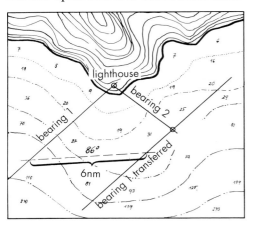

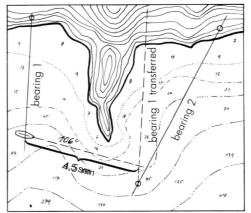

Left: Two bearings from one landmark from ship's position, sailing past. Right: If the first landmark is later sailed past and so hidden, it can still be used and combined with another bearing.

Tips for working with charts
● Only work with HB pencils, and rub out old course lines. Do not use use an eraser if the chart is damp.
● Only one chart at a time on the chart table, otherwise you will risk reading off distances from the chart underneath.

● Every trip should be reconstructed from the chart. You should therefore draw in the course(s), and mark on the chart the ship's position [in square brackets] with the time each time you write up the log. Never write compass courses on the chart, you always navigate with 'actual' measurements.

Question 9
At 0430 with a log reading of 44.37, the skipper measures with the sextant the height of the Punta Imperatore navigation light above water as 2°25'. A bearing taken with the steering compass, with which a course of 300° is being steered, gives 114°. What is the ship's position?
(Write the log in square brackets and the time next to the ship's position on the sea chart.)

Question 10
After getting the exact position, the skipper now sails close-hauled (wind ENE 2) and is on a heading of 20° on the compass. What is the estimated ship's position at 0525 with a log reading of 49.47?

Question 11
To check the ship's position, the horizontal angle between Punta Imperatore and a light just visible to the east, giving a double flash every ten seconds, is measured at 65°. A bearing taken with the steering compass from a flashing light on the NE corner of Ischia: 125°. Does the fix correspond to the ship's position in question 10?

Question 12
The course of 20° can be maintained. At a log reading of 53.25 the Capo Miseno navigation light comes into sight. At 0716 – log 59.75 – the bearing of the flashing light at the mouth of the Volturno with a hand-bearing compass is 67° (no deviation). What is the ship's position, which we can get by using the bearing taken earlier on deck of Capo Miseno?

Question 13
At 0830 – log 67.01 – the church of San Vito lies straight ahead, while the steering compass shows 10°. The reading on the echo sounder, whose transmitter lies one metre under the water line, is 19m. Ship's position? What sort of anchoring ground?

Question 14
At 1900 – log 67.01 – the anchors are weighed and a compass course of 264° is followed under engine towards the northern tip of Zannone.
● What is the estimated ship's position at 2400 – log 91.87?
● What was the average speed over this leg of the trip?

Question 15
Whilst the compass points to 270°, the following bearings are taken with the bearing disc: Zannone lighthouse 330°, Capo Circeo 58°, Gaeta St Erasmo 164°. What is the actual ship's position at 2400?

Navigation in tidal currents

Current presents particular difficulties because it can seldom be exactly established. Either a chart of currents will give details of direction and strength in 'normal' conditions, or you will have to find it out yourself. To do this, draw on the chart the position which you should be at without being affected by the current and given the course covered, and the position which you are actually at. To determine this you need the last position line obtained without using distance covered. From the change in current you can then calculate its speed over an hour.

If you want to reach a particular destination by the shortest and quickest route in the current, you will have to choose a course through the water which gets you to your destination despite the effects of the current on the course between starting and finishing points on the chart. You can easily solve this by drawing it. Draw a line from your starting point, to represent the current (direction and one hour's travel). The end of the line is your theoretical starting point. Set the dividers to your estimated speed through the water (one hour's travel). Where this arc crosses the desired course made good over the ground, you have a compass course to be sailed, taking into account deviation and variation (from right to wrong etc).

Question 16
How big was the effect of the current in 5 hours?

Question 17
Current's strength and direction?

Question 18
The skipper wants to steer towards Punta Madonna on Ponza (actual course?)

Question 19
Which compass course should you steer with an expected speed of 6 knots if, in spite of the current, Punta Madonna is to be reached by the shortest route (current triangle!)?

Question 20
• What would the speed be over the ground?
• What is the estimated time of arrival at Punta Madonna?

At 0402 the skipper gets a crossing point from distance covered; at the same time he gets a 'definite' ship's position from 2 land bearings (a fix). The difference between crossing point and fix is the drift in 111 minutes. After calculating equivalent distances over one hour, the current triangle can be drawn, giving all values per hour.

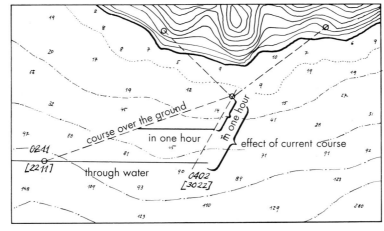

A current triangle should only be constructed from 2 fixes (shown as small circles on the chart) and a crossing point. The desired course over the ground is only reached after taking the current into account, if direction and strength of current remain the same, and the 'expected' speed is achieved.

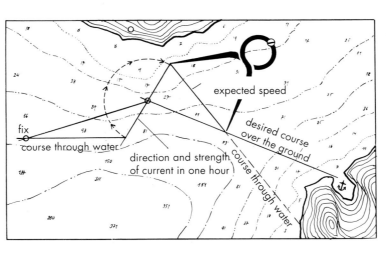

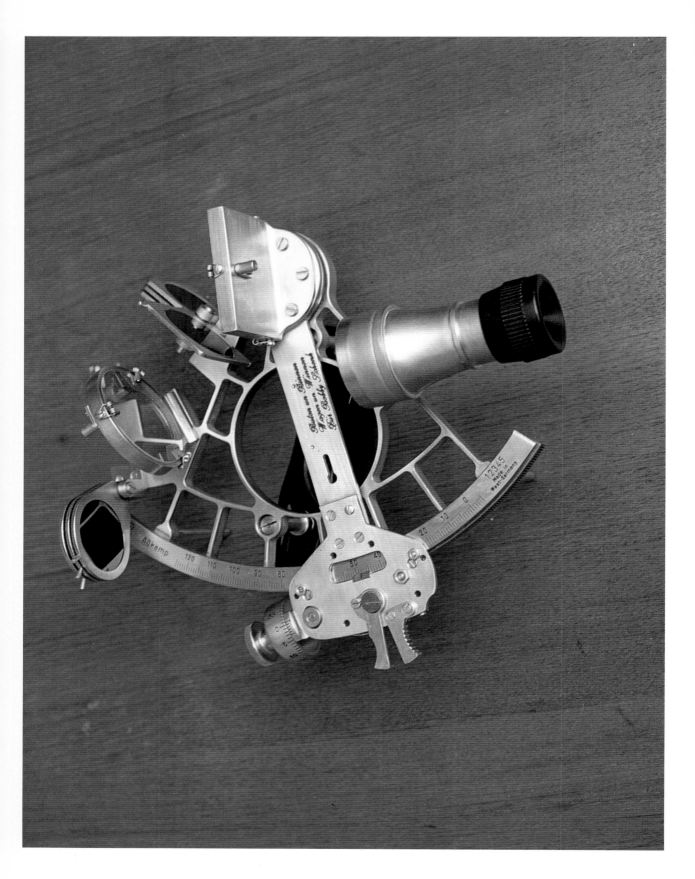

Astronavigation

Anybody who can solve the following question is in a position to make astronomic calculations using modern charts:

$$244°\ \ 31.7'$$
$$+\ 118°\ \ 44.9'$$
$$=\ ?\qquad ?$$

If you consider here that 60 minutes make one degree, and – if possible – 360° are to be taken from the answer, the answer must be:

3 degrees 16.6 minutes

In principle astrononavigation works just like measuring an angle using a sextant in coastal waters (see diagram below). There it is a matter of a vertical angle between the tip of a lighthouse or something similar and its base. In astronavigation you measure the angle between a star and the horizon.

As in terrestrial navigation, you have to know the exact position of the bearing objects (sun, moon, stars), which change constantly, at the time you measure it. You will find these in the Nautical Almanac. There is only one small difference to coastal navigation: if you want an exact astronomic position line (this is what you will get from a measurement, never a whole position), you have to measure the angle much more precisely than is necessary in terrestrial navigation. An inaccu-

racy of half a degree, which would do no harm if you were measuring the horizontal angle between two landmarks, would cause an error of 30 nautical miles when taking a measurement from the sun.

Which sextant?

Obviously, a cheap plastic sextant (about £35 ($50)) which is quite sufficient in coastal waters for a horizontal angle, should at the most be used for practice and never be used seriously in astronavigation. You will have to dig deeper in your pocket and get a drum-sextant, which will probably cost you more than £350 ($520).

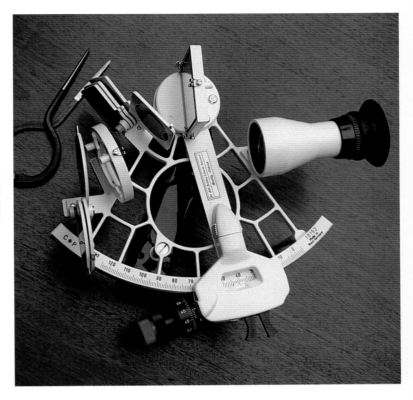

A modern sextant with total-view mirror and index adjustment.

Opposite page: This special model of a sextant illustrates the peak of building sextants. With a maximum error of two seconds, this must be one of the most exact sextants ever made. Of course in practice the achievable accuracy will not exceed one minute or one nautical mile.

Height of light above the shore

The angle in terrestrial navigation is based on: light – observer – shore.

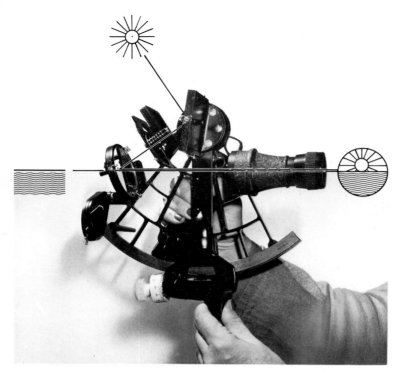

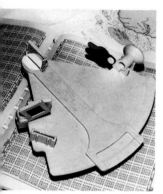

Astronavigation
The angle is based on: sun – observer – horizon.

Cheap plastic sextant, suitable for practising.

Plath drum sextant with lighting built in.

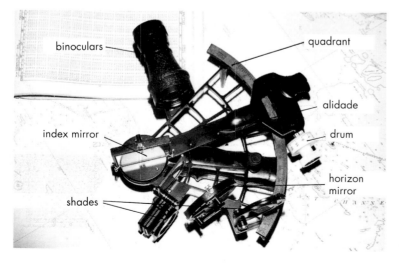

binoculars

quadrant

index mirror

alidade

drum

horizon
mirror

shades

Sextants come in different designs, and it is often difficult for the beginner to judge which additional gadgets are really necessary. As well as the standard equipment (such as shades, drum, and binoculars with a magnification of four at the most) a sextant should have graduated lighting. In the author's opinion a spirit level attachment is much too inaccurate on yachts.

The drum sextant as we know it today has been made the same way for forty years. There has been only one significant innovation in recent times, and that is the total view mirror, built onto sextants for several years by the firm Cassens and Plath. I would always recommend a total view sextant to a newcomer. Handling is much easier, because stars and horizon can all be seen at once. A hint: the classic sextant made by C. Plath can be fitted with a total view mirror from Cassens and Plath, if the sextant was made before 1972.

Metal sextants as made by Plath, Freiburger and Japanese manufacturers (Tamaya) usually leave the factories with a certificate in which its outstanding measuring capacity is listed. Naturally, these precision instruments should be handled with the utmost care. A slight knock on the degrees scale can make the sextant unusable. Every navigator should also be capable of testing his instrument for faults which can occur over time.

Faults in a sextant

A fault in the index is not actually a 'fault'. Basically, it means that the sextant's indicator is slightly altered. If you simply take a bearing from an object (which must be more than 2 miles away), the indicator on the drum should, if without defects, be at zero degrees, zero minutes, as no angle was measured.

This will usually not be the case, and the sextant will be faulty. If it is less than two minutes, you don't correct it, because moving the precision screws on the mirrors only does damage. It is often recomended that you take the index error into account in your calculations. In any calculations human error can occur, and I think it is wiser therefore to mark a new zero-point in permanent ink on the drum to avoid this. In my experience changes in the index error are hardly perceptible in the course of a trip. It should be checked at the start of a trip though.

To detect an error in the tipping mechanism of the horizontal mirror (the semi-circular mirror), proceed exactly as you would when testing the index error. Set your sextant to the horizon and fix the alidade so that the horizon is a straight unbroken line. If you turn the sextant about 45° around its binocular axis, the horizontal line should remain unbroken if there is no fault in the horizontal mirror. A fault can easily be remedied by slightly adjusting the screw in the middle of the upper edge which presses against the horizontal mirror from behind, with the key that comes with it.

A similar fault on the *index mirror* (the square one) is determined by setting the alidade in the middle of the quadrant and holding the instrument so that you can look straight down with your eye onto the index mirror, whilst you can look at the inner edge of the index mirror after the zero point of the index mirror. The part of the quadrant you are looking at directly and the part you are seeing indirectly should run into each other without a break. You can also put this fault right yourself, by slightly turning the screw in the centre of the upper edge which presses from behind on the square mirror.

The *index error* should always be set again after any changes to your sextant, particularly to the mirrors. If it still lies within two minutes, mark the new zero point again. Bigger index errors should be removed. To do this,

Marking the zero point with a felt pen, as shown by the arrow.

there is usually a screw in the side of the horizon mirror (the semi-circular one) with which you can swivel the mirror vertically a little on the axis level with the instruments. Be careful: tinkering with the screws too much will damage the instrument.

Measuring techniques

This is the only difficult aspect of astronavigation in my view. Beginners should not be satisfied with calculating a few position lines in winter, but should practise making a fix by stars. Bad measurement is the usual cause of inaccurate position lines. Professional seamen accept an inaccuracy of two angle minutes (two nautical miles) in good conditions as normal. On a small pitching yacht you won't be able to

If there is no fault in the tilt of the semi-circular mirror, the line of the horizon should remain unbroken in the binoculars. Any error in the tilt is removed by adjusting the arrowed screw.

no index error

error in tilt of horizon mirror

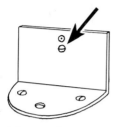

Adjusting tilting errors with the appropriate screw.

achieve this degree of accuracy. Beginners should reckon with an error of five angle minutes, and they can only improve through practice.

The best opportunity for practice is to measure the midday sun at its highest point. At this point the sun can apparently be seen at the same angle for a few minutes. Another proven method of measuring stars is to measure the sun five times in quick succession in the morning or the afternoon, and then to draw up the results in view of the time difference to scale. If the five results make a straight line, you can be confident about your ability to use a sextant even in an emergency.

One of the most common mistakes in measuring is not holding the sextant exactly vertical, thereby getting much too large an angle between the horizon and the sun. You can only avoid this by swinging the sextant slowly while you are taking a reading. At its lowest point the sun should just touch the horizon, but never actually break the line of the horizon.

Beginners will find when they start

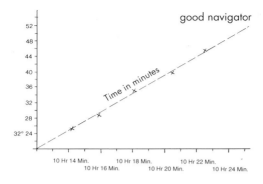

With the 'bad' navigator the readings clearly lie some way from the true line.

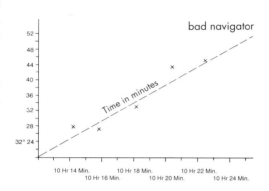

If the sextant isn't held exactly vertically, the angles you get will be far too large.

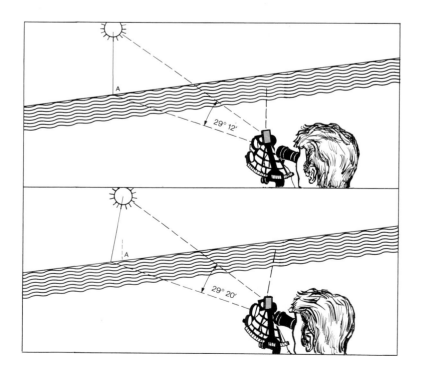

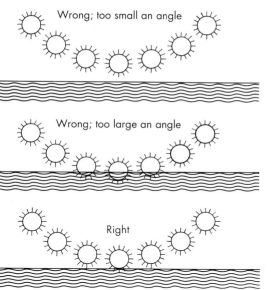

Wrong; too small an angle

Wrong; too large an angle

Right

Just a slow swinging movement guarantees a correct reading.

to practise that it isn't at all easy to get the sun and the horizon in the sextant at the same time. The following method, if it can be called a method, has produced the best results for me. Hold the sextant towards the sun and look at the horizon at the same time. Then move the alidade rapidly back and forth, into which the second strongest smoked glass has been put, whilst looking slowly along the horizon with the binoculars until you get the yellow disc. You have got plenty of time to make this more exact with the drum.

You can also put the alidade at 0°, look at the sun and move the sextant down at the same time until the horizon appears in the glass. The danger with this is that you won't be able to see the horizon if you are using too strong a smoked glass, or if you want to avoid this that the sun pierces you in the eye so that you aren't in a position to take a reading in the next few minutes.

If you have practised your skills of reading the sun and stars and have gained enough confidence, you will soon be in a position to judge the qual-

ity of each reading. An archer can also tell exactly if he has deviated up, down, or to the left or right.

The exact time

An important principle: in astronavigation you only calculate with Universal Time 1 (UT1): UT1 = central-European time minus 1 hour, i.e. GMT.

A few years ago Greenwich Mean Time was replaced by Universal time 1. Nothing has changed in navigation because of this, as both times are identical for nautical purposes. If GMT is occasionally mentioned, you can substitute UT1 or UTC (Universal Time Coordinated) without a problem. UT1 differs from UTC by a few fractions of a second, so you can consider them identical for use on board.

As in terrestrial navigation you should know the exact position of the object you are taking a fix from (the stars). Since these move incredibly fast you need to know the exact time of your reading so that you can look up their position in the Nautical Almanac. Even years ago you had to spend a lot of money on a chronometer whose accuracy was never satisfactory on a long trip. The 'two seconds per day' were usually not achieved in the changes in temperature and mechanical vibrations on a yacht. An inaccuracy of four seconds already meant an error of one nautical mile.

Quartz clocks have however caused a revolution. Whether they cost £3 ($5) or £200 ($300) they all work on the same principle (either with a frequency of 32KHz or 4.19MHz). They are all accurate to within a second. Mechanical vibrations don't influence their precision but their mechanism can be damaged more easily by an impact than that of a sprung clock. It is obviously advisable to check it occasionally with your radio.

Constant time signals with announcements every minute are broadcast on the following frequencies: 2.5 MHz, 5 MHz, 15 MHz, 20 MHz, 25 MHz. You are recommended to set your navigation clock independent of any local time permanently to UT1. All the time signals broadcast on the above frequencies and the times given in the Nautical Almanac are all in Universal Time 1.

If you check your quartz clock daily – a quartz diving watch is most suitable on board – against the radio, you shouldn't adjust it every time. Either note the difference or mark it on the diving watch with the adjustable ring. Because reading the time is not as easy after this, you can set a stopwatch in motion at the point when you take a reading with the sextant with the command 'Now'. The navigator can then put his precious but sensitive sextant away and establish the exact time of reading the angle on his navigation clock using the stopwatch and write it down immediately.

The 'position' of the stars

Geographical position (GP)
As we have already said, as in terrestrial navigation you should know the exact position of the sun or the relevant object at the time of the reading.

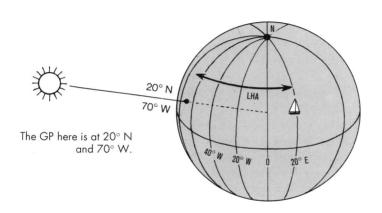

The GP here is at 20° N and 70° W.

Whilst you can determine the position of landmarks by their longitude and latitude, it seems there is a difficulty with the heavenly bodies since they are in space and we therefore have to work with three dimensional coordinates. A few centuries ago a genius found a way to get round this difficulty by setting the position of the stars using their GP. The GP is the key to the whole of astronavigation, and those who grasp this technique will have no more problems in establishing their ship's position using the stars.

Start from this observation: all stars are in practice at an infinite distance from the earth. It therefore isn't relevant if a star is really 'near' the earth like the sun, or if it revolves around others further out in space. You can leave the distance between the earth's surface and the stars out of consideration; and the distance of the 'near' moon is included in the horizontal parallax.

If you draw a line from the centre of the earth to the centre of the star, this line would cut through the earth's surface at a definite point. In other words, if you know the place where this line cuts through the earth's surface, you will also know the position of the star as it should be situated (in infinity) exactly vertically above it. All you need is the co-ordinates of the place on the earth's surface, and that is the complete GP, giving the position of the star.

You always work with the co-ordinates of the GP to carry out astronomic calculations. Everything happens on the earth's surface so to speak. You could quite simply give this GP with longitude and latitude like any place on the earth's surface. To avoid mistakes, the latitude of the GP is given as declination and the longitude as Greenwich Angle.

The GP latitude, the declination, is counted from 0° (equator) to 90° (pole) south or north, like the latitude of any

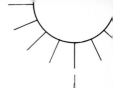

When you are taking a reading you must wait until the horizon is visible, and there are no waves in front of it.

other place on the earth's surface. A small but only superficial difference occurs in the longitude of the GP. Whilst the longitude of a point on the earth is counted from 0° to 180° East or West, the longitude of the GP is counted from 0° to 360° and always from Greenwich to the West. There is therefore no such thing as 167° West GP longitude, but just a GP longitude of 167°. 122° East GP longitude corresponds with a Greenwich Angle of 238°.

Nautical Almanac

Using this you can read the GP co-ordinates for every second on a particular day. All you need to do is to look up the relevant date and star. The Greenwich Angle is given first as the Greenwich Hour Angle because it is only given for every full hour on the white pages of the Nautical Almanac (don't forget: all the times are in Universal Time). As the sun moves quites steadily, it is easy to determine the Greenwich Angle for times between the hours using the auxiliary table in the green pages at the end of the Nautical Almanac. There are extracts on the back of the test chart inside the back cover of this book.

Example: On 1.8.75 we measured the

sun at 10h 28min 13s UT1. What are the GP's coordinates? Under the 'sun' column you will find for UT1 10 a Greenwich Hour Angle of 328°25.4'. Then you also have to look up how much further West the sun's GP has moved in 28 minutes and 13 seconds. For this calculation you don't really need an auxiliary table.

But we do know: The sun moves exactly once round the earth in 24 hours from east to west, that is, its GP races across 360 degrees of longitude. In one hour it covers exactly 15°, in 4 minutes 1° etc. Since we want to make things as easy as posible for ourselves in navigation, we don't actually calculate the values but look up the 'sun' column in the green table in the Nautical Almanac. On the page for '28min' we can read off the degrees and minutes longitude in the line for 13 seconds, which is 7°03.3', which the sun (or its GP) has covered since 10 o'clock. The Greenwich Angle is therefore 335°28.7'.

328°25.4'
7°03.3'
335°28.7'

With the latitude of the GP, that is declination, it is even easier because the differences between the full hours are usually less than a minute. I can say from experience that it is best not to waste a lot of time here, but to guess the declination. If the declination at 10 o'clock was N 18°07.7', and was only 0°00.6' less an hour later, (the difference between the full hours is in the variation column right at the bottom), we can guess that the declination was 18°07.4' at 10h 28min. This estimate is completely reliable, as the declination for our purposes is always rounded up or down to the nearest full minute. Now we have all the hand tools necessary for an astronomical position line.

Whether a star is 150 or 300 million miles from the earth, the angle in the sextant and the GP remain the same.

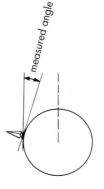

measured angle

Noon latitude

This is the simplest astronomical position line (and can almost be calculated in your head), and is still used today by professional seamen because of its accuracy. You don't even need both coordinates of the sun's GP, as the latitude (declination) is completely sufficient. As its name suggests, you have to shoot the sun exactly at noon. 'Noon' on board is always when the sun is at its highest. If you are on the Greenwich longitude, it is almost exactly at 12 o'clock. The sun races west round the whole earth (360°) in 24 hours, which makes 15° in one hour. At 15° West the sun, which must cover 360° from east to west in a day, is therefore exactly one hour later, so noon is at 1 o'clock in Universal Time. If you know vaguely the midday time, you only need to go on deck and observe the sun in the sextant. You will have to adjust the angle on the drum constantly, until the sun remains for several minutes at the same angle (or appears to), only then to sink again. This constant largest angle is the noon high point.

Depending where we or the GP are, there are different easy formulae for calculating the noon latitude. It would be wrong to learn these formulae, as all you need is to note the relevant one in the Nautical Almanac.

If you are in the Northern Hemisphere, the following variations work:

- The sun has a northerly variation (declination), at noon you see the sun in the South (which is normal with us), so: latitude = 90° *plus* variation *minus* (measured angle *plus* total correction).

- The sun has a southerly declination (never the case in summer with us), so: latitude = 90° *minus* variation *minus* (measured angle *plus* total correction).

- The variation is northerly, at noon you see the sun to the North (not the case in the Mediterranean or in Britain), so: latitude = variation *plus* (measured angle *plus* total correction) *minus* 90°.

As you can see, calculating the noon latitude is child's play. Only the total correction has not been mentioned so far. Roughly speaking, it occurs through the sun's rays being broken slightly by the different layers of air in the atmosphere, so that we are measuring the apparent not the true horizon ie the one we can see. You only have to look up the total correction in the table in the Nautical Almanac. It is unnecessary to calculate it to a tenth of a minute because you can't make that exact a measurement anyway.

Usually the eye level you need for the table in the Nautical Almanac lies at 2m on yachts. If you round the total correction up or down, you will arrive at the lower edge of the sun which you should always use if possible, managing with the following three values, thereby avoiding having to look up:

If a yacht sails north in European waters, the sun rises astern in the SE, is at its highest point (ship's noon) exactly in the South and goes down in the SW.

Local time

212

measured angle	total correction
from 20°	+ 11 minutes
from 25°	+ 12 minutes
from 40°	+ 13 minutes

Example: On 1.8.75 we are at about 39°44'N, 14°00'E. At 11 o'clock we measure the sun at its highest point with the sextant giving an angle of 68°17'. What is our latitude?

```
    89°60'
+   18°07' variation
–   68°30'
    39°37' N latitude
```

Question 21
On 1.8.75 we are south of Ischia. On a compass course of 62° the 164m high Punta Imperatore lighthouse lies straight ahead of us. At 11.11 UT1 we measure the latitude as 67°16'. What is our noon position? Use the table above in conjunction with the deviation table on the back of the test chart (found in the map pocket at the back of the book), taking eye level as 2m.

In practice this system has a slight disadvantage. As you don't know the exact time of the sun's highest point (midday), you have to go on deck fairly early with your sextant so that you don't miss the midday high. This doesn't do you or the sextant any good. You should therefore always be in a position where you know the midday time to within a few minutes. You can easily calculate this in advance, and I would ask the reader not to skip this as you can very easily determine the latitude later with this calculation.

You will see the sun at its highest point if it is exactly south of you in the northern hemisphere and the latitude of its GP corresponds exactly with your boat's latitude. Using the Nautical Almanac you can look up and calculate the Universal Time for the relevant Greenwich angle of the sun.

Suppose that on 1.8.75 we estimate our latitude as 13°22'E. This corresponds with a Greenwich angle of:

```
    359° 60'
–    13° 22'
    346° 38'
```

because whether the latitude of the GP is East or West is not expressed. The sun's GP reaches this latitude between 11h UT1 and 12h UT1. At 11h UT1 it is on a latitude of 343°25.4'. To reach our latitude it must therefore cover another 3°12.6'. You will find this difference in the green panel on the page for 12 minutes. At 11.12h the sun's GP is exactly on our latitude; it is noon. The sun stands at its highest point.

It doesn't matter that you don't know your longitude as the sun appears to remain at its highest point for several minutes, so an inaccuracy of twenty or thirty nautical miles matters little either.

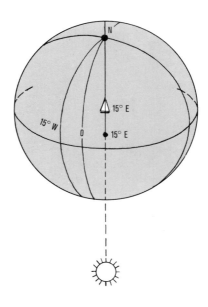

At noon on your boat the sun is exactly South (or North), its GP lies on the boat's latitude (see also diagram on page 217).

Question 22
When is noon on your boat at an estimated longitude of 9°09′E on 1.8.75?

Question 23
At this point in time we measure the sun at 68°44′, with the sun to the south . What is our latitude?

Noon longitude

Just as we have calculated the time at noon using our assumed longitude, it is also possible the other way round to calculate our exact longitude if we know the exact time of the sun's highest point to the second. Unfortunately we will come across practical difficulties here. The sun apparently remains at the same angle in the sextant for several minutes. This would however be much too inexact for determining longitude. We need to know our longitude within at least 3 or 4 nautical miles. There is a little trick which is useful here, used particularly by American sailors.

If you were to illustrate the sun's route at noon graphically, you would get the curve below:

You can easily see that the sun remains 4 minutes at the same angle of 67°29′ at 11h 22, and 4 minutes before and 4 minutes after is one minute lower. On the other hand you can also see that the curve is almost symmetrical. To determine the noon time to the second, you only need to take a reading some time before midday, while the sun is still climbing fast and steeply, and wait after midday until the sun appears again at the same angle.

Noon was the exact second between both times measured.

Just as we calculated earlier the time at midday from the ship's longitude, we can determine the exact ship's longitude from the exact time at midday which we now know how to calculate.

Question 24
On 1.8.75 in the Mediterranean (estimated ship's position: 40°20′N and 9°40′E) we measured the sun at 10h 28min 38sec at 63°50′, at 11h 29 at 67°10′ and at 12h 28min 24sec again at 63°50′. What was our position at midday?

Despite being so easy to calculate, the 'noon longitude using two similar heights' is very exact, particularly if we are going east or west. If on the other hand our position is more than 5 miles to the south or north between the two readings, minor errors will appear. To make these good, a German sailor called Albrecht invented a supplementary correction which doesn't complicate the noon longitude at all. It runs as follows:

For every mile the boat moves towards the sun between the two read-

The sun's curve at midday; it remains in the same place between 11h 22 and 11h 26. At 11h 46 it is sinking at a speed of 1 minute of angle in 20 seconds of time.

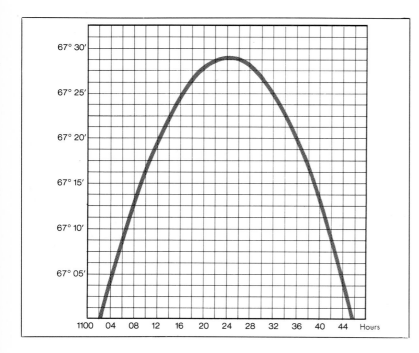

ings, you should add an extra minute to the angle on the sextant to the second reading. If the boat moves away from the sun, for every mile a minute should be subtracted from the reading.

With noon longitude as with noon latitude you must take into account the disadvantage that you can only carry out your readings to a particular time. For noon longitude you even need two measurements for a position line, and the whole position can be spoilt if a cloud appears at the wrong time. The methods in HO 249 tables do not have these disadvantages any more. They are sufficiently accurate for sailing and extremely easy. They are used all over the world not only by sailors but also by ocean-going ships where they have – particularly with young officers – replaced the notorious semiversus formula with its boring trigonometry calculations.

How to use HO 249

These tables consist of three volumes, of which only volumes II and III are of interest to us. You will use volume II if you are between the equator and 39° latitude (South or North), whilst volume III is used for the rest of the world (extracts on the back of the test chart).

Estimating the altitude from the HO 249 tables works on the following principle: Imagine that you are are a short distance from a lighthouse. If you know the height of the lighthouse and measure the angle 'foot of lighthouse – observer – tip of lighthouse', you can easily calculate your distance from the lighthouse with the formula on page 200 and from that draw a position line (which will be a circle around the lighthouse with a distance as diameter).

The higher you have to look up at the light of the lighthouse, the nearer you are to it. Or the other way round, the smaller the angle, the further you are away from it. If you apply this simple observation to measuring the stars,

imagine the light on the lighthouse to be the sun. The foot of the lighthouse corresponds exactly with the sun's GP. You can use somewhat more complicated formulae here to calculate the distance from the sun's GP, because you are dealing with an uneven surface. Theoretically all you have to do is draw a circle round the sun's GP with this distance as diameter, and you would get a position circle just as with the comparison with the lighthouse.

In practice this obviously isn't possible as the distance from the GP often covers thousands of miles. A chart covering such a large area, so that you could draw in a circle like this, would be of little use in navigation.

However, if you use a normal sea chart, you would only break a relatively tiny part of this circle around the GP. This section would be so small that on the sea chart the position line would not be recognisable as an uneven line because of the huge radius of the circle, but it would almost be a straight line.

It would not be a bad thing to get only a tiny section of the circle on the chart, because we are only interested in this part. We would only fail if we couldn't draw this small section of the position circle without the starting-point for the circle.

The astronomical position line is a circle with such a large diameter that the section in question only appears as a straight line. This isn't the case for angles greater than 75°, which should therefore be avoided.

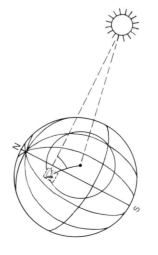
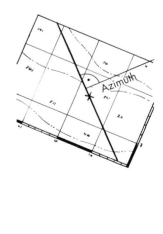

To repeat: we have said that the distance from the GP can be calculated from the angle measured and the sun's position. At the same time we have established that this position line, the circle with the calculated diameter, cannot in practice be drawn onto our sea chart.

Therefore one can choose a slightly altered technique: instead of calculating the diameter, start from an estimated ship's position and calculate (don't worry, the tables take care of this work) how big the angle horizon – observer – star must be if the boat really were at the estimated position. At the same time calculate in which actual direction the sun should be at this moment. If you really were to measure the predicted angle, the position line would be easy to draw: it would run through the estimated position and simultaneously stand perpendicular to the actual direction to the star, that is to the GP, because it is a part of a huge circle around the GP.

Of course it never happens in practice that the calculated angle is identical to the actual measured angle. You will therefore find that you are not exactly in the log position. Think of the comparison with the lighthouse: if the measured angle is greater, that is if you have to look up further to the light, then you are nearer the sun. The difference between the measured and the predicted angle tells you how far you are from the estimated ship's position. One minute of an angle corresponds with one nautical mile on the earth's surface. For instance, if the measured angle is 5 angle minutes smaller than the predicted one, you are 5 nautical miles further away from the GP than your estimated ship's position.

Transfer the 5 nautical miles to the actual direction to the sun's GP (azimuth) from this (and therefore from the sun). Now you only need to draw the position line vertically on the azimuth through the point you have got, a

straight line which is actually a piece of a huge circle.

We have now seen what is needed for drawing an astronomic position line:
• The direction to the star (azimuth);
• The estimated ship's position, for which the angle is predicted, which we would measure if we were at the exact estimated position;
• The difference between the measured and the predicted angles (intercept), which is the distance transferred either *to* or *from* the estimated position of the azimuth to the sun.

The once dreaded calculations of angle and azimuth with the semiversus method is now taken care of by the HO 249 tables. Angles and azimuths for countless points on the earth are predicted in them. The only 'skill' needed in using these tables is finding the nearest point for which the HO 249 tables have predicted angle and direction to the star (azimuth), instead of the estimated ship's position which is probably wrong anyway.

If you now open volume III of the HO 249 tables, you will find the latitude at the top of each page right and left. Since the pages of the tables always refer to latitudes in round minutes, the latitude of your estimated position should also be at a round minute. As the estimated position should be as near to us as possible, choose the next suitable latitude (for an estimated ship's position of 45°31′N, 46°; for 45°29′N, 45°). Another entry in the tables is declination (GP's latitude). If you are in the northern hemisphere and the declination is 'North', the only relevant pages are those marked '*declination same name as latitude*'. If the declination was South, the relevant pages are marked '*declination contrary name as latitude*'.

With this we have got two of the three entries in the tables. We now know the latitude of the predicted position, but what about its longitude? Take another look at the tables: so far we have looked at the entries for declination and latitude. The third entry is the LHA (Local Hour Angle). To come to the most important point first: Both the longitude of the calculated point and the longitude of the star's GP are contained in this LHA:

> **Very important:** The LHA is the number of degrees and minutes longitude (counted west from the calculated position) to the GP.

For instance, if you are at 10°W and the GP is at 20°, the LHA is exactly 10°. If however the GP is at 0°, and the sun is about to catch up with us, the LHA is 350°. Strangely enough, even the concept of LHAs and their calculation causes great difficulty for beginners. I would therefore recommend going into the calculation of LHAs thoroughly.

To be able to work out the LHA, first of all you need the exact longitude of the GP: see pp.214–15 for method.

Example: If you have measured the height of the sun on 1.8.1975 at 17h 28min 11sec UT1 (don't forget that only Universal Time is used in navigation, not local time), you can look up in the Nautical Almanac that the sun's GP was at 73°25.6′ at 17h. The green table works out for you how far the sun has covered in exactly 28 minutes and 11 seconds, at a speed of 15° in 60 minutes. The result is 7°02.8′. If you add these 7°02.8′ to the Greenwich Angle at 17h (the Greenwich Hour Angle), you will find your GP's longitude at 80°28.4′. If your log position were now 22°02.4′W, you only need to subtract your longitude from from the GP's longitude to get the LHA. Don't forget: the LHA is always counted west from the observer. In the above example the LHA would be exactly 58°26′.

Right: for the LHA it is a matter of the difference in longitude between ship's position and GP, while the Greenwich Angle is the difference in longitude between Greenwich Meridian (0°) and GP.

Below: the LHA is counted W from the ship's position to the geographical position.

Left: LHA = 10°
Right: LHA = 350°

If you were on an easterly longitude you would have to add on to the longitude of the GP to get the exact LHA.

> **Remember:** LHA = longitude of GP *minus* observer's longitude , if you are on a westerly longitude.
> LHA = longitude of GP *plus* observer's longitude if you are on an easterly longitude.

If your westerly longitude is greater than the GP's longitude and you therefore can't subtract it from it, just add 360° to the GP's longitude.

Example: longitude of GP = 10°24.4′; observer's longitude = 40°12.2′W, so you must add 360° to 10°24.4′ turning it into 370°24.4′. Now you can subtract 40°12.2′ from it. Result: LHA = 330°12.2′.

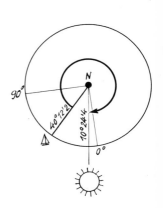

It is always better for the beginner to make this clearer by drawing a small sketch including the North Pole for every measurement.

If we now think back: The HO 249 tables only predict for positions which fulfil certain requirements. This calculated position must:
- Have a latitude rounded to the nearest degree,
- make a LHA with the star's GP which is also a round number of degrees.

How do you fulfil the second requirement? Of course you can't change the GP's longitude since the GP's longitude had a certain value at the time of the reading. But what you can change is the calculated position. For just as the estimated ship's position you started from is inaccurate, the calculated position will not correspond accurately to the actual ship's position. It should just be as near as possible to the actual ship's position.

You should therefore choose your calculated position somewhat differently, just as we did when calculating the LHA. When doing this, your calculated longitude should be changed as little as possible in order to get an LHA to the nearest degree. In the above examples, instead of a calculated longitude of 22°02.4'W we will therefore take one of 22°28.4', giving a LHA of 58°; or instead of 40°12.2'W we take 40°24.4'W, and therefore a LHA of 330°. To find the right calculated position you must either make your calculated longitude bigger or smaller depending on which calculated longitude our estimated longitude is nearer to (study the examples on the left carefully!).

Now we have all the entries in the HO 249 tables together. First the calculated latitude, second the LHA which also has to be to the nearest degree, and finally the declination. You will find the declination (variation), like the GP longitude, in the Nautical Al-

manac. Remember here that unlike latitude and LHA you don't choose the nearest declination entry in the HO 249 tables, but always round off the declination first. If you have a declination of 15°59', go to column '15°' in the tables. Obviously you can't ignore these 59'. For this reason there is a correction at the end of the tables which takes into consideration the fact that only declinations to the nearest degree are entered in the tables.

As a result you will find three values in the tables:
1. The calculated height (Hc).
2. The correction for rounding off the declination, which is then added to the declination (d).
3. A figure which gives us finally the azimuth or the direction of the star (Z).

Suppose that our calculated latitude is 41°N, our declination is 18°07'N, and our LHA, which we have made a complete degree by changing the calculated longitude, 357°. On the page for *'Lat 41° – declination (15° – 29°) same name as latitude'*, we will find in the 18° column:

Hc	d	Z
66 51	+ 60	173

66°51' is therefore the angle made by horizon – observer – star, if we were exactly at the calculated position and the declination was exactly 18°00'N. The third figure shows us how to get the azimuth. To do this we have to correct Z depending on whether we are in the northern or southern hemisphere. This is in order not to make the tables too thick, because they are used in both hemispheres. If you've got the tables in front of you ready to use, you will find the easy rule for changing Z into Zn (azimuth) on the left above and below. In our case we would use the rule above left *'N Lat'* (North Latitude). There are two columns: 'LHA greater than 180°' and 'LHA less

Examples of LHA calculations to find the angle:

First example
Greenwich Angle :
68°39.2'
estimated longitude:
97°01'W

$$\begin{array}{r} 360° \\ + 68°39.2' \\ \hline 428°39.2' \\ - 96°39.2' \\ \hline \end{array}$$

LHA = 332°00.0'
It would be wrong to subtract 97°39.2' because this longitude is about 38' from the estimated and is therefore further away than 96°39.2'.

Second example
Greenwich Angle:
68°39.2'
estimated longitude:
34°58'E

$$\begin{array}{r} 68°39.2' \\ + 35°20.8' \\ \hline 104°00.0' \end{array}$$

34°20.8' would be wrong because it would be more than 30' away from 34°58'.

than 180°'. In the first case, which concerns us because our LHA is 357°, the azimuth (Zn) is equal to Z, which is 173°.

Only the correction is left, which is necessary because the table has only 18° not 18°07'. A small auxiliary table at the end of the HO 249 tables helps to calculate this. Table 5 is needed here. Find 7 at the top of the table and next to 60 you will find the correction for 7. Watch your signs! In this case you add 7 minutes to the calculated height ('d' was '+ 60'), so that the calculated height is now 66°58' not 66°51'. What you still don't have is the number of nautical miles you have to carry the position line from the calculated position. To do this you need only compare the calculated height with the measured height. You also have to add the total correction to the measured height as with the noon latitude (see pp. 212–13). Only then can you finally establish the difference. Think of the picture of the lighthouse:

If the measured height is greater than the calculated, you have to look up further to the light, and are nearer to the lighthouse. In this case, transfer the difference in angle minutes to nautical miles towards the star, which is on the azimuth which runs through the calculated position at 173°; finally set the position line perpendicular to this.

Getting a position line using the HO 249 tables

1 Measure the height of the sun, noting the exact time (Universal Time)	UT1 14h 29m 22s
2 Correct the measurement with the total correction	Sextant angle = 42°18' + 13' 42°31'

3 Establish the latitude and longitude of ship's estimated position 40°40' N / 13°33' E

4 Round the estimated ship's latitude up or down (= calculated latitude) 41° N

5 Determine the declination from the Nautical Almanac 18°05' N

6 Using the Nautical Almanac determine the GP longitude for the exact time the measurement was taken
28°25.5'
7°20.5'
35°46.0'

7 Change the observer's longitude so that you get a LHA to the nearest degree when adding the GP longitude (observer looking East) or subtracting the GP longitude (observer looking West)
+ 13°14' E
49°00'

8 Fill the calculated position in on the chart (latitude to the nearest degree, calculated longitude corresponding with the longitude which has made the LHA a full degree)

9 Look in the table where the declination is rounded off to the nearest degree

	15°			16°			17°			18°		
LHA	Hc	d	Z	Hc	d	Z	Hc	d	Z	Hc	d	Z
40	46 44	+42	115	47 26	+42	114	48 08	+41	113	48 49	+40	112
41	46 03	42,	114	46 45	41	113	47 26	41	112	48 07	40	111
42	45 22	41,	113	46 03	41	112	46 44	40	111	47 24	40	110
43	44 40	41	112	45 21	41	111	46 02	40	110	46 42	39	109
44	43 58	41	111	44 39	40	110	45 19	40	109	45 59	39	108
45	43 15	+41	110	43 56	+40	109	44 36	+39	108	45 15	+39	107
46	42 33	40	109	43 13	40	108	43 53	39	107	44 32	39	106
47	41 50	40	109	42 30	40	108	43 10	39	107	43 49	38	106
48	41 07	40	108	41 47	39	107	42 26	39	106	43 05	38	105
49	40 24	39	107	41 03	39	106	41 42	39	10	42 21	38	104
50	39 40	+40	106	40 20	+39	105	40 59	+38	104	41 37	+38	103
51	38 57	39	105	39 36	39	104	40 15	38	103	40 53	37	102

10 Look for the three results in the right lines (calculated height = Hc, correction for declination = d and Z)

13°E

41°N

calculated position
41°N
13°14'E

d/'	1	2	3	4	5	6	7	8	9	10	11	12	13	14	15	16	17	18	19	20	21	22	23	24	25	26	27	28	29	30	31	32	33	34	35	36	37	38	39
0	0	0	0	0	0	0	0	0	0	0	0	0	0	0	0	0	0	0	0	0	0	0	0	0	0	0	0	0	0	0	0	0	0	0	0	0	0	0	0
1	0	0	0	0	0	0	0	0	0	0	0	0	0	0	0	0	0	0	0	0	0	0	0	0	0	0	0	0	0	0	1	1	1	1	1	1	1	1	1
2	0	0	0	0	0	0	0	0	0	0	0	0	1	1	1	1	1	1	1	1	1	1	1	1	1	1	1	1	1	1	2	2	2	2	2	2	2	2	2
3	0	0	0	0	0	0	0	0	0	0	1	1	1	1	1	1	1	1	1	1	1	1	2	2	2	2	2	1	2	2	2	2	2	2	2	2	2	2	3
4	0	0	0	0	0	0	0	1	1	1	1	1	1	1	1	1	1	1	1	2	2	2	2	2	2	2	2	2	2	2	2	2	2	2	2	2	▼	2	3
5	0	0	0	0	0	0	1	1	1	1	1	1	1	1	1	1	1	2	2	2	2	2	2	2	2	2	2	3	3	3	3	3	3	3	3	3	3	3	3
6	0	0	0	0	0	1	1	1	1	1	1	1	1	1	1	2	2	2	2	2	2	2	2	2	2	3	3	3	3	3	3	3	3	3	4	4	4	4	4
7	0	0	0	0	1	1	1	1	1	1	1	1	2	2	2	2	2	2	2	2	2	2	2	2	3	3	3	3	3	4	4	4	4	4	4	4	4	4	5

11 Using the rules above left and below left calculate the azimuth

360
– 104
256°

12 Using table 5 establish the correction for rounding off the declination and either add or subtract this depending on the sign in front of the calculated height

42°21'
+ 3'
42°24'

13 Determine difference between the calculated and the measured height (with total correction)

– 42°31'
7'

14 Draw the azimuth through the calculated position

15 Transfer the difference in nautical miles to or from the star to the azimuth

7nm
towards
it

16 Set a position line vertically through this new point to the azimuth

Left: the azimuth is drawn through the calculated position . . .

Centre: the intercept is then measured off on it . . .

Right: and the position line is drawn at a right angle to the azimuth.

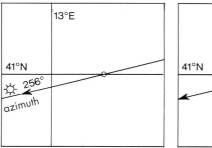
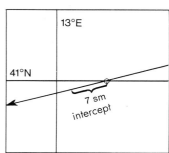
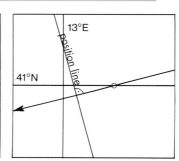

To repeat: Even if the procedure sounds complicated, a position line like this can be calculated and drawn in 5 minutes by anyone capable of simple arithmetic.

Using an astronomical position line

Up until now we have only talked about one position line. Apart from exceptional cases, a single position line won't be much help to us. In navigation we need our ship's position first of all, and this can only be got by the intersection of two or more position lines. As already shown in coastal navigation, you can combine any position lines, if they have a reasonable intersection point, ie not too flat. You could therefore combine your position line of the sun with any terrestrial position line. But what do you do on the open sea, when in the day you have no objects to take a bearing from apart from the sun? It is quite simple: Since the sun moves fairly fast, wait a little after the first reading and take a second one. Your position line stands perpendicular to the sun's azimuth, so you will get a position line from the second reading which intersects the first position line more clearly the more the bearing to the sun has changed.

Of course, the sun doesn't change its position much in a couple of minutes, but if you wait two hours – especially around midday – you will see that the two position lines intersect at a very good angle. Today it is still practice even on ocean-going ships to observe the sun's altitude in the morning and make this into a position line using the HO 249 tables, and to use the noon latitude later as the second position line. As long as you don't bob up and down in a calm between these measurements, you will still have to take into account that you have changed your position somewhat during the two measurements. As with double bearings in terrestrial navigation (see p. 201 'Position lines already passed'), all you need to do is transfer your first position line in the course direction over course covered.

I know from the wide experiences of my well-travelled friends that the position lines on the sun are part of the daily bread of navigation, and that measurements from stars are carried out relatively infrequently. If you sail on the open sea for a long period of time, you will only need your exact position once every 24 hours. Only when you sail nearer to the coastline should you get your exact ship's position as often as possible. Only in cases like this does one resort to the stars.

It is not a bad idea to prepare a simple plan for your calculations for frequent use. You can use a plan like this in two ways. Either you produce the necessary number of photocopies or stick the plan on a box and cut out the places where figures have to be entered. After this you can lay the template on any clean piece of paper and then put the figures in. I would recommend that everybody makes up their own plan depending on how they envisage it.

You should always ask yourself the question : What do I need to draw a position line?

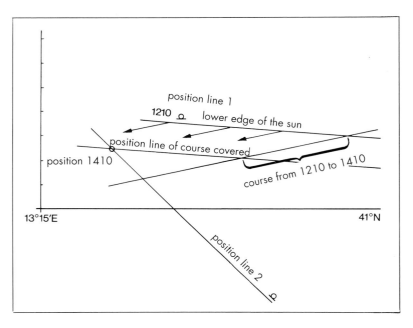

- The calculated position
- The azimuth
- The intercept.

You should emphasise these answers, which give you the plan, in different colours. To make your work easier still, it is a good idea to mark the entries in the HO 249 tables in colour as well. A plan as I would do it is on page 280.

Checking astronomical deviation

Just as we established the deviation of our compass in terrestrial navigation using an object on land, we can also use the sun to do this. It is an extremely easy method and much more reliable than taking a bearing from an object on land. The only extra thing you need is a so-called shadow-pin, which should stand vertically above the centre point of the compass.

Since the sun's azimuth (the actual bearing) naturally changes, take a time during the day for this where this change occurs slowly, which is morning or afternoon. As with terrestrial bearings let your boat turn slowly around a specific point and write down

Shadow pin. Compass with a pin in the centre; its shadow shows the compass bearing to the sun.

the sun's bearing every 10° of the compass course. You can easily read this off using the shadow pin on the compass. At the same time you must establish the time when determining the deviation in this way. Writing down the time in whole minutes is enough. The only calculation which you have to make now is the LHA (to a degree) for your first measurement. You do this in exactly the same way you got a position line from the sun.

To repeat: The LHA changes by exactly 1° in 4 minutes, as the sun needs 4 minutes at its speed (360° in 24 hours) to cover 1°. To make 36 measurements all you need to do is write down which LHA was valid, and using that finally read off the azimuth (the actual bearing of the sun) from the tables. The deviation can then be calculated exactly as in terrestrial navigation (page 196).

But even if you don't produce a new deviation table, a careful navigator will test occasionally with spot checks on the sun's bearings whether the navigation chart tallies with the actual deviation on the the course at the time. This is especially important on a steel boat, as the deviation can change drastically even after a storm.

The moon

Quite simply, the fear that many navigators have of using the moon (even experienced yachting folk) is unfounded. A position line is calculated and drawn from the moon on exactly the same principles as from the sun. You use volumes II and III of the HO 249 tables here as well. There are three small differences for the moon compared with using the sun's altitude.

Calculating the GP longitude

Whilst you could rely on a steady speed of 15° per hour for the sun in a westerly direction, there is a difference with the moon in that its speed is not as regular as this. The calculation remains the

Question 25
On 1.8.1975 at 0630 UT1 (log: 02.44) you get a definite ship's position from compass bearings of 40°31.5′N, 14°20.0′E. After that the compass course changes to 283°. At 9h 29min 55sec (log: 18.54) the navigator measures the sun's lower edge at 58°41′.
● What is the estimated ship's position?
● What are the three table entries for LHA, latitude and declination?
● What calculated angle and which azimuth do we get from the HO 249 tables?
● How big is the difference between the calculated and the measured angle?
● Should the sun be drawn 'towards' or 'away'?
● What were the co-ordinates of the calculated position, which you now need as 'reference position'?

Question 26
At 0946 UT1 the sun's bearing is taken at 146° using the shadow pin on the compass. Does the navigation chart agree with the continued compass course of 283°?

Question 27
At 1112 UT1 (log: 26.44) the sun is measured at its peak at 67° 21′. What is the noon latitude?

Question 28
What is the ship's position now (noon position) if you use the position line from the course covered since 0930 UT1?

same in principle. Establish the hour angle for the hour itself and then add on the course covered in the minutes and seconds remaining. For the sun we used the green table, which then showed us the remaining degrees and minutes taking a speed of 15° per hour as a basis. The green table cannot of course be used for the moon, because the moon has different speeds. The moon's slowest speed has been taken as a basis for the tables: 14°19'. We can first of all read this 'increase' from the table, but we have to add a correction to it which results from the fact that the moon probably wasn't travelling at its slowest speed on this day, but was a bit faster. You can tell how much faster by the difference given for the moon at every GHA. You can read off the correction for this difference from the relevant page of the green table, and add it on.

> **Example**: On 1.8.1975 at 19h 28min 12sec the Greenwich Angle was
>
> | | 181°57.6' | (diff. 10.2) |
> |---|---|---|
> | + | 6°43.7' | (increase) |
> | + | 4.8' | (correction for 'diff. 10.2') |
> | = | 188°46.1' | |

Declination of the moon

This is not as easy to estimate as the sun's. We need the declination in whole minutes, but table 5 in the HO 249 tables doesn't work any more for us, as the moon's declination changes so fast that we have to calculate the declination for the exact time the angle was measured. The green table helps do this. First you must establish the difference between the declinations for the preceding and following hours, which is given in the tables as 'diff' under the relevant day next to the 'var'. Then you can read off the 'corr' for the extra time. For example, on the page for '28 minutes' in the green table, if you have taken the measurement at 19h 28min and 12sec, the correction is 2.3 minutes for a 'diff 4.8'.

There is one thing to watch out for. In calculating the moon's Greenwich Angle the correction was always added; the declination can be either added or subtracted. We can only take this from the declination figure for the preceding and following hours. If the declination for the following hour is smaller, then you have to subtract the 'correction'. If the declination is greater than in the above example, you add it.

Total correction

With the sun we took the eye level and measured angle into consideration and were therefore in a position to reduce the total correction table for our use to a few figures. The horizontal parallax also has to be considered for the moon. You don't even need to know what this is. In the Nautical Almanac it is given with 'HP' for for every 'UT1 4h, 12h, 20h'. Look in the total correction table for the moon with the HP under the relevant angle ('distance from horizon') and 'horizontal parallax'. If you have measured the moon's upper edge, the subsequent correction to the latter table is definitive. The eye level must also be taken into account and it is found at the bottom of the same table.

It is difficult to understand why the moon is used so seldom in navigation, as it really only differs from the sun in these three additional corrections. The moon is an excellent object to use because it never superimposes on the horizon during the day. At half moon, with the sun's position lines you get an excellent intercept and therefore accurate positions.

A word of warning: You should not use the moon at night. This is because the moon reflects so strongly on the water that the horizon behind it cannot be seen by the observer.

The planets

If you can make these out during the day – which would only be Venus and Mars – they are just as good to use as the moon. In order to find them more easily, it is a good idea just before taking the fix to calculate the angle for the presumed time of observation from the nautical tables, and to find the horizon during the time of calculation with the sextant angle in the relevant direction (azimuth). Calculating the planets is done in exactly the same way as a sun position line, but you have to remember to look in the 'planets' column for the total correction for the co-ordinates of the GP (declination and Greenwich angle).

The stars

Navigators need not know individual stars. Volume I of the HO 249 tables will help you here. The angle and azimuth of selected stars is included in them. The best way to get the star in question in the sextant is as follows: since all stars in the heavens hardly change their positions in relation to each other, you can choose a certain point arbitrarily and give all further positions in relation to this point, the 'Aries' or 'vernal point'. It has the great advantage for us that to use volume I of the HO 249 tables you need only calculate the GP longitude of this spring point from the Nautical Almanac. The difference in longitude of the LHA between the longitude of the calculated position and spring point longitude is also given (counted westwards from us).

If you want to measure the chosen stars in volume I at 19h UT1, you need only calculate the time of the LHA for the vernal point, and you will find on the page for the longitude of your calculated position (without any further calculations as for the sun) the angle and azimuth for all seven chosen stars. If you put this angle in the sextant and look for the horizon in the relevant

direction (azimuth), in good observation conditions you will be able to see the star clearly in the sextant, even though it is not visible to the naked eye. It is extremely unlikely that you would look at the wrong one and this would be picked up when you drew in the position lines anyway.

Unfortunately there are a number of problems which occur in practice. This stems from the fact that observing the stars is only possible at dusk or at dawn, and that they can only be observed for a short time. At night you can't see the horizon and by day you can't see the stars. I find the following method the best:

Calculate in advance the LHA (observer – vernal point) for a whole hour during which the observation will probably take place at dusk. It sounds a lot more complicated than it actually is. You need only calculate the LHA once, for the beginning of these 60 minutes.

Every 4 minutes the LHA increases by exactly 1°. You need someone to help you by sitting at the chart table in the cabin during observation and putting a ruler in the HO 249 tables under the relevant LHA. The ruler is moved one line lower every four minutes (watching the clock). The angle and azimuth can be called out whenever you want them, and you can test whether the star can be seen by looking in the direction given by the azimuth at the angle given. If you can see a small black dot in the sextant, measure it as usual and establish the exact time by calling to your helper. Of course you try to measure as many stars as possible in the short time available.

It is useful to know that you can more easily make out stars which are higher in the sky than those which are lower. At the same time you look for the first stars to the east, where the heavens are darker, whilst the last ones appear in the west. The 'selected stars' are not the brightest fixed stars, but they are chosen from amongst others because their position lines give the best intersects.

Where is the total correction if you read the stars' altitudes directly from the HO 249 tables? One look in the total correction table in the Nautical Almanac will show you that all the values are generally around 4 minutes. You can ignore this figure with an easy conscience so as not to complicate the calculation, as what you must do next is find the star where the four minutes are irrelevant. You must also subtract the total correction, which is always negative for stars, from the calculation.

You only use the above method for looking for stars. To get the position line, proceed as with the sun, only you need your latitude and the LHA to the Aries for chart entries. There is no entry for declination, and there is therefore no 'same' or 'contrary' for your latitude. It is important to remember that whilst volumes II and III are al-

ways valid, volume I is only calculated for one year. You can however work with it in other years if you move your given position line a certain number of nautical miles in a certain direction. Table 5 gives you both values in an appendix to the HO 249 tables and an extract of this is printed on the back of the test chart.

LAT 41°N

LHA ϒ	*CAPELLA		ALDEBARAN		*Diphda		FOMALHAUT		ALTAIR		*VEGA		Kochab	
	Hc	Zn	Hc	Zn	Hc	Zn	Hc	Zn	Hc	Zn	Hc	Zn	Hc	Zn
0	35 07	056	26 46	091	30 03	168	17 41	195	26 16	258	30 10	297	28 46	348
1	35 45	057	27 32	092	30 12	170	17 29	195	25 32	259	29 30	297	28 36	348
2	36 23	057	28 17	092	30 19	171	17 17	196	24 48	260	28 50	298	28 27	348
3	37 01	057	29 02	093	30 26	172	17 04	197	24 03	260	28 10	298	28 18	349
4	37 39	058	29 47	094	30 32	173	16 50	198	23 18	261	27 30	299	28 09	349
5	38 17	058	30 33	094	30 38	174	16 36	199	22 33	262	26 51	299	28 01	349
6	38 56	059	31 18	095	30 42	175	16 21	200	21 49	263	26 11	300	27 52	349
7	39 35	059	32 03	096	30 46	176	16 05	201	21 04	263	25 32	300	27 44	350
8	40 13	059	32 48	097	30 48	177	15 49	202	20 19	264	24 53	301	27 36	350
9	40 52	059	33 33	097	30 50	178	15 32	202	19 34	265	24 14	301	27 29	350
10	41 31	060	34 18	098	30 51	179	15 14	203	18 48	265	23 35	302	27 21	351
11	42 11	060	35 02	099	30 51	181	14 56	204	18 03	266	22 57	302	27 14	351
12	42 50	060	35 47	099	30 50	182	14 37	205	17 18	267	22 19	303	27 06	351
13	43 29	061	36 32	100	30 48	183	14 18	206	16 33	267	21 41	303	27 00	351
14	44 09	061	37 16	101	30 46	184	13 58	207	15 48	268	21 03	304	26 53	352

Stars lead sailors over the sea as they did a hundred years ago.

Calculators and computers

When the first efficient calculators appeared years ago, many people believed that navigation would be revolutionised shortly by these magic boxes. We know today that this isn't true. Calculators have not brought a single new procedure, apart from changing the navigator's method of working. But given electronic calculators' efficiency they have made navigation

> - safer
> - faster
> - more exact

Calculators are fantastic gadgets, but they have to be made for their purpose. In the same way that you cannot saw through metal with a woodsaw, it is stupid to use a basic calculator for astronavigation, if it has no keys for trigonometric functions. On the other hand, the person at the chart table must be able to use the instrument, just as for example not everyone is able to use a lathe.

So which calculator should you use? Basically, calculators fall into three categories for navigational use:
- Simple calculators
- Programmable calculators, pocket computers
- Special programmed navigation calculators.

Simple calculators

In every household there is one of these, which is capable of the four basic calculation methods. It therefore also belongs by every chart. When you buy a calculator like this, make sure it is solar-powered (because of the problem with electricity on board). It must have a memory, be able to do square roots and if possible be able to calculate sin, cos and tan. More important than the latter would be a built-in quartz clock with alarm, stop-watch etc. A few years ago these would still have been quite expensive, but these days they don't cost much more than a slide rule.

What do you need it for? The navigator must be able to key in the first three formulae at the end of the chapter (sin, cos and tan are used in all navigational formulae), calculate the fuel he has left, find out the boat's speed from distance covered in a certain time (stop-watch function), convert £ sterling into the relevant currency, calculate harbour fees and so on. Only your imagination limits the uses it has. A calculator's limits are apparent when you come to difficult formulae such as the azimuth calculation for astro-navigation in the footnote opposite.

Anyone can get the right answer with one of these if they have patience, but be warned, a calculator does not work with degrees, minutes and decimal minutes but just decimal minutes, so you must convert them first. However, keying in is less safe and slower,

Basic calculators belong by every chart, and are best if they have a built-in clock.

because of the high number of buttons, than looking up in the HO 249 tables. Basic calculators are not suitable for this.

Programmable calculators

A programmable calculator or pocket computer is just the thing for those who enjoy games of logic and playing with figures. These gadgets can repeat a series of transactions in one push of a button, which makes them not only fast but safe to use. However, they are hardly necessary if a navigator never spends any time on astronavigation, because this is their domain on board a yacht. Their efficiency is measured according to their programming capacity, which is the steps of programming that they can remember. For example, '2 x 3 =' totals already 5 steps.

A few years ago 100 programming steps would have been a sensation, but today there are calculators with several thousand steps (one kilobyte corresponds to about 1000 steps), and there are programmes which use this high number. This expects too much of the 'average user' in sailing, and there usually isn't enough time to draw up such a labour-intensive programme. There are however plenty of people who can produce programmes like this, for a fee of course.

Computers

The time has already passed of special navigation calculators, which in the past almost revolutionised navigation before they were applied to satellite technology. Computers are now used on board which, loaded with the right software, can take over any naviga-tional calculation. It just depends on the software.

A computer without software is like a record player without records. If you instal a DOS computer you will have no problems, as the biggest software library in the world is available to the DOS system (Disk Operating System). There are countless navigation programs amongst them, so the navigator must decide for himself to whom he wishes to entrust the safety of his ship. But before you buy your software, ask about the author of the program. Good programs are extremely complex pieces of work, which the author or the publisher will usually have spent years making. Since computers have become more and more capable, manufacturers have been required to come up with programs which will do as much as possible for you. When installing a navigation program always remember that the experts say there is no 'faultless software'.

Any DOS computer which can be run on batteries at less than 13 volts is suitable for use on board. Electricity consumption is then not a major problem as this additional burden is no problem for your big battery on board. My preference always lies with computers which don't run on an electri-

With the program *Navtools* the actual starry sky can be illustrated for any point in a century. You can click on each star and ask for its name.

1. HC = arcsin ((sin declination × sin estimated lat) + (cos declination × cos estimated lat × cos LHA))

2. Z = arccos $\left(\dfrac{\text{sin declination} - \text{sin estimated lat} \times \text{sin Hc}}{\text{cos Hc} \times \text{cos estimated lat}} \right)$

3. Azimuth = Z, if sin LHA smaller than 0
   Azimuth = 360 *minus* Z, if sin LHA greater than 0

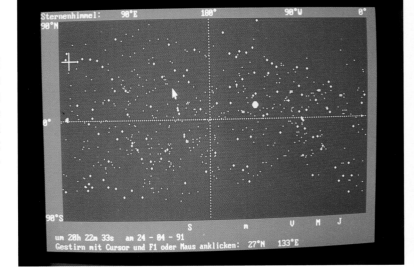

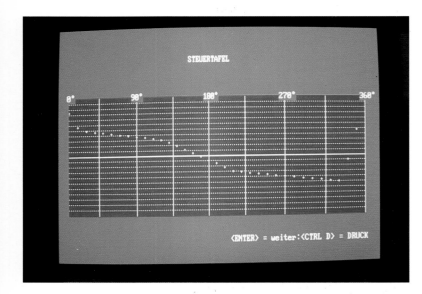

working a DOS system, and look at the size of its screen. It should show the full textual screen of 25 lines and 80 figures all at once. If it can't, it is not worth the fact that it can work any DOS programme.

Of course, you should be able to solve any questions on higher (astro-) navigation by pushing few buttons and without any tables. It can also be used with a modem to send or receive a fax from the telephone box in the harbour ordering spare parts.

Computers are being used more and more to receive weather forecasts (weather charts, and even satellite photos) from the radio receiver on board. The computer can be connected to a GPS receiver with the programme *Gpstools*, to take down the log of the trip or to have a big backup chart in the navigation section of the boat. With the software *Bordtools* voltages at several points on board can be checked at once. An electronic barometer (Baromodul) can also be used as a voltage source so that the computer can work as a barograph, showing, storing, and printing atmospheric pressures on a whole trip.

A deviation curve calculated by *Navtools*.

city supply network but on normal personal stereo batteries.

Computers are becoming smaller and easier to use all the time. Notebook computers are out, and hand-held computers are now becoming the standard aboard yachts. They can't get any smaller than this. You also couldn't make the keyboard any smaller because they would be difficult to use. When you buy a computer like this, make sure it is capable of

The Sharp PC-3000 lap-top computer is an adequate DOS computer. It can do graphics, weighs less than a pound and lasts for 30 hours with three batteries. Its price is just as small: just under £250 ($375).

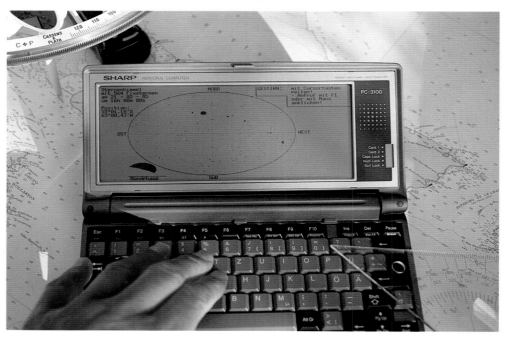

The PC-3000 is connected
to a GPS system with the
software *Gpstools*, which
logs the trip, shows the
continuing course and
variation on its clear
display.

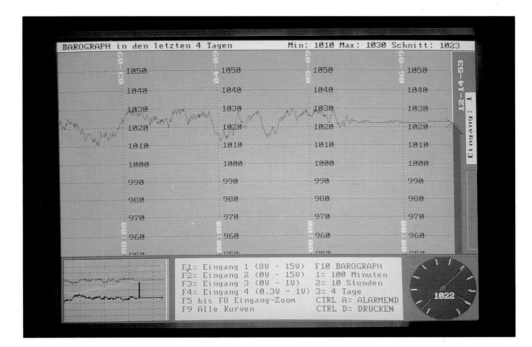

The programme *Bordtools*
can watch up to four
voltage sources at once,
give the alarm and store
values. For instance, the
engine temperature and
the bilge level can be
controlled with it. A
Baromodul is connected
here, so that the computer
becomes a barograph. The
curves can be stored and
printed off.

Important formulae for calculators

● Measurement of distance with the sextant (object this side of the horizon)

Distance in miles = $\dfrac{13 \times \text{altitude of light above shore horizon (m)}}{7 \times \text{angle minutes}}$

● Distance of a navigation light on the horizon when the 'heart' of the light – not the apparent light – can just be seen.

Distance in miles = $2.075 \, (\sqrt{\text{altitude of light (m)}} + \sqrt{\text{eye level (m)}}$

● Distance of a shore object the other side of the horizon; in areas with few navigational aids, eg the Mediterranean, mountains are suitable.

Nautical miles = $\sqrt{3.71 \, (\text{H} - \text{EL}) + (\text{w} - 1.76 \sqrt{\text{EL}})^2} - (\text{w} - 1.76 \sqrt{\text{EL}})$

H = Height of mountain in metres
EL = Eye level in metres
w = sextant angle in minutes
Example: H = 1239 metres
         EL = 2 metres
         w = 114 angle minutes
         Result: 18.96nm distance

● Calculating (great circle) distance between two objects. Latitude and longitude must be given in degrees and the minutes follow in decimal degrees, so 15°30′ should be given as 15.5°. 'West' and 'South' are given as negative values:

Distance in nautical miles = 60 × arc cos [(sin lat of departure point × sin lat of arrival point) + (cos lat of departure × cos lat of arrival) × cos (long of departure – long of arrival)]

● Calculating course between two places:

Course =

$\text{arc cos} \left\{ \dfrac{\text{sin arrival lat} - [\text{sin departure lat} \times \cos (\text{dist}/60)]}{\cos \text{departure lat} \times \sin (\text{dist}/60)} \right\}$

Subtract 360° from the calculated course if sin (departure long – arrival long) greater than 0, ie positive.

The distance must next be calculated as for the distance between two objects, so that the actual course can be found. If departure and arrival points lie on the same degree longitude, the course is 0° or 180°.

Modern navigation electronics

Over the last few years there has been a lot going on in the area of electronics on yachts. Suddenly navigation technology has become available which for a long time only appeared in ocean-going ships. It has all become very efficient and within one's means.

Loran C

Loran C is still the standard method in many parts of the world. Its only disadvantage is that not all areas are covered by Loran C transmitters. It therefore can't be used in the North Sea, but this should change. Negotiations are being held with the former Soviet Union to be able to use their Loran C transmitters. This method could then come into use in the Baltic and the North Sea. For Loran C you need a main transmitter and several additional transmitters. The Mediterranean, for instance, is completely covered.

With modern receivers exact navigation to within several hundred metres is always possible. The receivers cost less than £700 ($1,050), depending on ease of operation. Everything is fully automatic. The machines search for a suitable chain of stations, measure the difference in running time and continually display the exact ship's position. Not only that, some machines are capable of storing points along the way, from which the course and the distance can always be shown digitally. Electricity consumption is no great problem any more, as receivers don't have to be turned on continually.

It has to be said though that particularly in the Adriatic there have been problems because some machines chose fully automatic transmitters which stood in an unfavourable line-up to the ship's position. This happened especially when machines were installed which had not been modified for use in Europe.

Until now there has never been a question of whether Loran C or Decca had the advantage because there are hardly any areas where both systems can be used. This could change in the future.

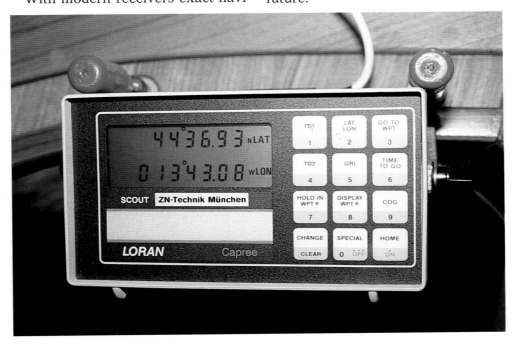

A Loran C machine. This was brought by a guest onto a charter yacht and fixed temporarily in the navigation corner with two clamps. This shows how easily these machines can be installed. It operates automatically, and you don't need to calculate anything or look up any tables. The ship's position appears on the display, exact to a few hundred metres.

Decca

This method has been around for over 25 years, but has only just been made available for yachts. This is also a hyperbolic method of navigation in which the relation between the phases of the main and additional transmitters is measured. These transmitters are maintained by Decca, who have given their receivers to sea-going ships and fishermen for a corresponding fee. Receivers now cost less than £700 ($1,050). Operation could hardly be easier, thanks to the most modern electronics: the approximate ship's position is first fed into it, and the machine then continually produces a ship's position every 20 seconds in longitude and latitude, exact to 200 metres.

Has every navigator's dream of always having an exact ship's position everywhere, come true? Not quite. This machine can only work in the region of Decca chains, for instance not in the Mediterranean. However, the whole Western European coast from the North Pole to the South of Spain is covered, so it is ideal if you are in these waters, as long as the transmitter is working.

Decca is used in the Baltic and the North Sea, including by cruising yachts over 6m long. The ship's positions are exact to 50m, and are usually more precise.

Global Positioning System (GPS)

GPS is the navigation system for the near future. It will replace all other electronic navigation systems such as Decca and Loran C. It has great advantages. GPS continually produces the position exact to the nearest 100m. No more and no less!

Don't be deceived by the confusing number of GPS receivers on offer. From the 18 satellites which circle the earth in 12 hours on 6 different orbits 20,000km high, the receiver only gets the exact position. Depending on the receiver, further calculations are then done from that, for instance course and speed by comparing the current position with an earlier position. When buying a receiver, everyone should choose how luxuriously it is kitted out. There will soon be receivers for £350 ($520) on the market which give the position as exactly as much more expensive machines.

GPS positions are more exact than it was thought possible when most sea charts were produced. So there is always some variation between the GPS position and places on the sea chart. New sea charts usually point out differences like this. The variations are in practice so negligible that they don't have to be taken into account in navigational practice.

GPS is an extremely exact and reliable system. However, there are several areas where faults can occur. The receiver can break, and the whole GPS system can be turned off (which has happened). It is therefore good seamanship to have a system in reserve on board. For instance it would be stupid to sail across the Atlantic with GPS and not have a sextant on board. The GPS digital display only helps to bring the yacht into the desired coastal waters. Yachts have run aground because of this, because the skipper has relied totally on GPS and not even looked up from the sea chart.

A word of warning: Even with extremely exact electronics, in coastal waters you should only navigate by sight.

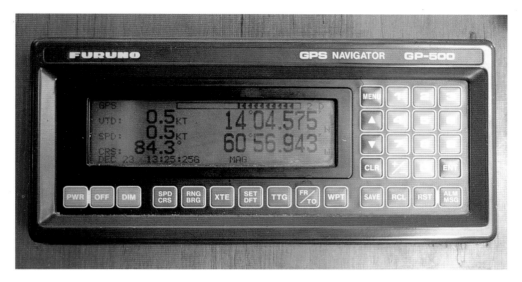

A GPS receiver shows the position to the second. It also shows speed and course over the ground.

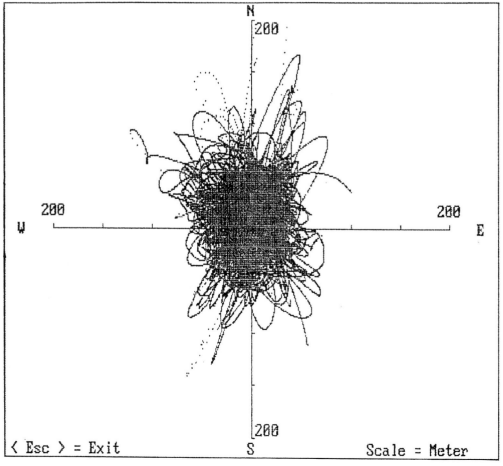

A GPS receiver's variation in accuracy over 24 hours. To be safe you should reckon on possible inaccuracies of 200m and more.

Radar

Over the last few years cruising yachts have become not only much more expensive but bigger. With this a reservation against one of the most worthwhile navigational aids has lapsed. Earlier, radar was only rarely fitted on yachts because the radar antennae were just too big for boats under 10m. Today you quite often see the round radar dish (antenna!) on yachts' mizzens and rightly so, because radar eases navigation greatly. The skipper can see his surroundings in a circle of up to 16 or 24 miles, whether there are other boats in the fog or a narrow entrance to a harbour.

Everyone who has ever experienced using radar is amazed by the help it gives. Radar is also invaluable if you are in waters which are usually spared fog. This is because the distance to (identified) objects on shore can be measured to within 50m on the radar screen. This allows you to plot first-class position lines on the chart, that is circles around an object with a radius of the distance.

The high electricity consumption (up to 10 amps) is not a convincing argument against a radar, as for navigation it is enough to turn the radar on occasionally for a few minutes. Colour radar is not absolutely necessary, because the colours are not natural and the echos are coloured by the computer with a particular colour depending on the intensity. Colour radars are extremely expensive. On the other hand there is another innovation which I find useful.

The radar picture can be 'frozen' at the press of a button. If the radar antenna is mounted on the mast, the picture is not ideal with every revolution of the antenna because of the strong ship's movements on the open sea. Occasionally the yacht's surroundings are shown in particular detail on the screen. This picture can then be 'frozen', so that the skipper can analyse the screen at his leisure with the chart in his hand.

Radar machines are unfortunately still very complicated machines which go wrong fairly frequently. It is not always possible to repair them in every

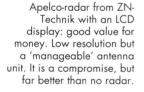

Apelco-radar from ZN-Technik with an LCD display: good value for money. Low resolution but a 'manageable' antenna unit. It is a compromise, but far better than no radar.

harbour. It is best to ask fishermen which make has proved the best. Radar is the only electronic navigation system which is not made superfluous by GPS. GPS shows figures and radar shows the ship's position.

Preparing for a trip at sea

'Haste is the biggest enemy of the seafarer.' This is why I think it is wrong to work out a trip from the beginning to an exact schedule. It is always possible that bad weather can change the dates you have set, which is a violation of the laws of seamanship. For this reason a more relaxed plan is better, where you can leave one or another harbour as you need to.

Sea charts There should be plenty of these on board for all the areas you plan to visit. It is easy to say that you should take all the charts with you that there are for this region, and those who can afford to do this are lucky. We should establish which sea charts are absolutely necessary.

The whole area of the trip should be covered by regional charts. Even if they don't show every detail they are enough in an emergency. By emergency I mean the possibility that you are forced by a hurricane to put into harbours which aren't on your schedule. You need every 'sea' chart of course. It is difficult to decide which detailed charts and harbour charts you should get in addition. If you put into harbours by day, in most cases you won't need any harbour charts. I have known only very few harbours where I would definitely recommend a harbour chart.

Every book advises that you only use sea charts which have been published recently. Apart from exceptions, I would not hesitate to use older sea charts if I could get them cheaply or borrow them from a yachting friend. Naturally we also give charts away if we don't need them anymore. Our friends usually mail them back once they have been used. Another thing which is useful to know is that seagoing ships are required by law to have the latest charts on board. The old ones usually end up in the engine room as insulation. An understanding navigation officer will certainly give you the material which has been taken out of service if you look him out on his ship in the harbour and ask him.

If you can afford new charts, sea charts produced by the government are always the best. Only these guarantee that they really are the latest state. In my experience Yugoslavian maps of the Adriatic are much more exact than foreign ones. Watch out for the fact that older British maps still give depth in fathoms. There are British (Admiralty) sea charts for all parts of the world. Their quality compared with American ones is much disputed amongst yachties. I personally find British charts better because the detail is worked out better on them. There are more detailed American charts available on the other hand. Harbour plans and Silhouettes for coastal navigation are often included on British charts.

To conclude, I would always recommend British sea charts as long as my eyes are good. Unfortunately not all charts use the same symbols. You should therefore have a relevant list of symbols and abbreviations on board. This is included in the American 'Chart No.1' and the British Admiralty's number '5011'. In France and Germany there are even special sea charts for racing yachts. These include everything you need to know (navigation light signals etc), so that you don't need any other nautical documents.

Handbooks and pilots Most of these are unfortunately published so rarely that the information in them and especially the diagrams just don't correspond to the actual conditions anymore. Almost every sailor has at one time searched helplessly for the 'small church with a red roof' in the handbook, which of course disappeared behind skyscrapers decades ago.

Handbooks do however give some good advice, especially if you put the supplements in order before your trip. Handbooks are written for sea-going ships. When they talk about 'space for one or two small ships' it can happen that you will find 20 yachts on this anchorage. By 'small ship' they mean ships of 1,000 tons and under. The anchorages recommended in the handbooks also seldom correspond with what we expect from a peaceful anchorage. A 2m high swell hardly bothers a tanker at anchor, whilst we would only spend any length of time there in an extreme emergency.

Over the last few years more and more handbooks have been written especially for sailors of yachts, and these should obviously be made use of as they are geared towards the needs of offshore cruising. The good ones will tell you where to find water, go shopping, get fresh bread in the mornings, a good bar and so on.

One thing should be pointed out: whilst handbooks for sea-going ships are as exhaustive as possible and only professional seamen have worked on them, handbooks for offshore cruising almost always touch on the experiences of holiday makers. A harbour which has still not been 'discovered' will be missing from a handbook like this, whilst a misunderstood breaker observed by a short-sighted skipper goes into the handbook as 'reef at the entrance'. The details are generally very reliable in my experience, although extreme care won't harm a skipper here either.

The list of lights This is the most important navigational document besides the sea chart. It should always be kept up to date, and corrections to it should be made before starting out on a trip.

Tide tables You should also take with you the tide tables valid for the relevant area and year even if the differences between high and low water are not great (as in the Mediterranean). A special current often occurs in coastal waters at 'high water' or 'low water' which you can see from the handbook in many cases.

Nautical Radio Service If you have a radio direction finder on board, you will usually have a book on the yachting radio service in the North Sea, Baltic or Mediterranean in your navigation area. I would get Volume II of the Nautical Radio Service and leave it at that. This contains all the sea navigation signals in the world and air navigation signals which have any meaning for shipping. Volume II of the Nautical Radio Service should also be brought up-to-date from time to time. In the Western Mediterranean for instance, almost all the navigation signals have changed over the last few years. 'Radio direction finding charts' are practical, and are printed for yachts, especially in France. On an outline chart the navigation signals are shown with signal, range and frequency.

I would also get Volume III of the Nautical Radio Service, as all the weather services in the world are to be found in this, as well as a very good introduction on how to draw weather charts, the key for FM 46 and a list of meteorological expressions in different languages so that you can work with a weather forecast in a foreign language in an emergency.

Pilot charts These are indispensable for long distance sailors. They include the prevailing wind directions and strengths for particular months. If you want to sail across the Atlantic, for example, you take the pilot chart for

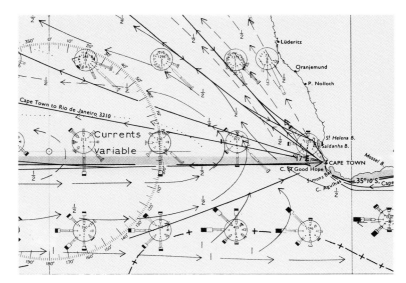

A section of a pilot chart for the South Atlantic in May.
The fatter the line for the wind, the stronger it is (the thick end of the line means force 8–12).
Its length gives the percentage frequency. The three values in the circle give you (from top to bottom) the number of observations, wind from changing directions and calms by percentage.

the relevant month, and you will find the following details for each of the special squares which cover 5°.

Number of observations, probability of storms and calms by percentage, and probable wind directions and strengths. The probability of tropical hurricanes in the West Indies is also given and, if one has taken place during this time it gives its path (and you should avoid this month). There are pilot charts for every ocean in the world, and usually a chart for each month.

Essential volumes You should definitely get *Ocean Passages for the World*, which has been published by the British Admiralty for many decades. You will find the recommended sailing boat routes and the best seasons for the whole world in this inexpensive book. The prescribed routes for steamships are also interesting for trans-oceanic sailors, who should pay great attention to these.

The skipper who wants to navigate by the stars should have a Nautical Almanac and the HO 249 tables on board of course.

Reading up All the nautical documents mentioned are obtainable from book-sellers or chandlers. From studying the documents you will discover which wind and weather conditions you must reckon with, and with that which distances per day. There can be no general rules if you move out of the trade winds areas. You should expect distances per day of 100 miles on average, no matter what the size of the boat. On the other hand in the Mediterranean or the Baltic you should prepare yourself for calms or 'unsuitable' wind directions. If you want to spare the engine, you can be grateful for an average of 70 miles in 24 hours.

You should prepare the documents themselves for your use. You can highlight dangers more clearly in the handbooks by underlining them. I have always found it particularly useful to write the symbols of navigation lights from the list onto the sea chart, as long as they are relevant before a trip. You can go wrong equally with navigation lights. If you don't know morse letters, write the symbol in dots and dashes. In an emergency, such as navigating towards a harbour at night, you will be glad if you can find all the necessary information on the sea chart and you don't have to search around in lots of books at the same time on your pitching boat.

Offshore cruising on charter yachts

Holidays on a charter yacht usually mean more carefree sailing than on your own yacht.

There are more and more enthusiastic people going offshore cruising on charter yachts. The advantages of a holiday like this are obvious: you can charter a yacht in almost all sailing areas of the world, and you don't get the arduous journey there in your own boat. And if you charter a yacht with other sailors or another family you can easily work this out as a really good value holiday as opposed to staying in a good hotel. Above all, if you take out the relevant insurance, on a holiday like this you are risking much less than if you sail your own boat. While the sailor on his own offshore cruiser might have to look up a shipyard after a trip to have repairs done, the guest on the charter boat can bring the boat back to the charter company and leave the yacht with no worries.

Of course you only have a successful charter holiday if you come across a good charter company which takes care of its boats. There are a lot of black sheep amongst charter companies, who save on the standard of equipment and condition of the yachts. You will only be able to tell this at the end of a trip, when it is too late. The best thing is, therefore, to rely on the opinion of previous customers. A good indication for the quality of a charter company is how long it has been in business. Shady firms don't last long luckily.

It is almost impossible to give an opinion on the quality of different charter areas. But a distorted picture and perhaps some prejudice will help you decide better than no advice at all.

From the point of view of the weather, the best charter area is the West Indies outside the hurricane period, in the winter. Some American charter companies have been going for decades in this area. If you find the charter prices high there, you should consider that most charter customers there are Americans who expect far more comfort on board than European sailors for example. So it can be said that you could get more for your money.

The main charter area for Europeans is the Mediterranean. It is however not an ideal sailing area even if there is enormous choice of boats to charter. In Spain, Italy and France you cannot count on wind during the overcrowded high season, so a sailing holiday can become a motorboat holiday (which also has its attractions). In spring and autumn there is often too much wind in these areas, and in the winter it is plain dangerous to sail around the Mediterranean on a yacht.

At the time of writing, former Yugoslavia is out of the question for political reasons. Greece and Turkey are the charter countries for the years to come. Particularly in Turkey you can find any number of beautiful coves which are not overcrowded even in high season. Sewage tanks are stipulated for charter yachts in this area, which makes a dip in the water before breakfast an unspoilt pleasure. The author finds Turkey by far the most beautiful charter area in Europe at the present time.

A luxury charter catamaran in St Lucia in the Caribbean.

239

There are special offshore regattas for cruisers. The different capacity and equipment of the cruisers is usually balanced out by 'heats' so that everyone taking part has a chance to win a place. But the fun of taking part still comes first.

Offshore cruisers at regattas

Charter companies make it possible for offshore cruisers to take part in events such as offshore regattas. If the ordinary holiday sailor has hardly any chance of sailing in a proper open sea regatta, more and more charter companies are offering this sort of opportunity. For instance, Ecker Yacht Charter organises a high standard racing offshore regatta with cruising yachts for a thousand miles across the Mediterranean. Private yachts and charter yachts on single bookings take part. This means that even individuals or small groups can take part and experience the adventure of an offshore regatta for several days and nights for comparatively little money. At the destination harbour in Tunisia or Egypt a party with 500 other offshore cruisers awaits them.

The 'Atlantic Rally for Cruisers' is quite a different event which has taken place over the last few years. It originated from one cruiser that wanted to sail across the Atlantic as part of a group. The thought that other yachts would be nearby to help in an emergency might have played a part in this. More than 250 cruisers start in November every year at the same time from the Canary Islands to sail to St Lucia or Barbados in the Caribbean.

The presentation ceremony of the Ecker-Cup, an open sea regatta from Turkey to Tunisia over 1,000 miles. Overall winner was Willi Lettner (below), who has been confined to a wheelchair for years.

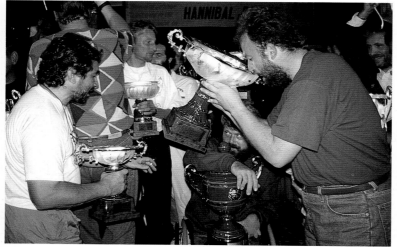

240

Important notes

Health on board

Dr Walter Dirr

The amount of medical knowledge and equipment called for depends on the conditions of each particular trip. If you take isolated routes away from the coast, you obviously have to make different preparations than if you are sailing from harbour to harbour, as the help of a doctor is always at hand on shore in an emergency. In the latter case, equipment such as a first aid box is really all that's needed, while for longer stretches, the level of knowledge and amount of equipment must be higher. The following pages contain suggestions only, and do not claim to be full advice. In particular, the first aid section on injuries has deliberately been kept very short. At the end of the chapter you will find a list of recommended reading on first aid. Before embarking on a longer trip with a larger crew, at least one crew member should have made themselves familiar with some basic medical terms, which they can do by taking a first aid course. It would, however, be much better to consult a doctor personally, particularly a doctor who also sails and knows the problems which can arise.

Preventive measures

When embarking on a trip, every crew member should be in optimum health so that you are confronted with the fewest possible medical difficulties. If this is not possible because of a chronic complaint, it might be necessary for the skipper to refuse their participation. The following are cases which will exclude someone from joining a sailing trip:

Marcel Bardiaux is living proof that sailing is a healthy activity. He hasn't spent one night on land for 40 years, and has sailed 350,000 sea miles. Already 80 years old, he will probably reach 100.

- coronary heart disease
- diabetes not under good control
- untreated high blood pressure
- bronchial asthma accompanied by frequent attacks

A thorough medical examination is recommended, and you must notify the doctor of your plans. A dental check-up is also recommended, as are inoculations, both for the country you will be travelling to, and advisable ones, such as sufficient tetanus jabs, which everybody should have anyway.

If your family doctor is unable to give you any information about the necessary inoculations, you may need to visit your local health centre. It might also be necessary to contact the Institute of Tropical Medicine in London, who will be able to tell you things such as what the latest anti-malarial pro-phylactic is.

Everybody must obviously take their own prescribed medicines with them, such as cardiac drugs or insulin. You can't expect items such as these to be available in the ship's pharmacy. Precautionary measures such as removal of the appendix are not necessary, since the risks of appendicitis are not very high, even on very long transoceanic trips. You can, however, take various preventive measures on board.

It must be taken into account that in a warm climate bacteria multiply extremely fast in food, and in drinks and water, though to a lesser extent. This can lead to diarrhoea, which is not only unpleasant but can also be very dangerous. It is therefore not recommended that you keep prepared foods for any length of time. The fresh water you take with you should be boiled before it is drunk. In an emergency you can use disinfecting additives according to instructions, which do, however, change the taste very noticeably. When you take over a boat, I strongly recommend that you disinfect the surfaces, which is most easily done with a spray.

Further things to avoid which are obvious, but ignored time and again are: too much sun, especially at the beginning; hypothermia from swimming or getting wet through; and excessive alcohol intake, which can encourage some illnesses to break out. Alcohol is certainly not a good method of fending off colds and flu, it has quite the opposite effect.

Injuries

Straightforward wounds, so-called minor injuries, need at the most disinfecting and covering with a sterile bandage or plaster. Stemming the blood-flow is usually not required.

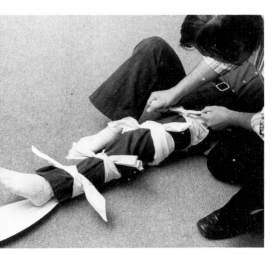
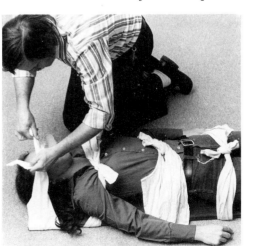

Left: immobilising a broken leg by securing it to a paddle.

Right: immobilising a suspected broken spine with the aid of a floor-board and a torn-up shirt; tie the head down as well.

Venous bleeding, which is recognisable by continuous oozing from the wound, can be stopped by applying pressure or a pressure bandage to the wound itself. Arterial bleeding spurts in time with the heartbeat, and can likewise be stopped by pressure to the wound area. It is only necessary to bind an extremity with thick bandaging in an extreme emergency, and with arterial bleeding. You must however be careful that an extremity is only left for half an hour at the most without any circulation. After this you must open it briefly, for 3 to 5 minutes. If necessary, it can be bound up again afterwards. A first aid manual will tell you the particular points at which to compress an artery, stemming the bleeding by applying pressure with your fingers or hand.

The main principle behind the treatment of **broken bones** is avoiding movement in the affected limbs. You must not set a fracture as it will only give rise to unnecessary extra pain. In almost all cases you should use a splint, so that the joints next to the injured part can be fixed to it, thus preventing movement. If the forearm is broken, this means that movement of the elbow or wrist must be made impossible. The bandages you use must be bound firmly yet loose enough not to prevent circulation. Check this by monitoring the relevant hand/foot occasionally – it should not appear blue or white.

Follow the same procedure for torn tendons or muscles. There are not generally any greater dangers.

A **spinal injury**, however, holds the possibility of paraplegia. Even in the case of reasonable suspicion the injured person should be tied to a rigid base lying on their back. Their head should also be tied to it.

In the case of **broken ribs** the best thing to do is to run sticking plaster right around the patient's chest, overlapping in layers, after they have breathed out hard. In order to protect the skin, it is recommended that you cover it with cellophane, or even toilet paper in an emergency. If breathing is badly hindered, cut the bandaging open with scissors on the other side of the body to the fracture.

With **open fractures** where the broken bone protrudes or there is a wound leading down to the fracture, you should mildly disinfect the wound as well as applying a splint. Following that simply apply a sterile covering and start a prophylactic course of antibiotics.

A satisfactory **painkiller** is very important in all bad cases of wounds, particularly broken bones, in order to prevent shock developing. Although the patient's life is rarely in any immediate danger, you must seek the help of a doctor quickly in all the above cases of complicated fracture, since irreparable damage can occur which could lead to amputation.

For **injuries to the stomach or chest areas** you must make do with a sterile bandage, antibiotics and painkillers. The patient's life will be in immediate danger, and medical help should be sought as soon as possible. Sadly, 24 hours after the onset of peritonitis the chances of survival are not great. You can extend this time somewhat by cooling the part with an ice-pack or a cold damp cloth.

Eye injuries, whether minor or serious, are treated by applying sterile eye

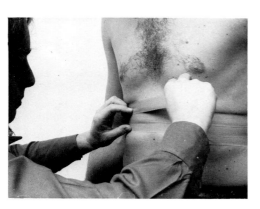

Broken ribs: use of an overlapping wide plaster.

ointment or antibiotic eye-drops, directly onto the cornea. Then close the eye either with a bandage or an eye-patch. In the case of a more serious injury apply stronger antibiotics and sufficient painkillers.

It should also be mentioned that **very deep wounds** might require stitching. However, stitches should only be carried out up to four hours at the most after the wound occurred. In an emergency you can use any needle or piece of thread as long as it has been boiled (if time allows). However, you can dispense with this if they have been kept in a clean enough place.

Technically, you begin by holding the edges of the wound together with one hand whilst inserting the needle through the skin about 1 cm away from and towards the wound. Stitch through the wound out through the skin on the other side, and knot the two threads together, so that the knot lies on the skin and not on the wound. Proceed in this way from one corner of the wound to the other, with the stitches lying about 1.5cm apart. The edges of the skin can then be further fixed together with sticking plaster. Apply a disinfectant powder to the wound if possible. This kind of stitching can be removed after 4 days. In these circumstances, a discharge of pus can occur from the wound, which can be treated with antibiotics and local dressings. Weeping wounds can also be cleaned effectively by applying ordinary caster sugar.

Nowadays the treatment for **burns** entails drawing the heat out of the skin fast by immersing it in cold water at about 12 to 16°C. Cooling down in the water should take about 10 minutes, after which take out the affected part for 2 to 3 minutes and immerse it again until the pain disappears. If larger sections of the body are affected such as the chest or back, the dinghy can double as a bath in an emergency. Then cover the burn with Metaline bandages, or apply a gel on smaller areas. Extensive burns can lead to very serious complications such as kidney failure, so medical help should be sought immediately. The body's fluid level should meanwhile be kept steady: as long as urine production is normal, give the patient plenty to drink, in the form of saltwater solution (2–3g per litre), and sweetened fruit juice; if urine production is reduced, in which case you should collect it and measure it, give the patient about ½ to 1 litre of liquid more than the amount of urine. The effects of **excessive heat or sun** can build up, and will be apparent either through heatstroke or heat exhaustion. Someone suffering from heat exhaustion, which is a relatively harmless manifestation, will feel increasingly weak and nauseous, will then vomit and break into a cold sweat. Lay the patient down flat and give them plenty of hot drinks. Heatstroke itself will cause sudden loss of consciousness from quite normal behaviour. Sweating stops completely and the body temperature can climb as far as 42°C. The skin will feel hot and dry. As the patient's life is in danger, call a doctor or a hospital immediately. In the meantime cool the body down with ice-packs or damp towels. It is a serious mistake to give an unconscious person anything to drink.

If the heart or breathing stops, the reason can be hypothermia, although there can of course be other causes. You should start resuscitation procedures at once. The first thing to do is to check whether the person is breathing, which you can do by putting one hand on the stomach and the other on the chest. If you feel no movement, breathing has stopped. If the heart has stopped pumping or is weaker, you will feel no pulse in the carotid arteries of the neck. To feel this, locate the voice box with one hand and press your thumb to one side of it and fingers on the other side of it with moderate

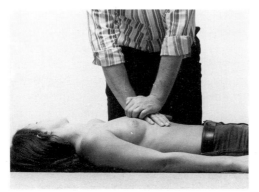
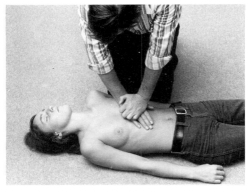

Heart massage should only be carried out on a hard surface.

pressure. External heart massage begins with a firm punch in the cardiac region. Sometimes this alone can restore a normal heartbeat, so you must then feel again for the carotid pulse.

The following points are important in heart massage:

• Lay the casualty flat on their back on a hard surface
• Kneel beside them facing their chest
• Put the ball of your thumb at the lower end of their breastbone and cover this hand with your other
• With your arms straight, press down about 4cm towards the spine
• Complete these chest compressions at a rate of 70–90 per minute

At the same time you must carry out mouth-to-mouth resuscitation, remembering the following:

• Clear the casualty's airways – clean the nose, mouth and throat of blood, water and anything else;
• Tilt their head well back, lifting their jaw up with one hand
• Blow firmly once into the casualty's nose, keeping their mouth closed, or alternatively into their mouth pinching their nostrils shut. If you have been successful you will see the chest rise and fall
• Continue giving breaths of mouth-to-mouth at a rate of about 15 times a minute

If you are the only person helping, give chest compressions 125 times followed by 3 breaths, then 15 chest compressions. If there are two of you, give a breath of mouth-to-mouth after every fifth chest compression, breaking off the chest compressions briefly to do so.

Heart massage even when carried out correctly can lead to broken ribs, particularly in the case of elderly people, and this must be taken into account. How long you should continue to resuscitate depends entirely on the individual situation. If the pupils are fully dilated and do not narrow after you have begun resuscitation, then after 15 to 20 minutes you can expect the onset of death. If the pupils do narrow, continue resuscitation until medical help arrives.

To sum up, the following three points are important: do not resuscitate unless it is obviously necessary; be absolutely sure of clear airways when giving mouth-to-mouth resuscitation; never administer any liquid orally to an unconscious person.

In the case of **exposure and hypothermia** warm the casualty up as quickly as possible in the heated cabin or in a hot bath. Smaller areas of frostbite/exposure should be warmed up in a bath at about 25°C, increasing to 40°C

246

within half an hour. After this apply vigorous motion to the frozen limbs and then put them up. You must seek medical help as soon as possible in order to avoid irreparable damage to the limbs.

Illness

This is such an extensive and difficult area that it cannot be covered fully in this book. Situations can obviously occur which aren't mentioned here. An amateur should not try to make a definite diagnosis where it is almost impossible for an expert, especially under the circumstances on board a boat. The following is an attempt to assess the types of illness and to show possible treatments, which derive from the given symptoms.

For almost every serious illness there are three distinct main symptoms:
- temperature
- pain
- malfunction.

By then you will generally already have established the method of treatment.

A **temperature** is caused in 90% of cases by bacterial infection. You will therefore need an antibacterial drug (antibiotic) which is available in your first aid kit as Amoxil and Penbritin. These are a pure penicillin preparation and a preparation deriving from penicillin, with a broad range of effects. The only time they should not be used is if the patient is definitely hypersensitive to penicillin. They can have the side effect of diarrhoea. Painkillers should be given according to the type and strength of the pain.

Any malfunction should be treated accordingly. We will now divide the body into the following regions: head, throat, chest, and stomach including urinary and reproductive organs. By region, the most common complaints will be dealt with first followed by the rarer and more serious ones.

Head

Sinusitis causes sneezing and a thick yellow secretion. There is pain in the upper jaw area and sometimes in the forehead. There is an unpleasant pressure behind the eyes particularly with eye movement upwards or to the side. The organisms occurring here are almost always sensitive to penicillin (Amoxil).

Nosebleeds are a common occurrence and usually stop of their own accord. To help relieve them place a cold compress on the neck. If the bleeding hasn't stopped after half an hour, administer Cyklokapron tablets and plug the nose with cotton wool. Nosebleeds are not generally dangerous.

Inflammation of the **outer ear** or eardrum is very painful. Use Amoxil and eardrops to help relieve this.

Toothache can be quite harmless. However, a dental sepsis will cause pain, then swelling (of the cheek) and finally a temperature. Ordinary painkillers are all that's needed at first. If swelling starts, give the patient Voltarol at once, which usually reduces the swelling very fast. Only use Amoxil if the patient has a temperature. Nosebleeds combined with a haematoma around the eyes can be a sign of a **fractured skull**. Besides making the patient comfortable, you can do little to treat them. If they become unconscious, the prospects of survival are not very good and a doctor should be called immediately.

Meningitis is equally dangerous. Symptoms are headaches, a very high temperature, and above all a stiff neck. The patient should be given antibiotics and a doctor should be called at once. Put the patient in a darkened room, as light is very unpleasant and painful, and give them painkillers.

Throat

Tonsilitis and laryngitis cause swallowing to be painful. Tonsilitis causes swelling of the lymph glands under the lower jaw, whereas laryngitis does not. In both cases use Amoxil and Tyrozets throat tablets and with laryngitis the patient should not talk or smoke. Swallowing problems create the danger of a blockage of the airways at the opening of the windpipe, the larynx. This will trigger a heavy cough as a reflex action, which will clear this up.

With small children small objects can slip through the larynx and get stuck in the windpipe, causing breathing to stop. The child will turn blue and will hardly show any signs of breathing. The only way to clear the windpipe is to hold the child up by its feet and hit it hard on the back.

Chest

Lungs and air passages Usually the problem will be bronchitis, which is the inflammation of the smaller air passages or of the windpipe itself. The main symptoms are coughing and producing phlegm. If the windpipe itself is inflamed, there will be pain behind the breastbone. As long as there is only a slight temperature, or none at all, you can make do with expectorants and cough medicines (Benylin).

If a high temperature (over 38.5°C) develops, you can suspect pneumonia, which is best treated at once with an antibiotic, Penbritin. Pleurisy can occur alongside pneumonia, or even on its own. This can be recognised by painful breathing, usually in the lower chest area, and rarely needs special treatment. If pleurisy occurs on its own, as painful breathing without a temperature, cough or phlegm, treat it with an anti-inflammatory such as Voltarol.

You usually won't be aware of your **heart** any more than any other internal organ. However, if someone begins to feel pain in the cardiac area, they will understandably be very worried. You will then have to distinguish between chest pain brought about by faulty circulation or a harmless functional complaint. Pains like this can also have a psychological cause. The following criteria will help you to differentiate:

- Chest pain which should be taken seriously worsens during manual work and in cold conditions. It usually disppears fast when the person relaxes.
- Real chest pain will disappear usually within a few minutes of taking a glycerol trinitrate tablet, whilst less serious functional complaints will not be affected by it.

Whilst serious chest pain requires rest and perhaps strong painkillers such as DF 118, the usual treatment is occupational therapy and work.

A **heart attack** is really only an intensification of a heart complaint caused by faulty circulation. There are severe pains in the cardiac area, combined with cramp in the chest and feelings of extreme agony. Circulatory collapse often occurs alongside, which can be recognised by breaking out in a cold sweat, going black before the eyes and a fast pulse. Keep the casualty absolutely still and give them painkillers and sedatives. You must obviously seek medical help at once. A heart attack can also lead to a severe state of shock or death within seconds. In this case start resuscitation procedures, as mentioned earlier.

It is quite conceivable that someone should have a heart attack on board when you think that there will be elderly people amongst your crew who are undertaking physical tasks which are completely new to them. Along with the main symptoms of pain and a high temperature, there will be problems in the stomach area, predominantly vomiting and diarrhoea.

Stomach

Vomiting will probably be the most common illness on board, considering seasickness. The cause of vomiting from seasickness is strictly speaking not in the stomach but in the vestibular apparatus of the ear.

Treatment is, however, the same as that for every other kind of vomiting. All appropriate drugs (eg Stemetil) have a central calming effect, and eventually cause tiredness. The sooner they are taken, the greater their effect, so you should take the medication at the first signs of heavy seas, and people who are prone to seasickness should do so even before that.

If heavy vomiting has already begun, you can't do much to stop it, mainly because tablets will quickly be brought up again. Suppositories would then have to be used, or in an emergency an intramuscular injection. As a prevention, do not overwork the stomach with large meals. Experience also shows that instant coffee aids the onset of seasickness. Once the vomiting is severe, it is best to abstain from any kind of food intake, but you must make sure that there is some fluid intake, even if in small amounts. The best thing to drink is unsweetened tea. In order for contraceptive pills not to lose their effect, they should be taken again if the vomiting started less than two hours after they were first taken.

Diarrhoea, particularly in warmer countries, can almost always be traced to a bacterial infection. It has already been mentioned that food, or even drinks infected with bacteria are usually responsible. Treatment must begin at the first signs of diarrhoea to prevent the patient from deteriorating dangerously. The best thing is to do without food completely.

It is vital however to keep up sufficient fluid intake, at least 1.5 or better 2 litres of liquid a day, best again in the form of unsweetened tea. Charcoal tablets and Imodium should be taken at the same time. Antibiotics can only be advised against, as they would worsen the diarrhoea, and they are not the right method for salmonella infections as they can weaken the body's own immune responses.

Heartburn is harmless in people who are prone to it. It often occurs after drinking a lot of alcohol, and responds well to Gelusil antacid tablets. At the same time, avoid food and drink such as coffee, alcohol and hot spices, which produce acid.

Bleeding in the digestive tract can complicate vomiting or diarrhoea, or trigger itself of its own accord. The vomit will look like coffee grounds, and the appearance in the stool will be variable depending on the position of the bleeding. You will only see red traces of blood in the stool if the bleeding is relatively close to the anus.

Otherwise another indication of bleeding in the upper digestive tract is a pitch-black stool, distinguishable from a harmless black stool (as after drinking red wine) by its nasty smell. The source of the bleeding is usually in an ulcer just behind the exit to the stomach in the duodenum. Treatment consists of Cyklokapron tablets, plenty of ice-cold drinks and Gelusil antacid tablets. This is always a case of serious illness and a doctor must be called immediately.

The **stomach and pelvic basin** are a peculiarity. These inner organs include the gall-bladder and bile ducts, the whole of the intestine, the kidneys and ureter, as well as the woman's fallopian tubes and womb. You must be careful with these organs because they can lead to a particular kind of pain, colic. Colic consists of pains which rise and fall in intensity, coming in waves. If these pains occur, the best antidote is Buscopan, taken as a suppository.

If the gall-bladder or bile duct are affected, there will often be a rapid rise in temperature, accompanied by shivering fits. The pains are always on the right hand side, usually radiating back from the shoulder blade. If the patient also has a temperature, they must be given antibiotics. With the kidneys and ureter the pain is more localised in the lower abdomen and is worst in the groin. Give the patient plenty of liquids along with Buscopan.

Almost half the population of Europe suffer from **constipation**, and almost all of these are women. Most of these are not real sufferers, because these are people who think you should produce a sizeable stool every day, which is absolute nonsense. Even if you don't pass a stool more often than every three days you are not necessarily ill. Laxatives ought not to be included on the list because they are often misused, but in some cases such as inflamed haemorrhoids or feverish illness they are indispensable. Otherwise eat plenty of high-fibre foods such as fruit, vegetables, salads and wholemeal bread, or cold fruit juice on an empty stomach.

An obstruction of the bowel or intestines will mean that bowel movement and passing wind will stop completely. Within two to three days, signs of peritonitis will appear, which is discussed below in further detail. Amateur treatment of this is not possible. Make absolutely certain in this case not to give the patient laxatives.

Inflammation of the fallopian tubes or the womb can cause colic pains in the lower abdomen, and will usually be accompanied by a temperature and painful pressure. There is no one distinguishing feature for the amateur between this and peritonitis. Give the patient antibiotics (Penbritin), painkillers (Buscopan in this case), and an anti-inflammatory (Voltarol).

Any illness in the abdomen except kidney stones can lead to **peritonitis**. As well as extremely severe pain across the whole abdomen, the stomach will feel as hard as a board. If the peritonitis is localised, as in the case of acute appendicitis, the stiffening of the stomach muscles will also be more or less localised, at least at first. It is a very serious illness at all times. You can only win time by applying ice-packs or cold compresses and giving antibiotics such as Penbritin. You will also find it necessary to give the patient the strongest possible painkiller, preferably DF 118 in the form of an intramuscular injection. But you must be careful not to administer any painkillers in the four hours before reaching a doctor or a hospital, in order that the right diagnosis can be made by the doctor as quickly as possible.

Inflammation of the urinary tracts, bladder and kidneys is accompanied by a varying high temperature. With a kidney infection, the temperature will rise rapidly, together with shivering. Another symptom in the urinary tracts is a frequent need to urinate and a burning pain on doing so, with very little urine being produced. Treatment for this is also antibiotics and painkillers.

Bleeding from the bladder is not common, and should be taken seriously. Apart from giving the patient Cyklokapron tablets, there is no other action to be taken.

The inability to pass urine occurs exclusively in men aged over 50, particularly with hypothermia and high alcohol intake, because of swelling of the prostate. An amateur would not be recommended to attach a catheter to the bladder if they haven't done this before. Aspiration of the full bladder is much easier, if you note the following points:

• No water should be passed for at least 12 hours, guaranteeing that the bladder really is full and increasingly so

• Shave the pubic hair and disinfect the skin above the pubic bone with Betadine solution

• Take a sterile cannula (size 1) and insert it vertically into the skin about the width of two fingers above the upper end of the pubic bone, letting the needle penetrate slowly under light pressure, until the urine begins to drip out of the cannula

With obese people it might also be necessary to compress the abdominal wall by pressing it inwards. If drops of blood start to appear, this is no reason to stop the process. Collect the urine in a measuring jug, as you should stop when about 1.5 litres of urine have been drained off. This is very important, as otherwise you can provoke bleeding of the bladder. After relieving the bladder in this way, withdraw the cannula quickly and close the wound with an ordinary sticking plaster. You can carry out this process as often as you like.

Phlebitis

Haemorrhoids are a particular kind of phlebitis which really can make your life a misery. As well as meticulous cleanliness, particularly after a bowel movement, and applying ointment such as Lasonil, it is worthwhile using an anti-inflammatory such as Voltarol.

For either surface or deep **varicose veins** the treatment is Voltarol. In a surface case, the inflamed vein will redden, swell up and harden, and pain will be felt. This is usually harmless. Cool the affected area and apply the relevant ointment or gel such as Lasonil. Keep the affected leg still until acute symptoms subside.

Deep varicose veins, which are not easily discernible apart from swelling of the leg, are a serious matter. Pain is felt particularly on standing and running. A typical sign is pain when applying pressure to the sole of the foot. There is danger here of blood clots spreading to the lungs. It is absolutely vital to keep the patient completely still. Give them Voltarol and Penbritin at the onset of a temperature. Make sure you give them plenty to drink. If within six hours of doing this the swelling of the foot doesn't go down significantly, call a doctor.

Skin inflammations are occasionally caused by insect bites or small cuts. A painful reddening of the skin under the wound occurs. Amoxil and cooling bandages are the best treatment.

Boils or abscesses are easily spotted. To treat them, wait first until they 'ripen'. Within a few days the skin over the abscess will become very red and tauten. The very tip will eventually become a bit white. Take a sterile knife or scalpel and make a small incision in the skin across the middle of the abscess. Pus will shoot from the wound as a result. Lay a piece of sterile gauze over the wound and cover it with a bandage. This will usually heal spontaneously, without complications. For safety's sake you can also give the patient an antibiotic, Penbritin.

A severe attach of **gout** is easy for an amateur to spot. The ball of the big toe begins to swell up and turn a blue or red colour, and is very painful. Voltarol is prescribed here as well, and plenty to drink (but no alcohol).

Allergies are very common, caused by oversensitivity to drugs, insect stings, food, washing powder and many other things. In milder cases the skin breaks out in an itchy, red and blistery rash, and the face might swell up. Calcium can help, and Medrone in serious cases. In very severe allergic reactions, extensive patches of hives can occur, as can signs of shock and asphyxiation. As long as the casualty is conscious, give them plenty of calcium and Medrone. If they lose consciousness and show signs of asphyxiation, the only thing you can do is give them an intravenous injection of Medrone soluble ampoules.

Injections

Neither intramuscular nor intravenous injections are difficult. It is absolutely essential here to give practical instructions rather than a lot of theoretical description. We have already covered situations where the necessity for injections arises. For example, you

Preparing a syringe: there should be no air in it, so press lightly on the syringe holding it upwards, until a drop of fluid appears.

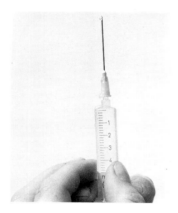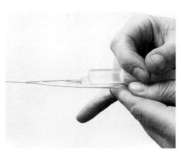

When carrying out an intravenous injection, imagine inserting the syringe in a plastic tube. In an emergency, draw the plunger back a little before injecting. If blood appears, you are in the vein. Bind the upper arm beforehand with a rubber tube.

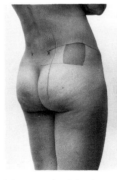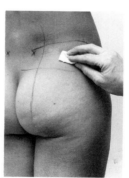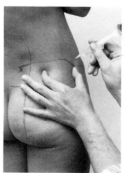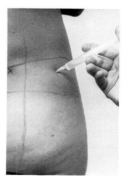

Intramuscular injections:
1 The point of injection
2 Clean the skin with an alcohol swab
3 Hold the syringe like a pencil whilst inserting it firmly
4 Slowly push the plunger in.

should never give an unconscious person liquids orally, as this will only lead to vomiting which again blocks the air passages and leads to asphyxiation. Also when diarrhoea and vomiting occur simultaneously, drugs can only be administered by injection.

An intravenous injection or even infusion is just as good for treating shock. You would be wise to take a blood substitute such as Macrodex with you. If you haven't mastered the technique of intravenous injections yourself, somebody else may come to the rescue with an infusion.

Collapse, shock, panic

Someone might **collapse** for one of several reasons: fluid deficiency, poor circulation following a feverish illness, and sometimes just from standing up quickly after bending down or from a lying position. Symptoms are blackness before the eyes, mild nausea, sweating and feeling weak. Symptoms can be so strong that consciousness will be lost very suddenly and the person will fall down heavily. It is important that the patient remains lying down. It is wrong to raise the upper body: you should in fact lift the legs above the level of the chest.

Most people regain their colour and consciousness within a few minutes. Many people who have collapsed tend to breathe very deeply and fast. If this is kept up for several minutes it can lead to severe cramp of the entire muscular system, which is easily recognised by the fingers forming a claw and an open gaping mouth. This is called a lockjaw attack (not to be confused with tetanus). A really easy way to stop attacks like this is to throw a handkerchief or jacket gently over the head. Calcium can also put a stop to these attacks.

The transition to **shock** is rapid.

Shock can be triggered by something serious such as a wound, an allergic reaction, bleeding, a heart attack or many other things. Most casualties are usually fully conscious. You can recognise shock by a cold sweat, a rapid heartbeat, pale skin and a marked drop in blood pressure which you can tell from a weak carotid pulse. The casualty's life is in danger. As well as lying the casualty flat and raising their legs, an intravenous infusion of a blood substitute can save their life. If they lose consciousness, their chances of survival are no longer great.

If somebody on board looks like going mad, you might find it necessary under the circumstances to calm them down with the help of drugs. Valium tablets are usually quite successful, and valium can be injected with force in an emergency. You can raise the dose to 40 or 60mg without running the risk of poisoning. Valium is also a tried and tested method of treating lumbago. Give the patient at least 40mg, which will of course make them very tired. In this case it is used to relax the cramped back muscles. Alcohol must not be taken at the same time.

Our list of recommended drugs purposely leaves out stimulants or so-called circulatory stimulants. There are no cases justifying their use, in fact using them gives rise to great danger. The body's self-protecting tiredness gets covered up, and after a short period of activity, the inevitable collapse is even greater. It brings to mind the death of a Danish racing cyclist during the 1960 Olympic Games in Rome, which was traced back to stimulants. Psychological reactions, the type and extent of which cannot be foreseen, but which definitely have adverse effects, are almost always caused. It can lead to overestimating your abilities, lack of discrimination and sometimes to dangerous depression.

What to do in distress

Inflatable life-rafts or life-boats should always carry a certain amount of medical aids. Since space is already confined, restrict yourself to bandages, painkillers and seasickness pills. Apart from these there is not much medically speaking you can take with you that will increase your chances of survival. You can only be advised most strongly against drinking seawater.

Any number of tests have already proved that even a small amount of seawater can lead to serious health problems, which reduce chances of survival. Only rainwater or water collected from precipitation on the foil should be drunk. In addition you should protect yourself against hypothermia, and avoid overexertion, for example from paddling.

Further reading

There are a few books which it is recommended you take with you on a long trip. They will give you some peace of mind in an emergency.

First Aid at Sea, Dr Douglas Justins & Dr Colin Berry (International Log Book)
All the appropriate information for dealing with medical emergencies on board.

First Aid Afloat, Dr Robert Haworth (Fernhurst)
Covers every eventuality with quick-reference information on immediate care, treatment of illness, survival and rescue procedures.

RORC Manual of Safety & Survival at Sea, Dag Pike (David & Charles)
Endorsed by the Royal Ocean Racing Club, the practical guide to safety precautions and dealing with emergencies, whether racing or cruising.

Safety & Survival at Sea (Greenhill Books)
Packed with eyewitness accounts of disasters at sea, this comprehensive manual covers the full range of critical situations and the essential action for survival.

Particularly in an extreme emergency – shelter in an inflatable life-raft (BFA-Pacific in this case) – the right medicines should be ready to hand. Make sure they are packed with everything else.

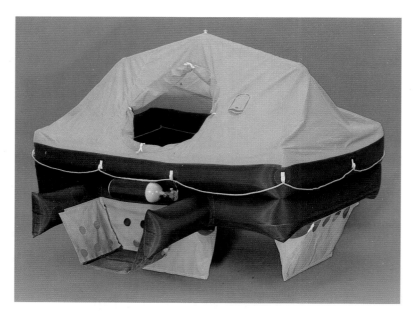

Ship's pharmacy

Karla Schenk, pharmacist

The 'mini' ship's pharmacy is just as important to an offshore cruiser's equipment as are sufficient tools and spares. There is no one single piece of advice, since the extent of the pharmacy depends on the circumstances of the trip, which must all be taken into account:

- The area the trip is taken in
- The length of the trip
- Number of crew members
- Children

First, you should be able to expect that all the crew members will join the trip in perfect health. If anyone suffers from a particular illness (such as diabetes, asthma or migraine) they will obviously have to bring their own medications with them.

The ship's pharmacy should be kept in a watertight plastic container, cool and easily accessible, for example against the hull below the water-line.

You must check your medicine box at regular intervals, and always at the beginning of the season and before a longer trip. You must check that it is complete, and that the medicines are in perfect condition. Some preparations have an expiry date printed on them (such as penicillins), so in this case it is easy to tell. But how can you be sure that the other medicines meet the regulations?

When should they be replaced by new medicines? The most important signs are:

- Tablets have disintegrated, the coating of sugar-coated pills is greasy or has flaked off
- Discolouring of tablets or solutions
- Precipitation or coagulation in clear solutions, liquids or drops
- Change in odour
- Ointments or emulsions, usually in homogeneous form, have decomposed.

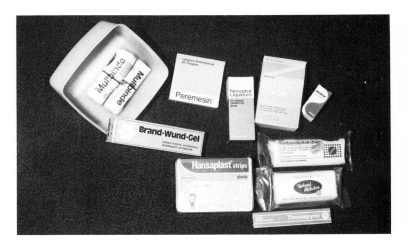

Throw them away if you see these warning signs. If you want to buy medicines abroad at a later stage, show the pharmacist the packaging and the instructions inside. From that, they will be able to see the chemical composition and sell you the corresponding preparation.

The following suggestion is for a yacht with a crew of 3–4 people, for a trip in, say, the North Sea, English Channel, Mediterranean or the Caribbean, where you can reach a harbour in 2–3 days in an emergency. The following checklist has boxes to tick off, so you can be sure that the medicines are all there.

The 'mini' ship's pharmacy should always be ready to hand on the bridge deck, even on a short trip.

Complete ship's pharmacy for a long trip; all the medicines fit in a plastic box.

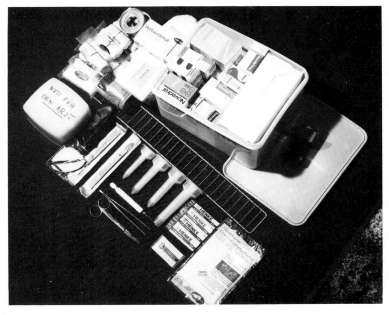

Medication

Medicine	Application
Valium tablets 2mg	Nervousness, insomnia
Voltarol Dispersible 50mg	Inflammation, swelling
Amoxil 500mg capsules	Infections of ear nose & throat region, skin, air passages, mouth, teeth & jaw areas
Penbritin injections 250mg	Infections of air passages, urinary tract & bile duct, blood poisoning
Benylin	Flu, fever, chesty coughs
Buscopan tablets Buscopan ampoules	Colic, cramps (gallbladder, kidneys)
Tyrozets	Sore throat
Dulco-lax	Constipation
Gelusil antacid tablets	Gastric complaints, stomach ulcers
Germolene cream	Boils
Imodium	Severe diarrhoea
Charcoal tablets	Diarrhoea
Lasonil cream	Sprains, bruises & contusions, piles
Betadine solution 500ml or Savlon liquid	Disinfection of wounds
Glycerol trinitrate tablets	Angina (pectoris)
Maxolon tablets	Severe vomiting
Maxolon syrup	Colic, cramps
Meclozine tablets	Seasickness
Stemetil suppositories 5mg	Severe vomiting
Rhinospray	Colds
Sandocal tablets	Allergies, itching
Panadol	Pain (headaches)
Chloromycetin ointment	Severe conjunctivitis, styes
DF 118 elixir and ampoules	Severe pain
Cyklokapron	Internal bleeding of the stomach, intestines & bladder, & nosebleeds
Otrivine-Antistin	Conjunctivitis
Savlon cream	Burns, sun-burn, grazes, insect bites

Instruments

1 thermometer

10 disposable gloves, steriles, large

1 pair tweezers

1 disposable scalpel

10 wound clips

1 pair dressing scissors

10×5ml disposable syringes

5×20ml disposable syringes

1 Safar tube

1 disposable catheter

100 ml isopropylalcohol 70% in a plastic bottle

Dressing materials

1 triangular bandage

50g cotton wool

3 large, 3 medium first aid kits

Dressing gauze, 1m

1 Lohmann Metalline bandage 60×80 cm

3 packets Metalline bandages

10 porous sticking plasters

Elastoplast strip in 5 sizes

Leukoflex 5m $\times$ 2.5 cm, 5m $\times$ 5cm (also for pressure bandage)

Gauze bandages 2×6cm, 2×8cm, 2×10cm

Ideal bandages 1×8cm, 1×10cm

1 eye-patch

Leather finger-cover, 1 each sizes 5 and 3

3 aluminium tubes, 25cm long, which may be inserted into each other

Safety pins

Drugs to be administered by the doctor only	
Medicine	**Application**
Marodex or other plasma expander in normal saline	Shock
Xylocaine with adrenalin 1:200,000	Local anaesthetic
Isoprenaline hydrochloride 6 × 2ml	Collapse, shock
Solu-Medrone	Severe allergy, insect sting inside the throat

A charter yacht in an idyllic bay in Turkey.

Keep drugs and bandaging materials which are in frequent use ready to hand on the bridge deck: first aid kit, adhesive strip (doubles as a pressure bandage), sticking plasters, gauze bandages, Betadine solution, sun block, painkillers and most important of all seasickness pills. This mini-pharmacy is also sufficient for day trips.

For longer trips you should also take with you drugs which only a doctor should handle. It is always possible that you will meet a medic on your island or receive advice over the ship's radio about how to administer these preparations yourselves. For practical purposes keep the 'doctor's medicines' in a separate small tupperware container clearly labelled 'Only to be handled by the doctor'. To avoid using them by mistake, seal the box.

If you are going to the tropics, your pharmacy should contain a malaria prophylactic and salt tablets for electrolyte balance. Dragees and capsules easily become unusable in the heat. You can cool down suppositories before use in water, in their container. The Institute of Tropical Medicine also provides leaflets on this.

If you have small children on board you will also need:
- Amoxil
- Penbritin
- Junifen syrup
- Imodium drops.

You could also keep a torch in your first aid box, attached to the lid, in case of emergency, but make sure you change the batteries every year.

You should consider very carefully where you are going to store your drugs, particularly in the tropics. Drugs are almost always sensitive to heat and it is difficult on board a cruising yacht to store them in a cool place. You can compromise by putting them in a box near the water-line, so that at least the temperature does not exceed 28°C.

Tools and spares

Probably the best advice that I received before sailing round the world was to take as many tools with me as possible. Even if you don't know how to use them you may meet somebody who does. I paid less for my entire tool kit than the equivalent of a single sheet winch. There are thankfully no special tools for yachts, so you can go into a department store to buy them like any other ordinary mortal. It is therefore astonishing how some sailors are so badly kitted out with tools, particularly when you consider the safety of the boat can depend on having the right tools. You can pay up to hundreds of pounds for an anemometer, which is not entirely necessary on a cruising yacht, and not have enough money left for a complete set of ring spanners at about £15 ($22).

You will naturally have to choose your tools according to your type of boat, as it would be stupid to buy a 32mm spanner if there are no nuts and bolts that size on the whole boat. On the other hand you will need to have double the amount of spanners on board if you're unlucky enough to use metric spanners and find that the machinery in the engine-room is made in England and is equipped only with screws in inch sizes. For this reason the following list is not exhaustive, and is only meant to give you a rough idea for choosing tools. It is meant for particularly long trips, although you need not strike too many items off it for shorter ones.

Tools

2 sets of spanners

The first set should consist of ring spanners, which have the advantage of needing very little space to turn a screw – very useful in the cramped conditions on board. If you have less than 60° to turn a bolt with an open-ended spanner, you have to twist the spanner round again fully the next time. You can loosen bolts which are stuck more easily with ring spanners, incidentally, as they cannot open as open-ended spanners often do when applying a lot of force, and slip off the bolt head, usually breaking them. Avoid adjustable spanners for this reason, even if they appear practical, because you can easily break the bolt head with them.

1 set of socket spanners
A rubber hammer
Pliers
1 large pipe wrench
2 flat nosed pliers
1 hack saw
2 mole wrenches

These are the most versatile tools on board. You just need a lot of strength to press the mole grips together, and they stay shut by themselves. They have many uses, eg taking the place of a crank which has gone overboard; unscrewing a screw head which someone has burred with a screwdriver;

The propeller-shaft is secured temporarily with a mole wrench.

preventing the propeller-shaft from slipping out if it has loosened itself from the flange, and more.

2 hammers

One of these must have a slightly rounded head.

Drill

If you have only a hand-operated drill, remember that you will often not have enough room to turn it in the cramped corners in the boat. You would be better off with an electric one. For very little money (about £20/$30) you can buy ones which are meant for use with a car's 12 volt battery, and which you can use just as well on board. They are very easy to manage and much stronger than your hands, and are usually sold with an 8mm chuck. You should try to get a chuck up to 10mm.

It would obviously be ideal if you could use a really powerful drill like ones you use at home for do-it-yourself. Electricity from either the shore or a generator is, however, a prerequisite. If you use a small Honda generator, you must remember that the small E 300 produces barely 300W, so you must buy a 250W drill. Naturally you should have high performance drill bits of all sizes on board. Small drill bits break easily if they are used by inexperienced people, which is the case on board.

A rivet gun

A wood saw

Handsaw and fretsaw with the appropriate saw-blades.

Vice

One of the most important tools, even though you seldom need it. But when you do use it you really have to depend on it. In an emergency you can file any piece of metal into shape with the aid of a vice in an isolated cove or even on the high sea. Setting it up will always be a bit of a problem. On small yachts you will usually find it possible to set the vice up on a step of the companionway. Put a board in between before you screw the vice on, in order not to damage the wood.

Metal shears
A sharp knife
A razor blade

Left: a battery-powered drill.

Screw clamp
Thread cutter
Chisel

Screwdrivers in all sizes. To be on the safe side take one or two screwdrivers for cross-head screws.

Files
Take these on board in all shapes and sizes. Remember that you will be working with steel as well as wood.

Scissors
These must be made of stainless steel and should be fitted with teeth. This is the only way to avoid slippery material sliding out of the scissors.

Shroud-cutters
These must be able to cut stainless steel wire to the thickness of the thickest shrouds. When you buy them, make sure you find out how many mm of stainless steel they will cut.

Blowlamp
This is a very practical item, powered by a small gas canister, which can also be used to fill gas lighters.

Lubricant/oil
Important for loosening rusted screws or threads which are stuck. You can also use diesel in an emergency. Usually, 'for electrical equipment' will be printed on the can, but I would advise against using this lubricant or rust prevention for this purpose. There are special things for sensitive electronics on board, which should only be used for electronic purposes. Whether this is effective is disputed.

Once when I sprayed my radio on the inside, it gave no sound at all any more. The oil had formed a thin film in the capacitors (a protective layer) which changed the space between the two plates. A lengthy adjustment was necessary. I have in fact used this oil since, but been very careful not to let it come into contact with capacitors. The oil evaporates anyway after a couple of months and so loses its effect.

Oil can
Grease gun
Sewing machine oil

Epoxy glue
This can be used for protecting screw threads as well as acting as a sealant which does not burn off in the exhaust.

Epoxy resin
You can't keep this any longer than about a year.

Plastic steel
This is also sold as 'cold weld'. It is nothing more than synthetic glue to which other fillers are added to reach a particular firmness. In no way does it reach the strength of metal, which you can easily tell if you use a file.

Superglue
This is one of those marvellous glues which promise everything. If you take just a drop between your thumb and index finger and hold them together for about 15 seconds, you won't be able to get them apart without tearing the skin. These glues are also used to stick wire cables in their terminals. The price is a disadvantage, as is the fact that in hot climates they don't last very long.

Adhesive
Pattex or Uhu.

Silicon rubber
Unlike natural rubber, this sealing compound doesn't age, and stays elastic forever. The disadvantage is that it doesn't stick to synthetic materials, and only to wood if the surface is treated first.

Vaseline
To grease battery contacts, and eggs,

which will then stay fresh for up to three months.

Tallow
This serves to grease lines or sheets which run constantly under strain over blocks.

Talcum powder
For rubbing into rubber seals on hatches and windows.

Sellotape

Insulating tape
You can also wrap this round open split pins on the shroud tensioners to protect yourself from injury.

Chewing gum
Not only for long night watches, but also to tighten a screw with a screwdriver when there isn't enough room for your fingers (or provisionally seal small leaks).

Waterproof smudgeless pen
These will write on any background, eg the time the oil was changed on the engine; numbers on parts of the starter, so that you can build it back together again in the right order; the turning direction next to the winches on the mast, etc.

Soldering irons
You can buy these in car accessory shops. The best thing to do is to clamp it onto the battery contacts when you need it. Of course you can also use a soldering iron which has been heated on an open fire, and a spirit or paraffin stove is sufficient for this. You must never poke about in electrical wiring with a soldering iron like this, as transistors and diodes are extremely heat-sensitive. The same goes for a soldering iron which is powered by a gas canister similar to those on the blow-lamp described above. These soldering irons are only usable for rough kinds of work, such as in areas where stray heat will not cause any damage. You will obviously need to take solder flux with you as well, containing the necessary soldering grease.

Tweezers (*pointed and flat*)
Hand mirror
Magnifying glass

Voltmeter or universal gauge
These are available in department stores from about £10 ($15). If you are not electronically minded, a cheap universal gauge is enough for use on board. An instrument with an indicator is better than one with a digital display.

Corks and rubber stoppers
For sealing possible small leaks. A set of rubber stoppers in different sizes is particularly good for this, and these should be found in every life-raft. If you go to a service station you can buy a set for very little money.

Sealing stoppers from an inflatable life-raft.

Sewing machine
This must be able to do zig-zag stitching if you are to use it for sewing sails. It is difficult to find a machine like this at a flea market, and modern machines raise the problem of electricity again. Over and above that the machine must be very strong to sew through sails. You can therefore hardly use it for this purpose, and it is best to resort to sewing by hand. However, if there is enough room, a sewing machine is always useful.

Adhesive tape
For makeshift repairs to the sails. Some modern tape, such as carpet or gaffer tape, has remarkable sticking power. Before you use it make sure that the surfaces are as dry and free of grease as possible. Incidentally its ability to stick can drop significantly in cold weather.

Tape measure

Diving mask and snorkel

Very important, because if you really want to master your boat, you must be in a position to go overboard to find out if there is something wrong. It is difficult to get round to cleaning the underwater part of the boat before setting off on long voyages. You can clean a 10m boat with a hard brush in about two hours on your own. But make no mistake, working on a moving boat on high seas is impossible, even for top athletes.

Wet suit

This is a very expensive 'tool' but it is recommended that you acquire one even if you are staying mainly in warm waters. You are only fit for action underwater with a wet suit. With one of these you can deal with your problems (rudder, propeller, speedometer, echosounder etc) for hours even in cold-water harbours.

Rubber gloves

Diving lamp

This is a help not only when you are unfortunate enough to have to go underwater at night to fix something. (Under no circumstances go underwater at night with a lamp if there is even the slightest possibility that there are sharks in the area). Often the range of these unwieldy lamps is overestimated. Even in quite clear waters you will not be able to see further at night than about 2m. But an underwater lamp is also a useful aid at night on board. The average torch usually lets you down very fast in bad weather and a lot of rain. The best thing is a floating diving lamp, which you can throw down to a person who has fallen overboard in the night, so that you can note the place through the beam.

Hose (about 30m long)

If you are filling your fresh water tank, it is often easier and less of a risk to attach a hose than to tie the boat up at the quay.

Folding bicycle

I would only take one of these with me if there was a lot of extra space. All harbours are on sea level, so it is usually uphill to the town centre.

A practical hose needs very little storage space.

Folding motorbike on board.

A surf board stowed on the rail takes up no room.

Small motorbike

This poses many problems: petrol on board, and questions of licensing and insuring. It is often easier and cheaper in the end to hire one each time you feel you need one.

Windsurf board

Although there is no need for one on a yacht over 10m long, it is a pleasant diversion in more southerly stretches, it needs no maintenance, is easy to stow on the rail and the sail can also be used as a sunshade.

Spares and reserves

Insulated copper wire

In different thicknesses for electrical work.

Stainless steel screws

In all possible sizes – better too many than too few.

Wood screws

Size and material depends on the inner panelling of the boat. If brass screws have been used, you must definitely have the same type in the right size on board. Brass screws corrode over a longer period in salt water, even if they are kept in a supposedly dry place. The screwdriver will no longer be able to grip the surface, so you are better off replacing them with new brass screws.

Stainless steel wire
Brass wire
Wire cable Stainless steel (small bits in 1, 2 and 3mm thickness).
Split pins in all sizes

Elastic springs

You will find all sorts in a hardware shop. They are usually made of a metal which rusts, but they can nevertheless be built into equipment for a short time, if one loses an important spring overboard when taking something apart.

Spare batteries

For all electrical appliances on board. For electronic gadgets make sure you use only leak-proof batteries, but these can only be stored for a certain length of time. Batteries in electrical appliances must be checked from time to time in their storage position. Even so-called leak-proof batteries can spring leaks and almost certainly destroy an appliance. Alkaline batteries last the longest, but are not suitable for torches.

Spare bulbs

For every light on board.

Spare sockets

Particularly for the navigation lights, where the sockets corrode because they get damaged the most by salt water.

Fuses

Many electronic appliances have their own fuse built into the casing.

2 Norseman terminals

In an emergency you can make a new shroud with these along with the wire cable. You must therefore have wire cable at least as long as the longest shroud or stay on board.

Notched loop

Stainless steel wire up to 6mm can be reliably worked with the 'Nauti Press', which has been used on American yachts for years. It is used for things such as shock cords, halyards, railings and emergency rig, and is one of the most all-purpose tools on board.

Shroud tensioner

For each type on board there must be at least one spare tensioner.

Bulldog grips

With these you can make an eye in the wire cable if need be.

Wooden plank About 40 × 200cm

A loose plank doesn't look very attractive on board a neat boat, and it would

There are many uses on board for a simple wooden board: gangway, table, work surface, protection against waves . . .

cause a few laughs to see one lying around on deck. An ordinary wooden plank with a couple of holes drilled in the corners is however of universal use, eg: a substitute for a chic gangway; you can use it as a float on the fenders on the side planking; if you lay it diagonally across the cockpit it makes a very comfortable dining table (which you can make more homely with a tablecloth); in an emergency you can use it to protect against waves in front of the cabin windows and if there is a catastrophe you can make a spare rudder blade from it.

Rings and blocks In all possible sizes.

Light cylinder For old petrol lamps.

Spare burners For the stove.

Sailing gloves

Rubber loops and the necessary hooks, ropes, hinges, tackle thread, canvas (2m sq is enough), stay rider, mast slider.

Sail needles protected from rust, by keeping different sizes of these in a screw-top jar filled with oil.

Sailmaker's palm.

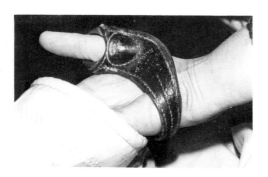

Alternator
If your alternator breaks down, you will certainly not be able to mend it afloat, so take a spare. If your engine drives an old-fashioned dynamo, giving direct current, the brushes will need to be replaced every three years.

Spare generator parts
These should be recommended by the manufacturers. You should take with you an oil filter, a drive for the water pump or better still a new water pump, and above all a spare gasket. For a diesel engine you must take lots of injectors (according to the number of cylinders) which are ready to instal. If you have a petrol engine it is imperative that you take spark plugs, points and an ignition coil.

Drive-belts
Fuel filters
Stainless steel hose-clips

Spare pump parts for all pumps on board, including the toilet. Neoprene membranes in particular last only one or two years in salt water.

If the skipper more or less follows this list, he will gather all sorts of odds and ends. Not that it would take up much room, the danger lies more in the parts disappearing somewhere in the corner. It is therefore highly recommended that you draw up a list giving the places where everything is kept, in which every spare part is painstakingly listed. Keep the tools in a tool box in a place where they are easily reached. You will need the tools much more often than you think.

This Fein generator produces 220 volts from batteries; ideal for short running times.

266

Hints and Tips

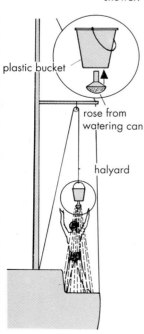

Topping lift

It often happens that the topping lift becomes too loose when the boom lifts, particularly on broad reaches, and catches on the backstay ball. This is a nuisance, if you find you have to use the topping lift in order to reef. To avoid this, you simply need to tauten a length of shock cord parallel to the topping lift, about 2m in length. This will keep the topping lift taut. The cord will last for two years in ultraviolet light.

A hose attached to the boom is an ideal freshwater shower on deck without any installation costs.

Temporary fresh water shower.

plastic bucket

rose from watering can

halyard

aerial ball

topping lift

topping lift

backstay

shock cord

topping lift

Drinking water

This is precious, but even so no one need go without a freshwater shower on deck. All you need is the rose from a watering can and a cheap plastic bucket. It is incredible how far 5 litres of water go.

Echo sounder

If you buy a new echo sounder, you can instal it temporarily if you don't have the opportunity to take your boat out of the water. This is because it also works inside a wooden or plastic boat if the sensor is close to the hull , and is surrounded by water. It is easy to test, by lowering the transmitter to the bottom of the bilge. However, it is best not to keep it there permanently because it does reduce its sensitivity.

Binoculars

These will get ruined quite fast on board, because they are used in all kinds of weather. It is all too easy to put them back in their case without cleaning off saltwater spray. It is therefore possibly cheaper to buy a cheap but good Japanese pair every 3 years. If you try them out before you buy them, you should buy exactly that pair, not another which is still in its packaging. It needs a lot of practice to be comfortable using binoculars on a magnification of ten, and it is probably better to stay on a lower scale than this.

Films and taking photographs

Temperamental on board. Without a wide-angle lens you shouldn't bother. Scarcely a single amateur is able to capture the weather or rough seas. If the observer sees the horizon as a straight line, he will assume wind-force three at most. That is why you should only photograph high seas in the trough of a wave.

When videoing, try to keep the horizon as closely parallel as possible to the top of the picture (similar to measuring the height of the sun), or best of all film on a tripod.

Unfortunately, almost all optical apparatus is particularly sensitive to damp and to seawater, which is why really dramatic pictures in bad weather are so rare. The best thing would seem to be underwater cameras, but these are mostly expensive and unwieldy. A good and cheap solution is to buy an underwater camera bag, which is available for all types of camera from super 8 to 6cm × 7cm). The manufacturer (Goedecke, Munich) guarantees watertightness down to 10m. Much more expensive is the small Nikonos camera, which is watertight up to 50m deep without protective casing.

But a danger lies within your valuable camera in the dark, a fungus which likes to grow in the glass of the lens. It thrives only on the damp and dark and covers the lens with a very fine net like a cobweb. The lens is then ruined as the fungus cannot be removed. As a precaution keep the camera in a dry place with lots of ultraviolet light. This is why cameras should be opened up to the air every so often, or even put in direct sunlight. The best place to keep them is in a sealed aluminium case or in a tupperware container, with a little linen bag full of silica gel. If this chemical turns pink, it is full of moisture and can be heated up on the stove until it turns dark blue again.

Polaroid camera with flash

This can be a great help if emergency repairs have to be carried out on complicated equipment which you don't really know much about. For example, if you photograph the open injection pump before dismantling it, you have a greater chance of putting it back together successfully. Close-ups are also possible with Polaroids.

Cassette recorder

This is indispensable for navigation as you can play back foreign language weather forecasts and decipher them at your leisure. You don't necessarily have to write your diary as a spoken account is much more alive. Letters home are much more interesting and thorough if they are taped rather than written down. Once you have overcome your shyness in front of the microphone, a 'letter' is drawn up very quickly.

A tape recorder is much better for playing music than a radio because reception of music stations is very bad even just a few miles from shore. A personal stereo helps enormously to pass a boring night watch in the cockpit. Cassette recorders are all sensitive to damp, but they will go on for years if they don't get damaged with a lot of sea water.

Television

Up until only a few years ago, a television on board a small yacht would have been thought an excessive luxury. But times have changed, and today there are mini TV sets hardly any bigger than a cassette recorder which have a straightforward power supply. They are not only good for entertainment in harbour, but also provide information. A television weather map is far more instructive than a spoken radio weather forecast. Make sure that your television is designed to receive various wavelengths, since with your TV from home you won't be able to receive foreign stations even from as near to home as Spain.

Video recorder

Don't turn up your nose at a small video recorder which you connect to a 12-volt battery. What you want is a video recorder which works off a car battery. A video will enrich life on board, particularly on a long voyage. Your friends can bring you the latest from home most impressively if they record the news or sport headlines. You will also have time to watch an old film on transoceanic passages or on days which have been rained off at anchor.

You should have a VHS recorder, as this is the most common type. But be careful, as foreign television sets won't allow you to play tapes even if they show the VHS sign. Video recorders are sensitive to damp like any other electronic equipment. Unlike cassette recorders, they are too expensive to change every few years, so it is best to afford yourself the luxury of a video recorder only on a really dry boat.

Camcorder

A video recorder has the same uses as a cassette recorder, but even more so. You could not make an account more alive than by videoing it as opposed to writing a boring letter. But this isn't

A watertight underwater camera bag for interesting photos in bad weather.

the only possible use. In the same way that you can use a Polaroid camera for photographing defective equipment, you can document a fault more impressively, such as a badly-set sail, water in the bilge, or smoke from the engine exhaust as proof of faulty equipment. All camcorders can be used instead of video recorders. A log book in moving pictures has the greatest sentimental value. Waterproof video cameras are already on the market, just made for the harsh life on yachts!

Fishing
Don't be under any illusions about the success you can have fishing. The Mediterranean has been emptied of fish over the last 3,000 years, so it isn't worth a try there. I have had bad experiences on the oceans with expensive reels (supposedly suitable for fishing at sea) as they were mostly too small. The Polynesians showed me how to do it: lay out 100m of nylon rope at least 1mm thick on board, put a steel cast and then a tuna bait (made in Japan) on the other end. The greatest chance you have of a bite is at dusk. Use a winch, as it will usually be a large fish such as mackerel or tuna.

Hand lead
You must have a hand lead on board as well as an echo sounder, because the latter could break down, and you can sound the depths of a narrow passage or around the boat if it is stuck, in the dinghy. A digital hand lead is even more practical.

The top of the mast
No member of the crew likes to go up here, but the rigging must be checked regularly. The cheapest and not the worst bo'sun's chair is made of a plank of hardwood (20 × 50 cm) which hangs from all four corners. It is more comfortable to work with than the 'posh' American ones which are like a trapeze, because you can move more

Use the bo'sun's seat for working on the mast even though there are rungs.

freely on the plank. Only go up with a safety belt on, which should be secured above the crosstrees to the chair and to the mast. There are metal rungs on the mast, to clear a halyard above quickly, or to look over the horizon.

Towed logs
Despite the electronics on board, the reliable old towed log will probably not be replaced. One great disadvantage of them is that the propeller towed behind is bitten off from time to time. If you dip the last few metres of the propeller line in epoxy resin, the rope becomes hard as rock, and fish will hardly be interested in it.

Dry dock
If so much vegetation has grown on the underside of the boat that its manoeuvrability and speed have been impaired significantly, you will have to take the boat out of the water. If you haven't worked with the shipyard in question before, you will have to give them a drawing to scale of the underside of the boat, or at least mark the beginning and end of the keel with tape on deck. Unfortunately, amateurs are not in a position to check the manufacturer's instructions about expensive underwater paints. Once when I ran out of paint a sympathetic fisherman gave me some dirt cheap antifouling paint which I used to finish it. This was much more effective, as one look at the underside after nine months showed. If you aren't fanatical about speed, leaving out unnecessary polishing will make work on the underside much easier. Scraping and brushing down, and washing with fresh water is enough, because the little bits of vegetation left behind act as an excellent key for the new paint.

Sea water for washing
Towels become stiff as a board, and pillows scratchy. You can beat and shake the salt crystals out more or less

270

completely, so if need be you can also use salt water for washing.

Sailing knife

Sometimes it is necessary to cut a rope in a matter of seconds. The sailing knife is usually under the oilskins. A seawater-proof diving knife with a sheath kept at the foot of the mast gives extra safety.

Stove

In an emergency when you run out of paraffin you can use your primus with pure diesel. It doesn't burn very cleanly,

but it works. You can even use diesel as a replacement for spirit for pre-heating if you wrap a broad wick which you have soaked in diesel beforehand around the burner. It produces a lot of smoke, but it's preferable to cold food. Warm up the cabin with the primus by using bricks which have been held over the flame.

But be careful: If there is no fresh air coming through, there is danger of poisoning with naked flames. The hatch should always be open. Condensation occurs as well.

Before taking a boat out of the water or entering dry dock, you must have plans of the underside.

271

Certificates and sailing clubs

The RYA training and certification scheme

Since more and more people are seeking pleasure and relaxation on the water, it is inevitable that it will become more crowded even on the open sea, and governments will not be able to avoid intervening even in leisure yachting. When I sailed round the world, I was not asked for my licence in any harbour I visited. These are surely times that will shortly belong to the past. In the Mediterranean, some countries have already gone over to a system whereby the skipper of an offshore yacht is required to prove his ability by producing an official certificate. France and Germany, for instance, have quite complicated systems of driving licences for skippers of powered craft.

In the UK, RYA certification schemes are graded: Competent Crew is the simplest, leading through Day Skipper, Coastal and Offshore up to Ocean Skipper. These are not yet a legal requirement (except for the purchase of certain sorts of radio transmission equipment) but they are highly recommended, even if you only intend harbour-hopping around these shores. This book does not contain enough information about the law, buoys or lights to act as preparation for the certificate, and you are advised to refer to the Royal Yachting Association brochure G4 for further details.

SSCA

The monthly Bulletins from the Seven Seas Cruising Association are probably the most valuable source of information about offshore cruising. You can only become a member of this exclusive club if you have spent a continuous year on a yacht. You then have to send accounts of your trips on a regular basis to the SSCA, where they are collected, printed and sent to all the members. Non-members can also receive them for a small fee.

It is also possible to obtain articles from past publications. There are accounts covering almost every place on earth where a yacht has been, especially written for yachties. Eric Hiscock, or Irving Johnson, who sailed round the world seven times, owe some magical anchorages to the SSCA's bulletins. Their address is: Seven Seas Cruising Association, Inc., 521 South Andrews Avenue, Suite 8, Fort Lauderdale, Florida 33301-2844 USA.

Magazines about offshore cruising

The American magazine *Sail* is the best. English magazines such as *Yachting World*, *Yachts and Yachting* and *Yachting Monthly* are very interesting in large part because of their classified advertisements. The sailing suppliers who advertise in them captivate you not only with the prices but also with the variety of offers. You can find yachting magazines at all major stations and large newsagents.

Offshore cruising shops

You will be able to find most things you need for offshore cruising in any shop that sells sailing equipment. A mail-order service based in Germany, and owned by round-the-world yachtsman Klaus Hympendahl, will supply all those odd specialised bits of equipment which even good chandlers tend not to stock, from irons which work without electricity to hand-driven desalination machines. The address: Blue Water GmbH, Im Rottfeld 23, 40239 Düsseldorf.

On the Atlantic under twin stay sails.

273

Opposite page: Sunbeam
37 (11.45m) from Schöchl:
an offshore yacht from
Austria, big enough for two
people to sail around the
world in.

Solutions

All exercises refer to the year 1975. From Q7 use the navigation table on the practice chart.

1 a) 41° 13.3′ N; 13° 04.2′ E
   b) 40° 54.5′ N; 12° 57.3′ E
   c) 40° 49.8′ N; 14° 25.7′ E
   d) 41° 00.7′ N; 13° 55.6′ E
   e) 40° 38.2′ N; 14° 36.7′ E

2 43.4 nautical miles

3 $(5 \times 0.5) - 11 =$ **−9°**

4
course	328°
var	+9°
compass course	337°

5
compass course	74°	
var	−9°	presumed position of boat: 40° 55.7′ N; 13° 04.3′ E
course	65°	

6 bearing: 344°
Example for 10°:
true bearing	344°	deviation curve
var	+9°	and navigation table on the practice chart
	353°	
compass bearing	−351°	
dev	+ 2°	

7
course	269°	
var	+9°	
	278°	
dev	+1°	(deviation for 280° = −1°, but will be wrong with the wrong sign)
compass course	**279°**	

8
course	282°
var	+9°
	291°
drift	+5°
dev	+3°
compass course	**299°**

9 $\dfrac{13 \times 164}{7 \times 145} = 2.1$ nautical miles;
compass course	114°	
dev	−3°	(compass course 300°!)
var	−9°	
	102°	

Ship's position: 40° 43.0′ N; 13° 48.6′ E

10
compass course	20°	Log:	49.47
dev	+3°		−44.37
var	−9°		
drift	−10°		5.10 nautical miles
course	004°		

Ship's position: 40° 48.2′ N; 13° 49.0′ E

11
Complementary angle	90°	compass course	125°	
	−65°	dev	+3°	(compass course = 20°)
	25°	var	−9°	
			119°	

Ship's position as 10.

12   compass course   67°   Log: 59.75

    var   –9°   –53.25

                                    6.50   nautical miles covered

    true bearing   58°

    Ship's position: 40° 58.3′ N; 13° 50.5′ E

---

13   compass course   10°

    dev   +2°   Ship's position: 41° 06.2′ N; 13° 49.7′ E

    var   –9°   Anchor ground: mud

                 003°

---

14   a) 41° 00.9′ N; 13° 17.7′ E

    b) Log: 91.87

             –67.01

             24.86   nautical miles: 5 hours = 5 knots

15

	Zannone	Capo Circeo	Gaeta St. Erasmo
bearing disc	330°	58°	164°
compass course	+270°	–270°	+270°
	600°	328°	434°
var	–9°	–9°	–9°
	591°	319°	425°
dev from 270	0°	0°	0°
	–360°		–360°
true bearing	231°	319°	65°

    Ship's position: 41° 04.7′ N; 13° 13.8′ E

---

16   5 nautical miles

17   1 Kn; 321°

18   227.5°

19   From current triangle:

    true course through the water   217°

    var   +9°

                                226°

    dev   –5°

    compass course   221°

---

20   a) From current triangle: 5.8 Kn

    b) $\dfrac{116.2}{5.8} \times 60 = 168$ minutes

        expected time of arrival: 02.48 hours

---

21   compass bearing   62°

    dev   +4°

    var   –9°

    true bearing   57°

                      90° 00′

    declination   +18° 07′

                     108° 07′

    measured angle   –67° 16′

                     40° 51′

    TL   –13′

    Latitude   40° 38′

    Ship's position: 40° 38′ N; 13° 41.7′ E

22
$$359°\ 60'$$
$$-9°\ 09'$$
GA $\overline{350°\ 51'}$
GHA $-343°\ 25.4'$ (= 11 o'clock)
$\overline{7°\ 25.6'}$ (= 29 min 42 s)
$\overline{\qquad 11\ hours\quad 29\ min\ 42\ s}$

23
$$90°$$
$$+18°\ 07'$$
$$-68°\ 44'$$
$$-13'$$
Lat $\overline{39°\ 10'}$ N

---

24 Measurement 1   10h 28min 38s
Measurement 2   +12h 28min 24s
$\overline{22h\ 57min\ 02s} \div 2 = 11h\ 28min\ 31s$

GHA for 11 hours   343° 25.4'
Increase for 28min 31s   +7° 07.8'
$\overline{350°\ 33.2'}$
$$90°\ 00' \qquad\qquad -360°$$
$$+18°\ 07' \qquad\qquad \overline{9°\ 26.8'\ E}$$
$$-67°\ 10'$$
$$-13'$$
$\overline{40°\ 44'}$ N

---

25 a) 40°32.7' N; 13° 58.8' E
   b) Lat: 41° N; decl: 18° N; (18° 08' N)
     GHA   313° 25.4'
     Increase   +7° 28.8'
$\overline{320°\ 54.2'}$
         +14° 05.8'   (nearest easting, to get integer LHA)
      LHA = $\overline{335°\ 00.0'}$
   c) computed altitude   58° 34'
     declination correction   6' (Azimuth = 130°)
$\overline{58°\ 40'}$

   d)   58° 41'
     TL   +13'
$\overline{58°\ 54'}$
$$-58°\ 40'$$
     measured altitude = $\overline{14'}$
   e) towards
   f) 41° 00' N; 14° 05.8' E

---

26 compass reading   146°   LHA at 9.30 GMT 335°
    var   −9°   at 9.46 (1° more LHA per 4 miles) 339°
    dev (from 280°)   −1°
$\overline{136°}$
Azimuth from HO 249: 136°
Navigational chart is correct for this course

---

27   90°
$$+18°\ 07'$$
$$-67°\ 21'$$
$$-13'$$
$\overline{40°\ 33'}$ N

---

28 Log: 26.44
$$-18.54$$
$\overline{-7.90}$ nautical miles covered, course 273°
Noon position: 40° 33' N; 13° 49.2' E

Opposite page: La Rochelle/Atlantic – gateway to the world.

279

1 Position line according to HO 249 tables

Estimated latitude	Estimated longitude	Date	UT1	Measured angle

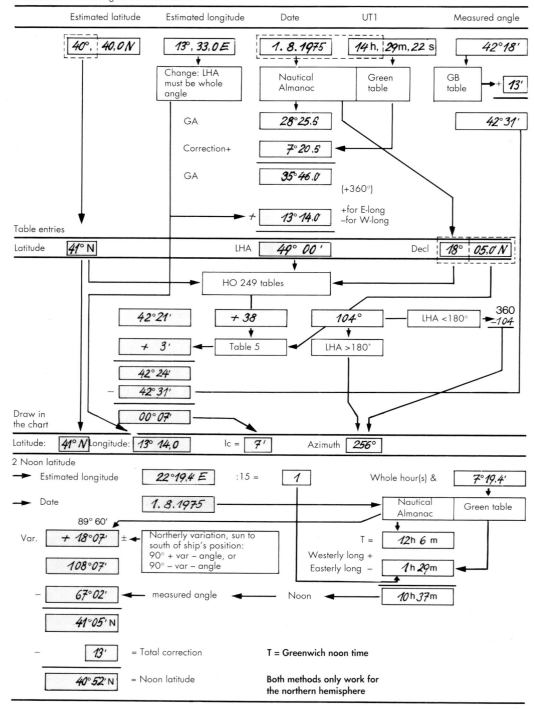

Estimated latitude: 40°, 40,0 N

Estimated longitude: 13°, 33,0 E

Change: LHA must be whole angle

Date: 1. 8. 1975

UT1: 14 h, 29 m, 22 s

Measured angle: 42°18'

Nautical Almanac

Green table

GB table → + 13'

GA 28°25,5

Correction+ 7°20,5

GA 35°46,0

42°31'

(+360°)

+ 13°14,0   +for E-long −for W-long

Table entries

Latitude 41° N   LHA 49° 00'   Decl 18° 05,0 N

HO 249 tables

42°21'   + 38   104°   LHA <180°   360 −104

+ 3' ← Table 5 ←   LHA >180°

42°24'

− 42°31'

Draw in the chart

00°07'

Latitude: 41° N   Longitude: 13° 14,0   lc = 7'   Azimuth 256°

2 Noon latitude

→ Estimated longitude   22°19,4 E   :15 = 1   Whole hour(s) &   7°19,4'

→ Date   1. 8. 1975

Nautical Almanac   Green table

89° 60'

Var. + 18°07' ±   Northerly variation, sun to south of ship's position: 90° + var − angle, or 90° − var − angle

T = 12h 6 m

108°07'

Westerly long +   Easterly long −   1h 29m

− 67°02' ← measured angle ← Noon ← 10h 37m

41°05' N

− 13' = Total correction

40°52' N = Noon latitude

T = Greenwich noon time

Both methods only work for the northern hemisphere

Important sailing terms – list of abbreviations

decl	=	declination
dev	=	deviation
diff	=	difference
GA	=	Greenwich Angle
GHA	=	Greenwich Hour Angle
GMT	=	Greenwich Mean Time
Hc	=	computed altitude
HP	=	horizontal parallax
Kn	=	knots
Lat	=	latitude
LHA	=	Local Hour Angle
LOA	=	length overall
Long	=	longitude
MET	=	Mid-European time
T	=	time of passage over the Greenwich Meridian
TL	=	total load
UT1	=	Universal time 1
var	=	variation
Z	=	Azimuth, given in semicircle
Zn	=	Azimuth, given in full circle

Measurements for sailors

1 nautical mile	= 1 minute of arc at the Equator = 1852m
1 knot	= 1 nautical mile per hour; speed measurement for boats, wind and current (but remember, the North wind blows *from* the North, and a Northerly current runs *towards* the North)
1 cable	= one tenth of a nautical mile =185.2m
1 inch	= 2.54cm (rope strength is given by circumference in the UK, by diameter in Europe)
1 foot	= 12 inches = 30.48cm; despite metrication, feet are still used in sailing. The length in feet is given for many types of boat in the description eg Carter 33
1 yard	= 3 feet = 91.44cm
1 fathom	= 6 feet =1.82m (older English sea maps give depths in fathoms)
1 ounce	= 28.35g
1 pound (English)	= 453.60g
1 PS	= 0.735 kW; since 1978 engine power has been given in kilowatts and no longer in horsepower (PS)
1 kW	= 1.359 PS

Further reading

Adlard Coles, K., *Heavy Weather Sailing* (Adlard Coles, 1991)

Bowyer, Mike, *The Concise Day Skipper* (David & Charles, 1989)

Buchanan, George, *The Boat Repair Manual* (Pelham, 1990)

The Glénans Manual of Sailing (David & Charles, 1993)

Hiscock, Eric C., *Cruising Under Sail* (Adlard Coles, 1985)

Howard-Williams, Jeremy, *Sails* (Adlard Coles, 1988)

Macmillan and Silk Cut Nautical Almanac (Macmillan, annual)

Pike, Dag, *RORC Manual of Safety and Survival at Sea* (David & Charles, 1993)

Pike, Dag, *Manual of Weather At Sea* (David & Charles, 1994)

RYA Navigation: an RYA manual (David & Charles, 1991)

Index

Page numbers in *italics* refer to illustrations

Index

Index

Index